INAPPROPRIATE

ALSO BY GABRIELLE BELL:

MY DOG IVY
GET OUT YOUR HANKIES
EVERYTHING IS FLAMMABLE
TRUTH IS FRAGMENTARY
THE VOYEURS
CECIL AND JORDAN IN NEW YORK
LUCKY
WHEN I'M OLD AND OTHER STORIES
GABRIELLEBELL.COM

Design: Tom Kaczynski
Production Assist: Az Sperry

UNCIVILIZED BOOKS
P. O. Box 6534
Minneapolis, MN 55406
USA
uncivilizedbooks.com

First Edition, Feb 2020

10 9 8 7 6 5 4 3 2 1

ISBN 978-1-941250-38-9

DISTRIBUTED TO THE TRADE BY:
Consortium Book Sales & Distribution, LLC.
34 Thirteenth Avenue NE, Suite 101
Minneapolis, MN 55413-1007
cbsd.com
Orders: (800) 283-3572

Printed in Canada

INAPPROPRIATE

GABRIELLE BELL

UNCIVILIZED BOOKS

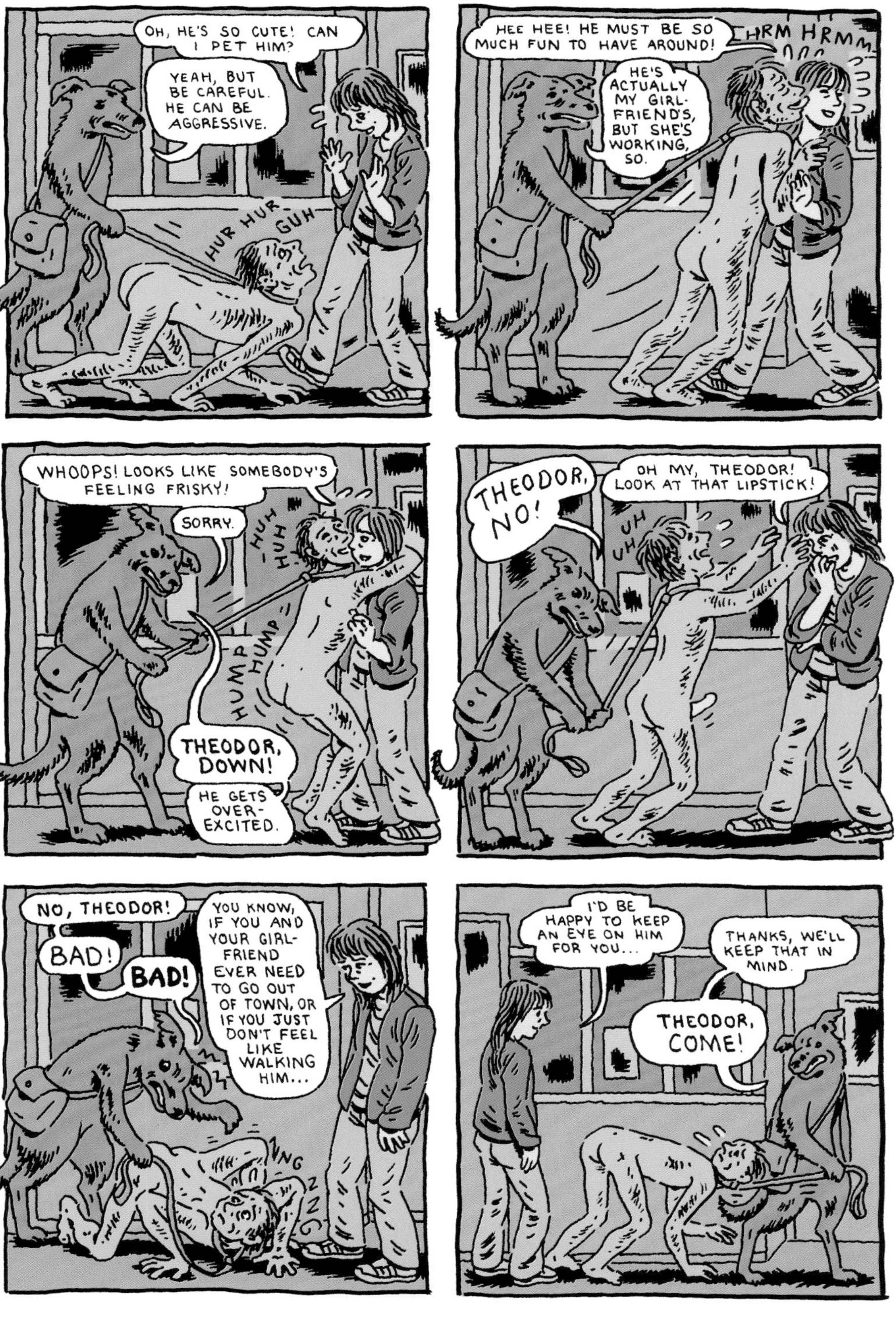

OH, HE'S SO CUTE! CAN I PET HIM?
YEAH, BUT BE CAREFUL. HE CAN BE AGGRESSIVE.
HUR HUR GUH
HEE HEE! HE MUST BE SO MUCH FUN TO HAVE AROUND!
HRM HRMM
HE'S ACTUALLY MY GIRLFRIEND'S, BUT SHE'S WORKING, SO.
WHOOPS! LOOKS LIKE SOMEBODY'S FEELING FRISKY!
SORRY.
HUH HUH
HUMP HUMP
THEODOR, DOWN!
HE GETS OVER-EXCITED.
THEODOR, NO!
OH MY, THEODOR! LOOK AT THAT LIPSTICK!
UH UH
NO, THEODOR!
BAD!
BAD!
YOU KNOW, IF YOU AND YOUR GIRLFRIEND EVER NEED TO GO OUT OF TOWN, OR IF YOU JUST DON'T FEEL LIKE WALKING HIM...
NG NNG
I'D BE HAPPY TO KEEP AN EYE ON HIM FOR YOU...
THANKS, WE'LL KEEP THAT IN MIND.
THEODOR, COME!

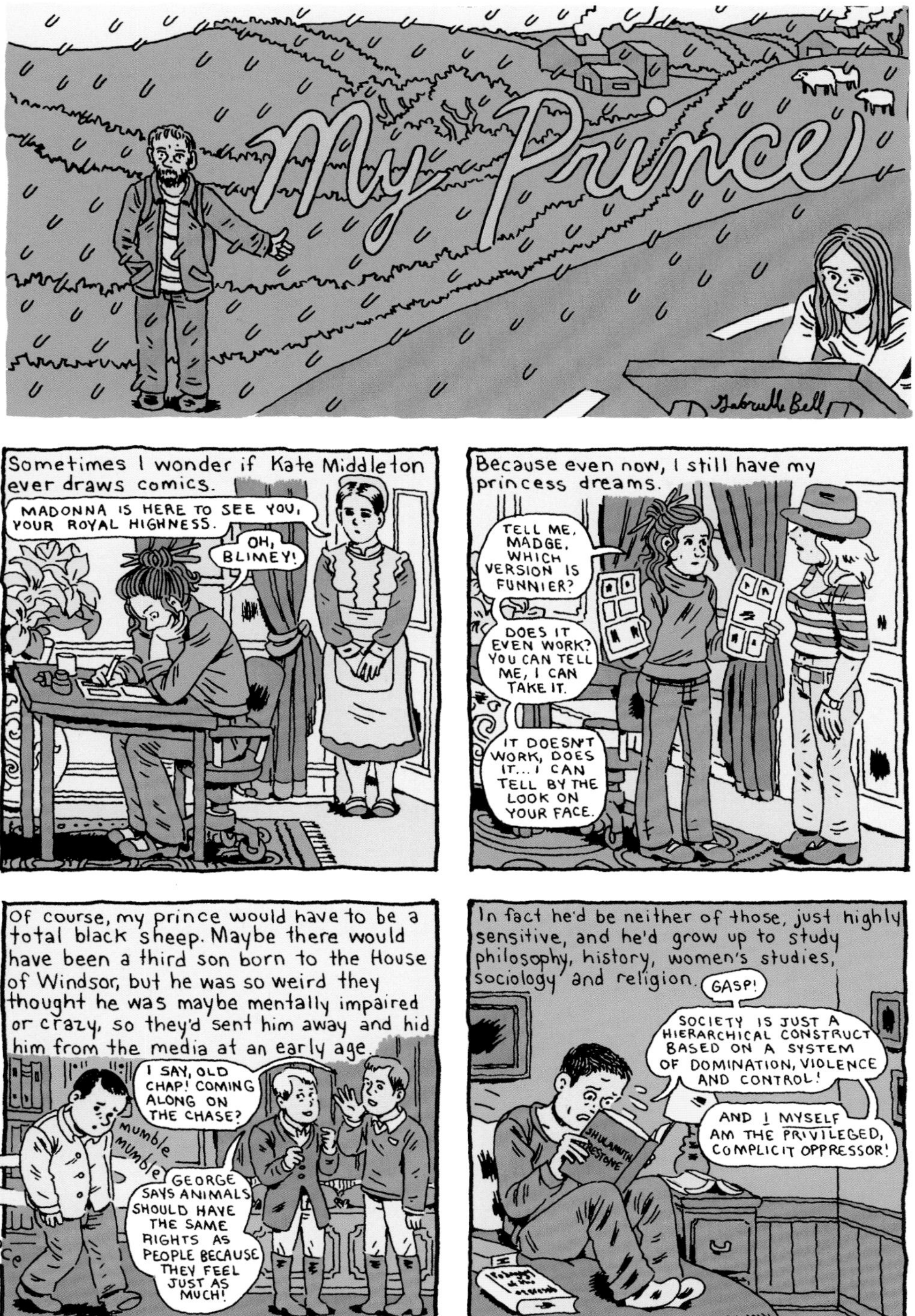
My Prince
Gabrielle Bell
Sometimes I wonder if Kate Middleton ever draws comics.
MADONNA IS HERE TO SEE YOU, YOUR ROYAL HIGHNESS.
OH, BLIMEY!
Because even now, I still have my princess dreams.
TELL ME, MADGE, WHICH VERSION IS FUNNIER?
DOES IT EVEN WORK? YOU CAN TELL ME, I CAN TAKE IT.
IT DOESN'T WORK, DOES IT... I CAN TELL BY THE LOOK ON YOUR FACE.
Of course, my prince would have to be a total black sheep. Maybe there would have been a third son born to the House of Windsor, but he was so weird they thought he was maybe mentally impaired or crazy, so they'd sent him away and hid him from the media at an early age.
I SAY, OLD CHAP! COMING ALONG ON THE CHASE?
mumble mumble
GEORGE SAYS ANIMALS SHOULD HAVE THE SAME RIGHTS AS PEOPLE BECAUSE THEY FEEL JUST AS MUCH!
In fact he'd be neither of those, just highly sensitive, and he'd grow up to study philosophy, history, women's studies, sociology and religion.
GASP!
SOCIETY IS JUST A HIERARCHICAL CONSTRUCT BASED ON A SYSTEM OF DOMINATION, VIOLENCE AND CONTROL!
AND I MYSELF AM THE PRIVILEGED, COMPLICIT OPPRESSOR!
SHULAMITH FIRESTONE

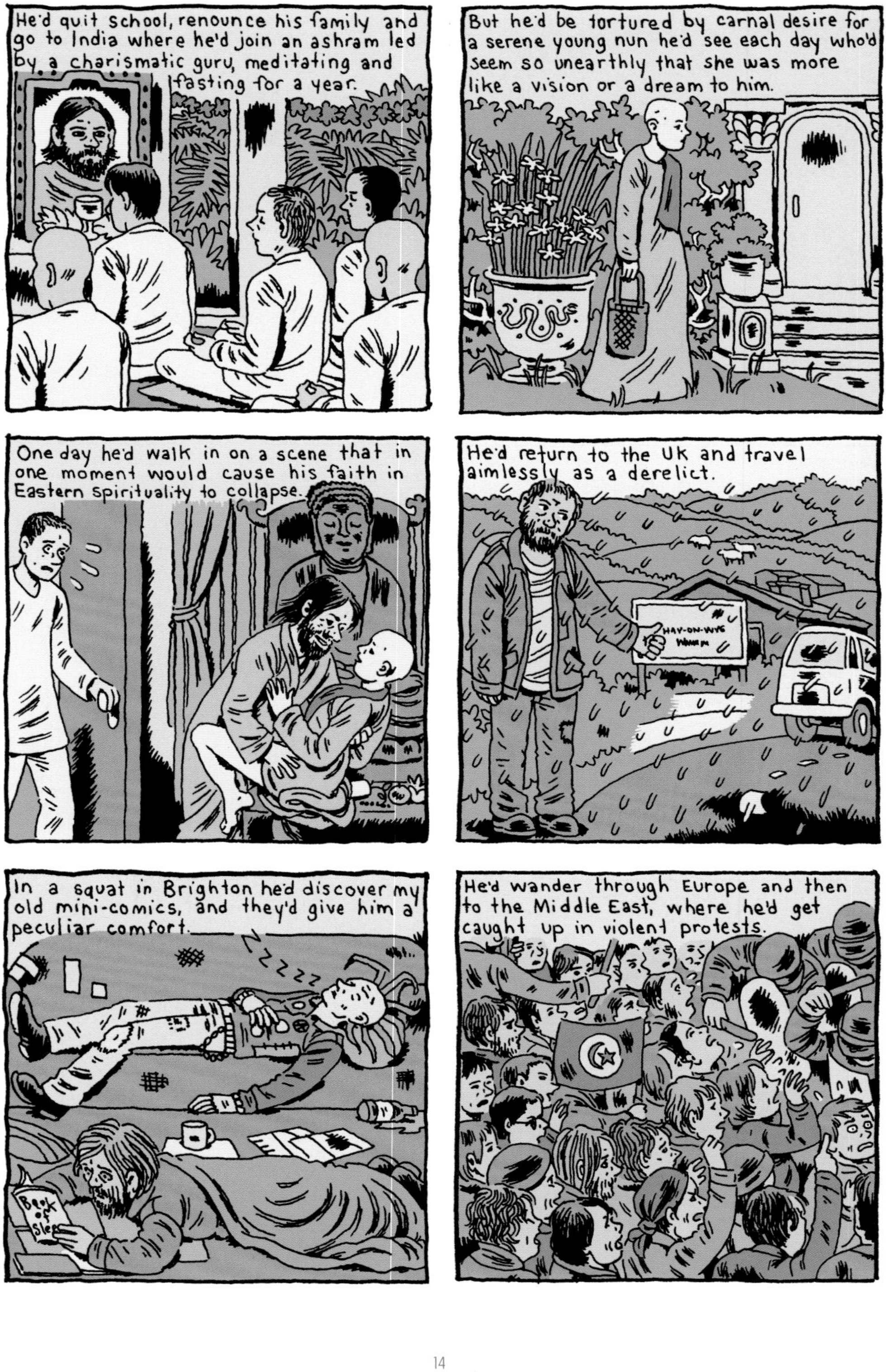
He'd quit school, renounce his family and go to India where he'd join an ashram led by a charismatic guru, meditating and fasting for a year.
But he'd be tortured by carnal desire for a serene young nun he'd see each day who'd seem so unearthly that she was more like a vision or a dream to him.
One day he'd walk in on a scene that in one moment would cause his faith in Eastern spirituality to collapse.
He'd return to the UK and travel aimlessly as a derelict.
HAY-ON-WYE
In a squat in Brighton he'd discover my old mini-comics, and they'd give him a peculiar comfort.
ZZZZZ
He'd wander through Europe and then to the Middle East, where he'd get caught up in violent protests.

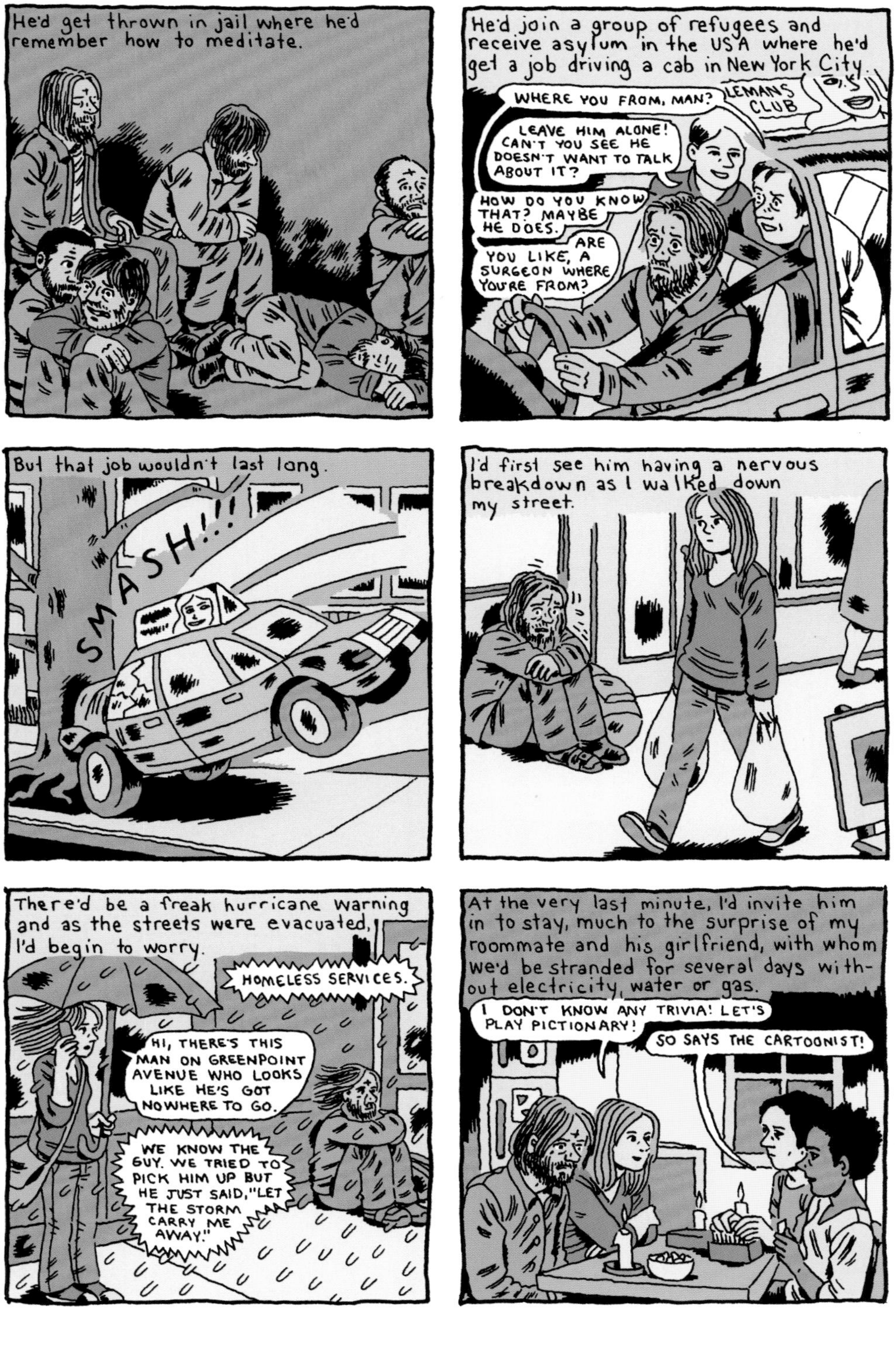
He'd get thrown in jail where he'd remember how to meditate.
He'd join a group of refugees and receive asylum in the USA where he'd get a job driving a cab in New York City.
WHERE YOU FROM, MAN?
LEMANS CLUB
LEAVE HIM ALONE! CAN'T YOU SEE HE DOESN'T WANT TO TALK ABOUT IT?
HOW DO YOU KNOW THAT? MAYBE HE DOES.
ARE YOU LIKE, A SURGEON WHERE YOU'RE FROM?
But that job wouldn't last long.
SMASH!!!
I'd first see him having a nervous breakdown as I walked down my street.
There'd be a freak hurricane warning and as the streets were evacuated, I'd begin to worry.
HOMELESS SERVICES.
HI, THERE'S THIS MAN ON GREENPOINT AVENUE WHO LOOKS LIKE HE'S GOT NOWHERE TO GO.
WE KNOW THE GUY. WE TRIED TO PICK HIM UP BUT HE JUST SAID, "LET THE STORM CARRY ME AWAY."
At the very last minute, I'd invite him in to stay, much to the surprise of my roommate and his girlfriend, with whom we'd be stranded for several days without electricity, water or gas.
I DON'T KNOW ANY TRIVIA! LET'S PLAY PICTIONARY!
SO SAYS THE CARTOONIST!

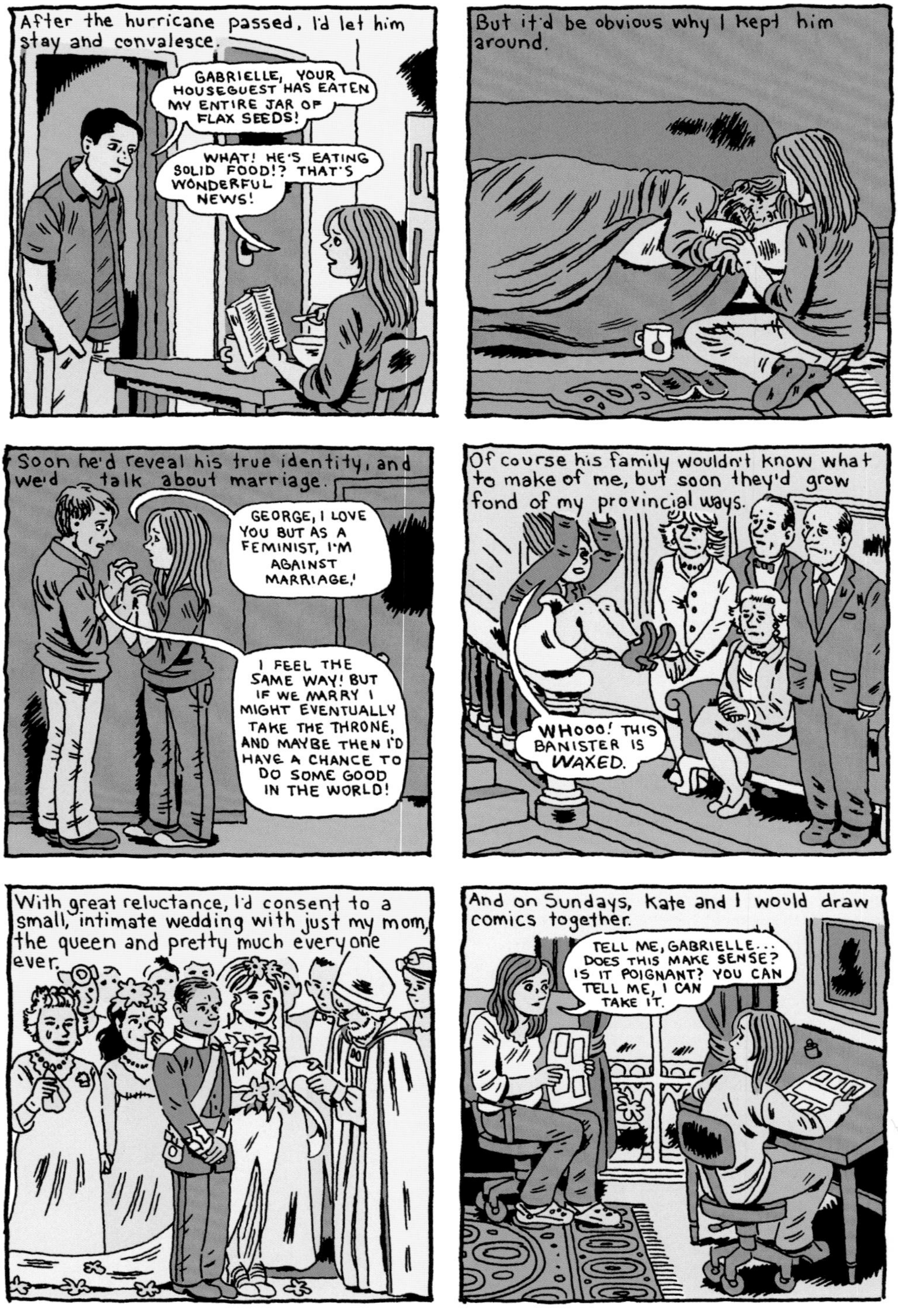
After the hurricane passed, I'd let him stay and convalesce.
GABRIELLE, YOUR HOUSEGUEST HAS EATEN MY ENTIRE JAR OF FLAX SEEDS!
WHAT! HE'S EATING SOLID FOOD!? THAT'S WONDERFUL NEWS!
But it'd be obvious why I kept him around.
Soon he'd reveal his true identity, and we'd talk about marriage.
GEORGE, I LOVE YOU BUT AS A FEMINIST, I'M AGAINST MARRIAGE!
I FEEL THE SAME WAY! BUT IF WE MARRY I MIGHT EVENTUALLY TAKE THE THRONE, AND MAYBE THEN I'D HAVE A CHANCE TO DO SOME GOOD IN THE WORLD!
Of course his family wouldn't know what to make of me, but soon they'd grow fond of my provincial ways.
WHOOO! THIS BANISTER IS WAXED.
With great reluctance, I'd consent to a small, intimate wedding with just my mom, the queen and pretty much everyone ever.
And on Sundays, Kate and I would draw comics together.
TELL ME, GABRIELLE... DOES THIS MAKE SENSE? IS IT POIGNANT? YOU CAN TELL ME, I CAN TAKE IT.

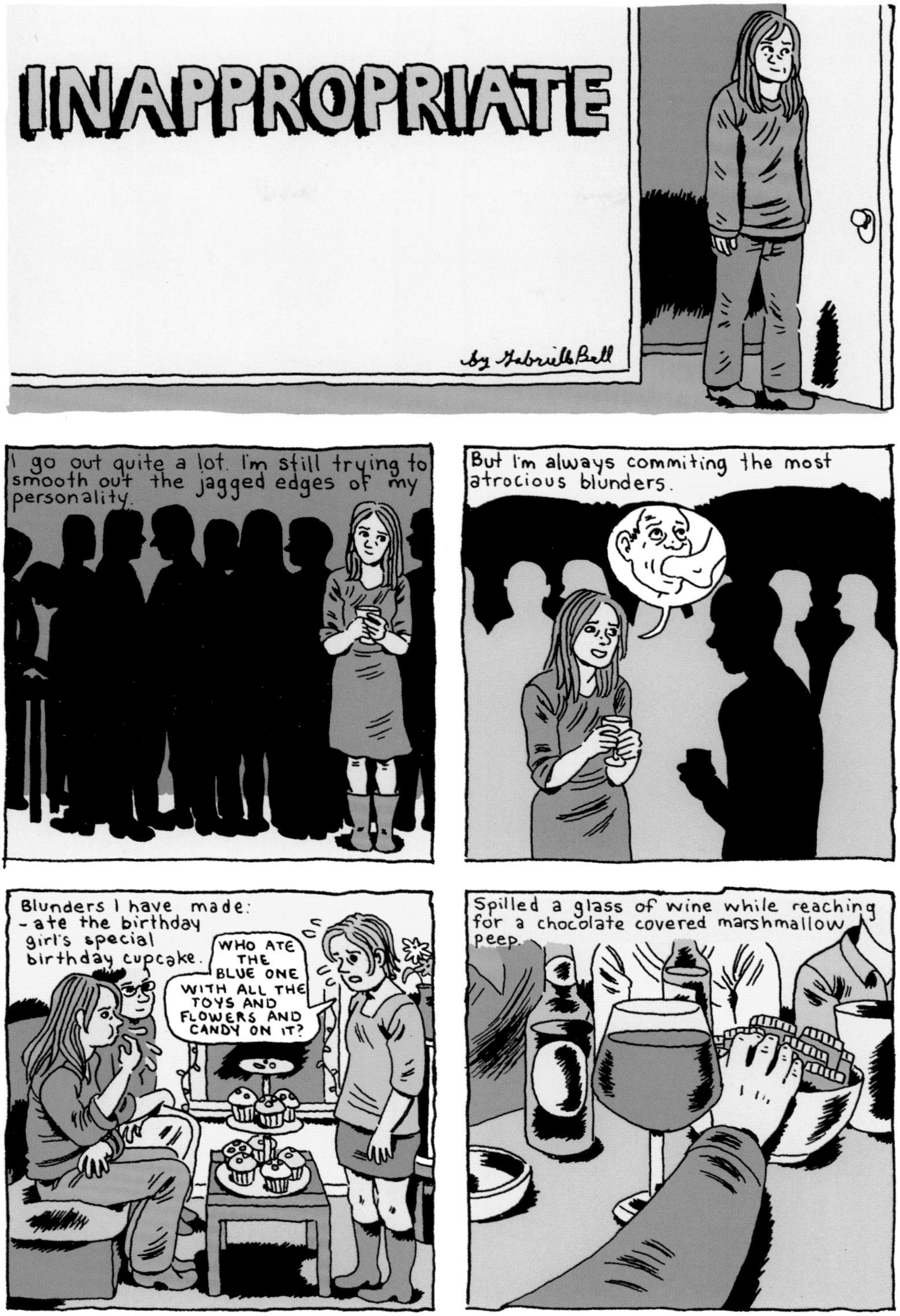
INAPPROPRIATE
by Gabrielle Bell
I go out quite a lot. I'm still trying to smooth out the jagged edges of my personality.
But I'm always commiting the most atrocious blunders.
Blunders I have made:
- ate the birthday girl's special birthday cupcake.
WHO ATE THE BLUE ONE WITH ALL THE TOYS AND FLOWERS AND CANDY ON IT?
Spilled a glass of wine while reaching for a chocolate covered marshmallow peep.

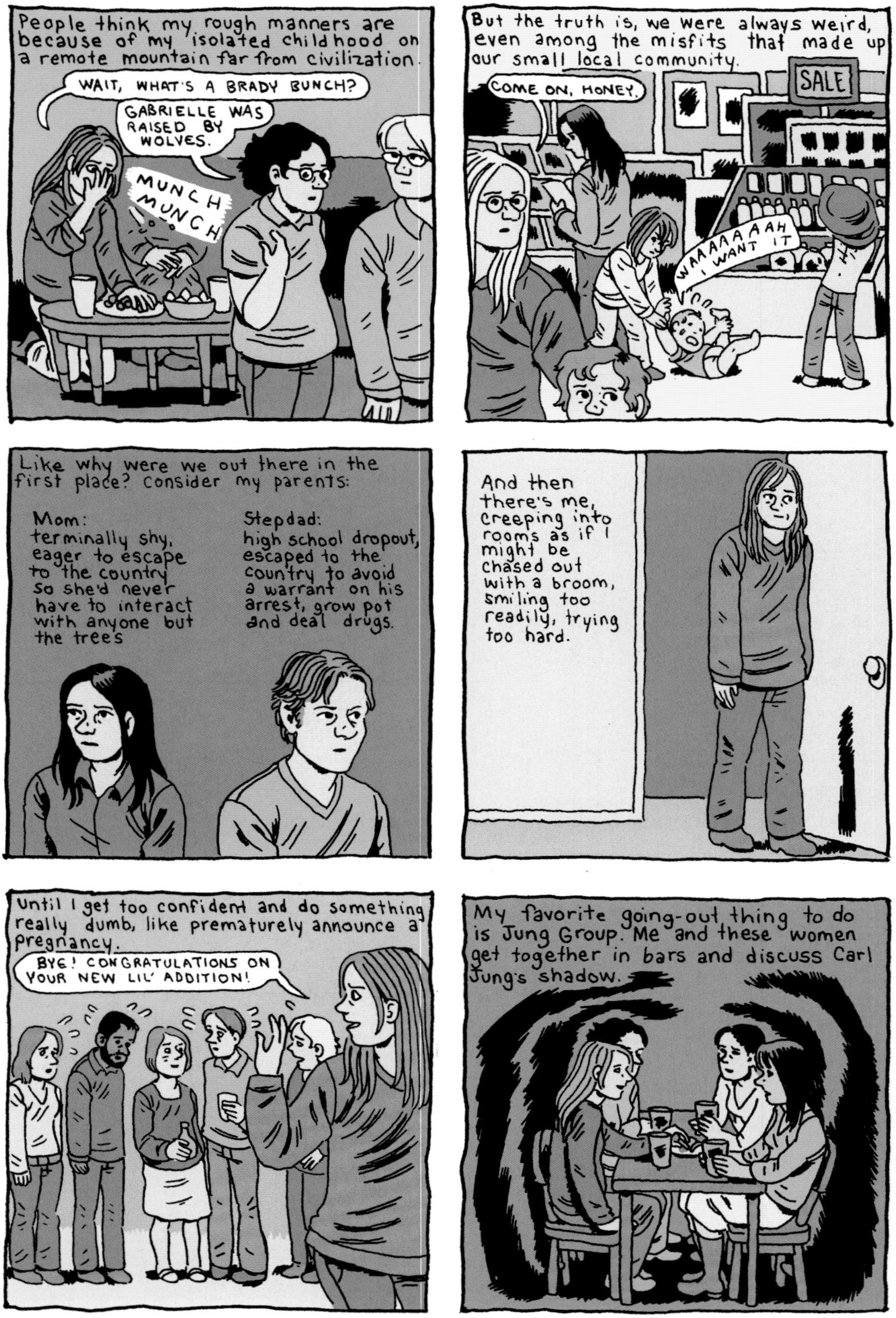
People think my rough manners are because of my isolated childhood on a remote mountain far from civilization.
WAIT, WHAT'S A BRADY BUNCH?
GABRIELLE WAS RAISED BY WOLVES.
MUNCH MUNCH
But the truth is, we were always weird, even among the misfits that made up our small local community.
COME ON, HONEY.
SALE
WAAAAAAAH I WANT IT
Like why were we out there in the first place? Consider my parents:
Mom: terminally shy, eager to escape to the country so she'd never have to interact with anyone but the trees
Stepdad: high school dropout, escaped to the country to avoid a warrant on his arrest, grow pot and deal drugs.
And then there's me, creeping into rooms as if I might be chased out with a broom, smiling too readily, trying too hard.
Until I get too confident and do something really dumb, like prematurely announce a pregnancy.
BYE! CONGRATULATIONS ON YOUR NEW LIL' ADDITION!
My favorite going-out thing to do is Jung Group. Me and these women get together in bars and discuss Carl Jung's shadow.

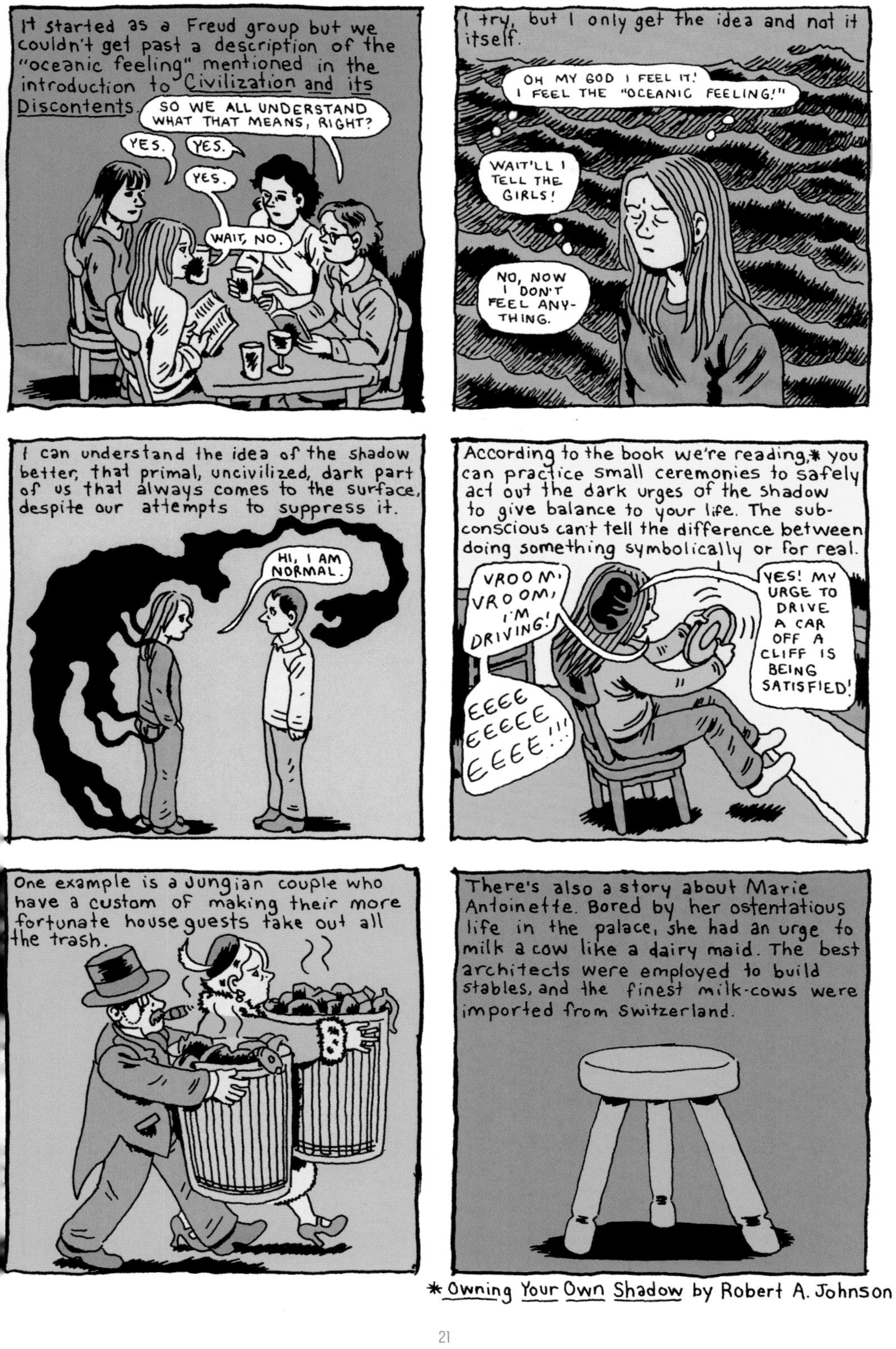

It started as a Freud group but we couldn't get past a description of the "oceanic feeling" mentioned in the introduction to Civilization and its Discontents.
SO WE ALL UNDERSTAND WHAT THAT MEANS, RIGHT?
YES.
YES.
YES.
WAIT, NO.
I try, but I only get the idea and not it itself.
OH MY GOD I FEEL IT! I FEEL THE "OCEANIC FEELING!"
WAIT'LL I TELL THE GIRLS!
NO, NOW I DON'T FEEL ANYTHING.
I can understand the idea of the shadow better, that primal, uncivilized, dark part of us that always comes to the surface, despite our attempts to suppress it.
HI, I AM NORMAL.
According to the book we're reading,* you can practice small ceremonies to safely act out the dark urges of the shadow to give balance to your life. The subconscious can't tell the difference between doing something symbolically or for real.
VROOM, VROOM, I'M DRIVING!
YES! MY URGE TO DRIVE A CAR OFF A CLIFF IS BEING SATISFIED!
EEEE EEEEE EEEE!!!
One example is a Jungian couple who have a custom of making their more fortunate houseguests take out all the trash.
There's also a story about Marie Antoinette. Bored by her ostentatious life in the palace, she had an urge to milk a cow like a dairy maid. The best architects were employed to build stables, and the finest milk-cows were imported from Switzerland.

* Owning Your Own Shadow by Robert A. Johnson

But when the time came, she was too grossed out to touch it.

If she had followed through with this earthly impulse, she would have ceremonially honored her shadow self, balancing the formalities of her courtly life, and perhaps wouldn't have been beheaded in the French Revolution.

According to Wikipedia, though, "The queen sought refuge in peasant life, milking cows or sheep carefully maintained by servants."

So what's true? The internet or a book? All I know is there is nothing I enjoy more than to get together with these women and discuss the shadow.

MY TEACHER SAID THAT EVERY NEGATIVE THOUGHT IS A BIT OF POISON WE GIVE OURSELVES, AND EVERY NEGATIVE THING WE SAY TO SOMEONE IS POISON WE GIVE TO THEM.

BUT HOW IS IT POSSIBLE NOT TO HAVE NEGATIVE THOUGHTS? EVEN WHAT YOUR TEACHER SAID HAS NEGATIVITY.

THAT'S WHAT THE MANDORLA IS ABOUT. IT'S A PARADOX.

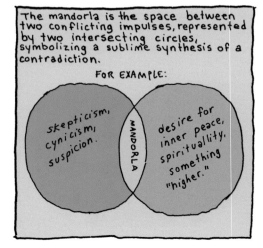

The mandorla is the space between two conflicting impulses, represented by two intersecting circles, symbolizing a sublime synthesis of a contradiction.

FOR EXAMPLE:

skepticism, cynicism, suspicion.

MANDORLA

desire for inner peace, spirituallity, something "higher."

So I recruited Jami from Jung Group to conduct a shadow ceremony before attending a birthday party at a bar.

I GUESS WE SHOULD JUST DO A THING NOW THAT WE ARE AFRAID WE WILL DO IN PUBLIC.

OKAY, I'M AFRAID I'LL KEEP TALKING ABOUT HOW I'M FORTY AND I HAVEN'T HAD SEX IN A LONG TIME. HAVE I MENTIONED THAT I'M FORTY AND I HAVEN'T HAD SEX IN A LONG TIME?

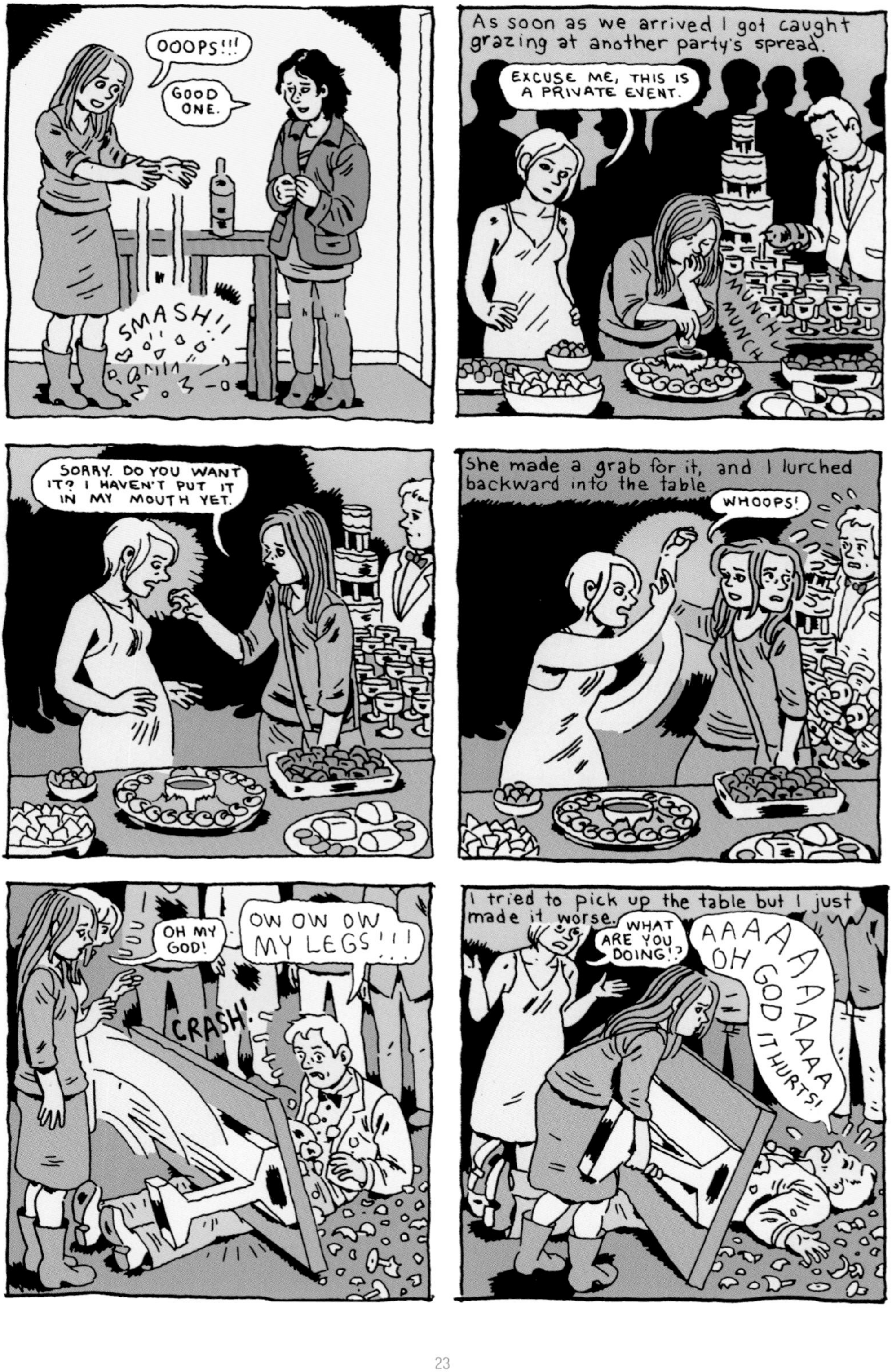
OOOPS!!!
GOOD ONE.
SMASH!!
As soon as we arrived I got caught grazing at another party's spread.
EXCUSE ME, THIS IS A PRIVATE EVENT.
MUNCH MUNCH
SORRY. DO YOU WANT IT? I HAVEN'T PUT IT IN MY MOUTH YET.
She made a grab for it, and I lurched backward into the table.
WHOOPS!
OH MY GOD!
OW OW OW MY LEGS!!!
CRASH!
I tried to pick up the table but I just made it worse.
WHAT ARE YOU DOING!?
AAAAAAAAAAAA OH GOD IT HURTS!

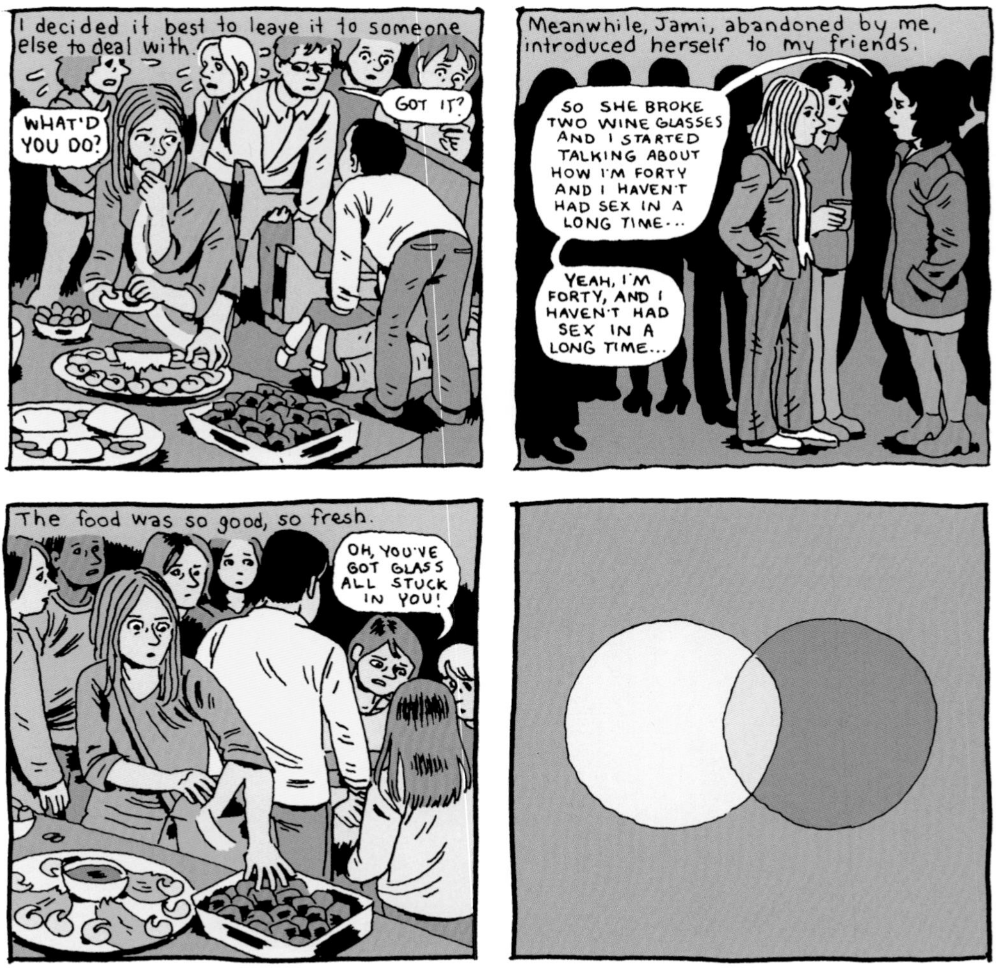
I decided it best to leave it to someone else to deal with.
WHAT'D YOU DO?
GOT IT?
Meanwhile, Jami, abandoned by me, introduced herself to my friends.
SO SHE BROKE TWO WINE GLASSES AND I STARTED TALKING ABOUT HOW I'M FORTY AND I HAVEN'T HAD SEX IN A LONG TIME...
YEAH, I'M FORTY, AND I HAVEN'T HAD SEX IN A LONG TIME...
The food was so good, so fresh.
OH, YOU'VE GOT GLASS ALL STUCK IN YOU!

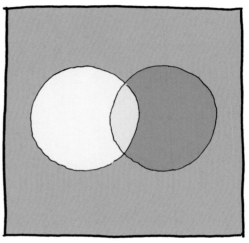

Dear Naked Guy In the Apartment Across From Mine, Spread-Eagled & Absent-mindedly Flicking his Penis While Watching TV,

I know that you know that I know that you see me seeing you seeing me back.

We have a silent conversation going. You are saying, "I'm just trying to watch TV," and I'm saying, "I'm just trying to wash my dishes."

...and organize my trash... ...And water my peperonia... ...and check to see if it's still raining...

Are you feeling disenfranchised, sandwiched in your tiny, roach-infested tenement for years on end, your wages stagnating, your expenses skyrocketing, and your neighborhood becoming unrecognizable with insufferable, rich brats?

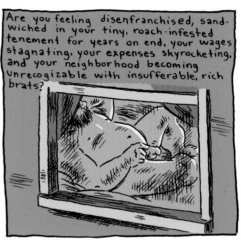

Or are you happy, warm and nude and alone in your cozy apartment, after a good day's work?

...and sharing with your ever-changing audience the generous size of your penis, even when only at half-mast?

DENTIST

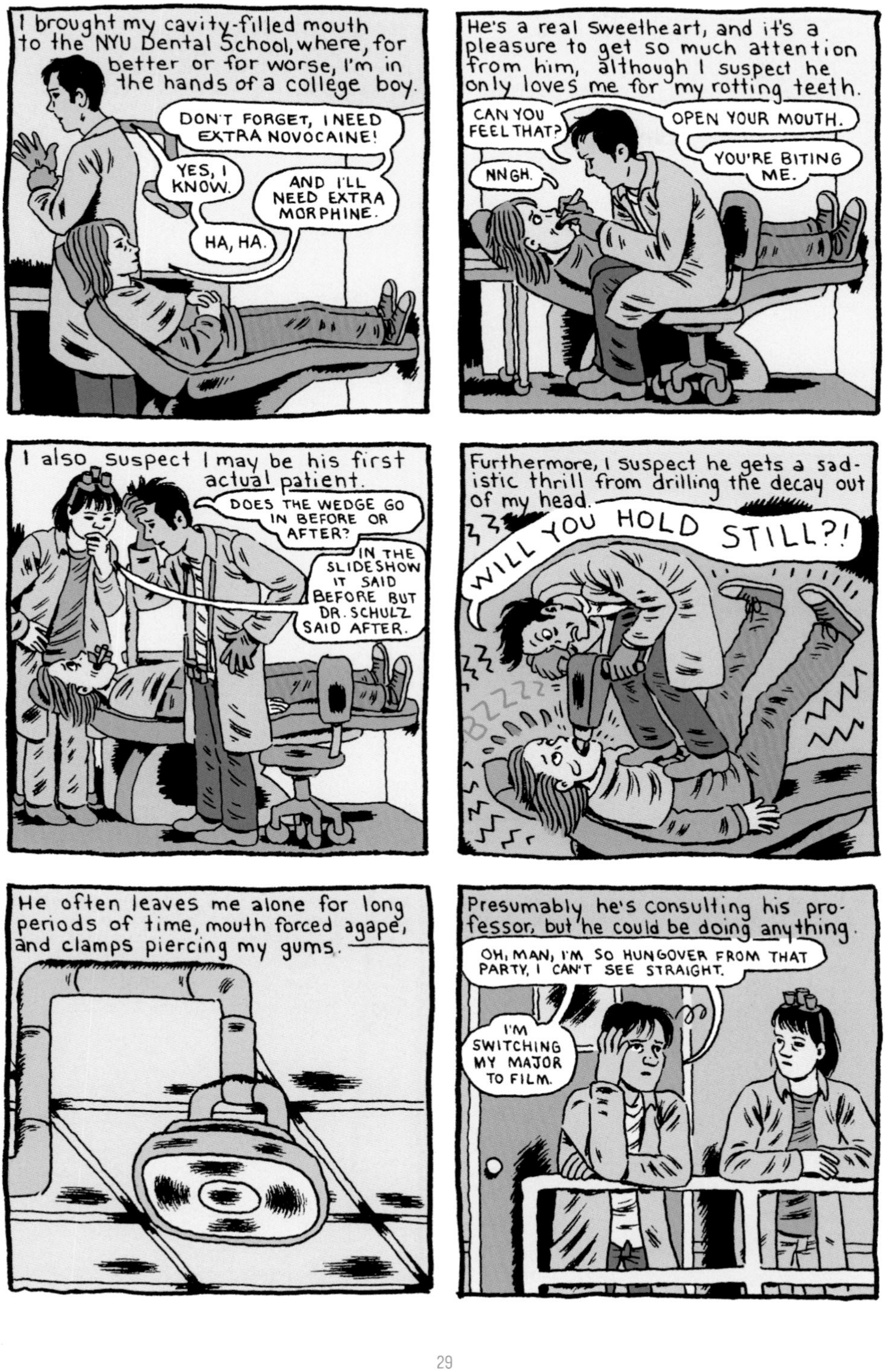
I brought my cavity-filled mouth to the NYU Dental School, where, for better or for worse, I'm in the hands of a college boy.
DON'T FORGET, I NEED EXTRA NOVOCAINE!
YES, I KNOW.
AND I'LL NEED EXTRA MORPHINE.
HA, HA.
He's a real sweetheart, and it's a pleasure to get so much attention from him, although I suspect he only loves me for my rotting teeth.
CAN YOU FEEL THAT?
OPEN YOUR MOUTH.
NNGH.
YOU'RE BITING ME.
I also suspect I may be his first actual patient.
DOES THE WEDGE GO IN BEFORE OR AFTER?
IN THE SLIDESHOW IT SAID BEFORE BUT DR. SCHULZ SAID AFTER.
Furthermore, I suspect he gets a sadistic thrill from drilling the decay out of my head.
WILL YOU HOLD STILL?!
BZZZZ
He often leaves me alone for long periods of time, mouth forced agape, and clamps piercing my gums.
Presumably he's consulting his professor, but he could be doing anything.
OH, MAN, I'M SO HUNGOVER FROM THAT PARTY, I CAN'T SEE STRAIGHT.
I'M SWITCHING MY MAJOR TO FILM.

There are two kinds of drills which create two different sensations. The skinny one makes a focused, narrow, shrill feeling that's almost satisfying.

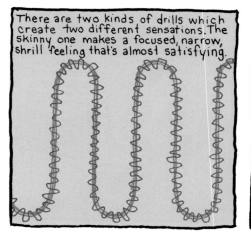

The fat one vibrates more slowly, and digs straight through my skull and into my brain. I worry about brain damage, and I wonder, where does the pain go? Will it resurface later? How are we able to circumvent this inevitable punishment? It defies nature.

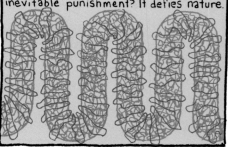

To pass the time, I try to imagine snuggling with polar bears. But it's not easy, because what are the chances that'd ever actually happen?

Like maybe I happen to be wandering around in the arctic, and a bear's only cub has just died, and in her deranged state of grief and shock, she comes to believe that I am her cub, and proceeds to raise me as such.

LICK! LICK! LICK!

TEE HEE HEE! GIGGLE!

Or better yet, a cub's mother dies, and I adopt it to raise as my own.

As he grows up, he'd protect me from predators, hunt for seal meat, keep me warm, snuggle when I'm lonely, and even carry me on his back when I'm tired. If you have your own polar bear you really don't need anything else.

But who am I kidding, when would a polar bear ever cuddle with me?

Instead I think about the town in Northern Canada where they leave the car doors unlocked, in case you ran into one walking down the street.

What would the likelihood be that the doors wouldn't be frozen shut?

And anyway, would a vehicle deter a starving bear?

BUT... I LOVE YOU!

SMASH!!!

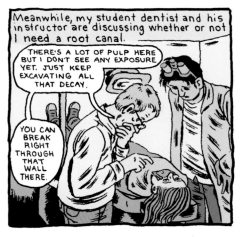

Meanwhile, my student dentist and his instructor are discussing whether or not I need a root canal.

THERE'S A LOT OF PULP HERE BUT I DON'T SEE ANY EXPOSURE YET. JUST KEEP EXCAVATING ALL THAT DECAY.

YOU CAN BREAK RIGHT THROUGH THAT WALL THERE.

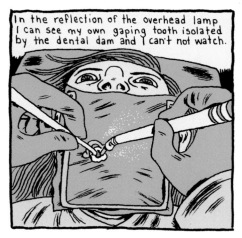

In the reflection of the overhead lamp I can see my own gaping tooth isolated by the dental dam and I can't not watch.

It's a cold, unforgiving world, and it only gets harder.

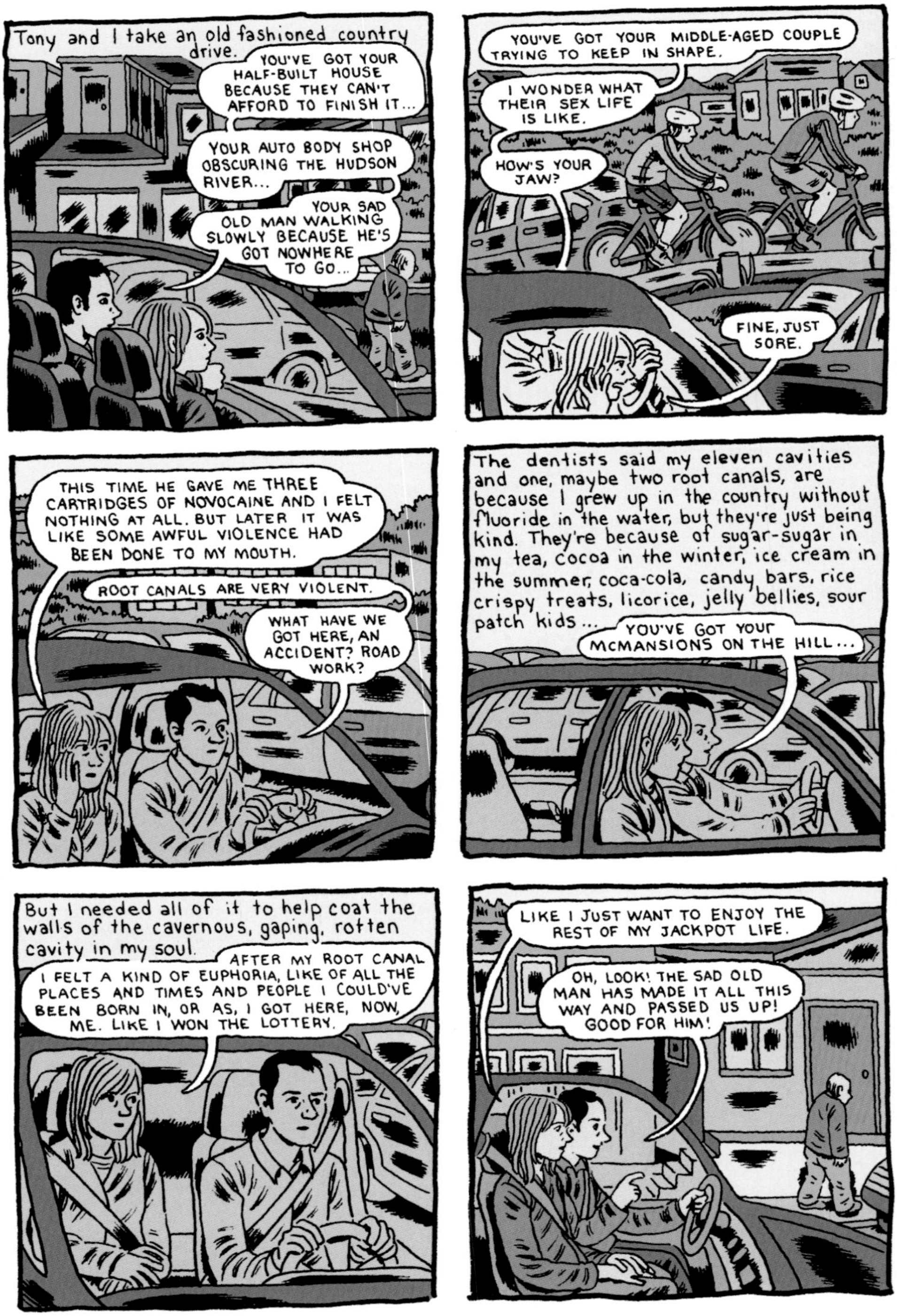
Tony and I take an old fashioned country drive.
YOU'VE GOT YOUR HALF-BUILT HOUSE BECAUSE THEY CAN'T AFFORD TO FINISH IT...
YOUR AUTO BODY SHOP OBSCURING THE HUDSON RIVER...
YOUR SAD OLD MAN WALKING SLOWLY BECAUSE HE'S GOT NOWHERE TO GO...
YOU'VE GOT YOUR MIDDLE-AGED COUPLE TRYING TO KEEP IN SHAPE.
I WONDER WHAT THEIR SEX LIFE IS LIKE.
HOW'S YOUR JAW?
FINE, JUST SORE.
THIS TIME HE GAVE ME THREE CARTRIDGES OF NOVOCAINE AND I FELT NOTHING AT ALL. BUT LATER IT WAS LIKE SOME AWFUL VIOLENCE HAD BEEN DONE TO MY MOUTH.
ROOT CANALS ARE VERY VIOLENT.
WHAT HAVE WE GOT HERE, AN ACCIDENT? ROAD WORK?
The dentists said my eleven cavities and one, maybe two root canals, are because I grew up in the country without fluoride in the water, but they're just being kind. They're because of sugar-sugar in my tea, cocoa in the winter, ice cream in the summer, coca-cola, candy bars, rice crispy treats, licorice, jelly bellies, sour patch kids...
YOU'VE GOT YOUR MCMANSIONS ON THE HILL...
But I needed all of it to help coat the walls of the cavernous, gaping, rotten cavity in my soul.
AFTER MY ROOT CANAL I FELT A KIND OF EUPHORIA, LIKE OF ALL THE PLACES AND TIMES AND PEOPLE I COULD'VE BEEN BORN IN, OR AS, I GOT HERE, NOW, ME. LIKE I WON THE LOTTERY.
LIKE I JUST WANT TO ENJOY THE REST OF MY JACKPOT LIFE.
OH, LOOK! THE SAD OLD MAN HAS MADE IT ALL THIS WAY AND PASSED US UP! GOOD FOR HIM!

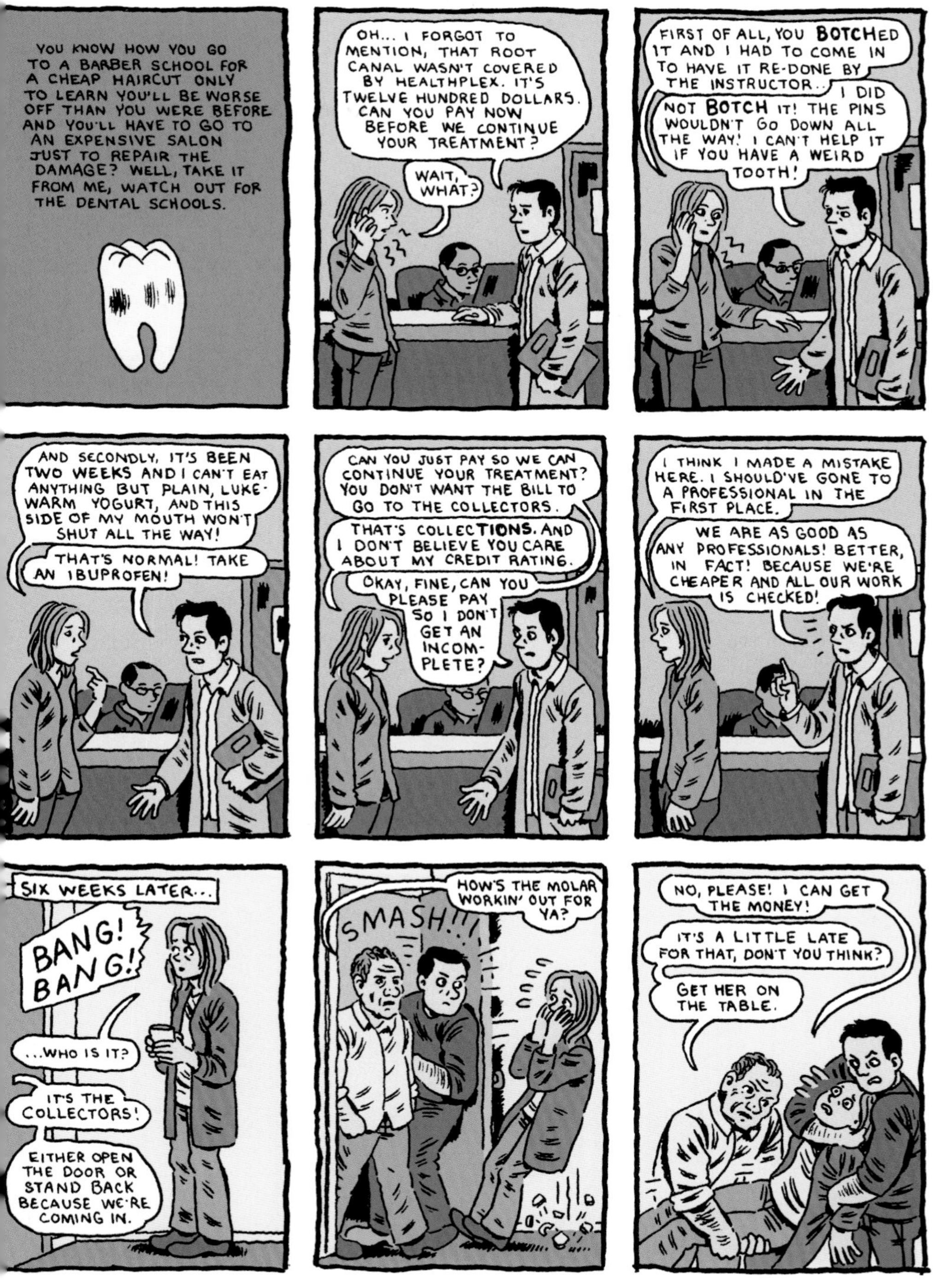
YOU KNOW HOW YOU GO TO A BARBER SCHOOL FOR A CHEAP HAIRCUT ONLY TO LEARN YOU'LL BE WORSE OFF THAN YOU WERE BEFORE AND YOU'LL HAVE TO GO TO AN EXPENSIVE SALON JUST TO REPAIR THE DAMAGE? WELL, TAKE IT FROM ME, WATCH OUT FOR THE DENTAL SCHOOLS.
OH... I FORGOT TO MENTION, THAT ROOT CANAL WASN'T COVERED BY HEALTHPLEX. IT'S TWELVE HUNDRED DOLLARS. CAN YOU PAY NOW BEFORE WE CONTINUE YOUR TREATMENT?
WAIT, WHAT?
FIRST OF ALL, YOU BOTCHED IT AND I HAD TO COME IN TO HAVE IT RE-DONE BY THE INSTRUCTOR..
I DID NOT BOTCH IT! THE PINS WOULDN'T GO DOWN ALL THE WAY! I CAN'T HELP IT IF YOU HAVE A WEIRD TOOTH!
AND SECONDLY, IT'S BEEN TWO WEEKS AND I CAN'T EAT ANYTHING BUT PLAIN, LUKE-WARM YOGURT, AND THIS SIDE OF MY MOUTH WON'T SHUT ALL THE WAY!
THAT'S NORMAL! TAKE AN IBUPROFEN!
CAN YOU JUST PAY SO WE CAN CONTINUE YOUR TREATMENT? YOU DON'T WANT THE BILL TO GO TO THE COLLECTORS.
THAT'S COLLECTIONS. AND I DON'T BELIEVE YOU CARE ABOUT MY CREDIT RATING.
OKAY, FINE, CAN YOU PLEASE PAY SO I DON'T GET AN INCOM-PLETE?
I THINK I MADE A MISTAKE HERE. I SHOULD'VE GONE TO A PROFESSIONAL IN THE FIRST PLACE.
WE ARE AS GOOD AS ANY PROFESSIONALS! BETTER, IN FACT! BECAUSE WE'RE CHEAPER AND ALL OUR WORK IS CHECKED!
SIX WEEKS LATER...
BANG! BANG!
...WHO IS IT?
IT'S THE COLLECTORS!
EITHER OPEN THE DOOR OR STAND BACK BECAUSE WE'RE COMING IN.
SMASH!!!
HOW'S THE MOLAR WORKIN' OUT FOR YA?
NO, PLEASE! I CAN GET THE MONEY!
IT'S A LITTLE LATE FOR THAT, DON'T YOU THINK?
GET HER ON THE TABLE.

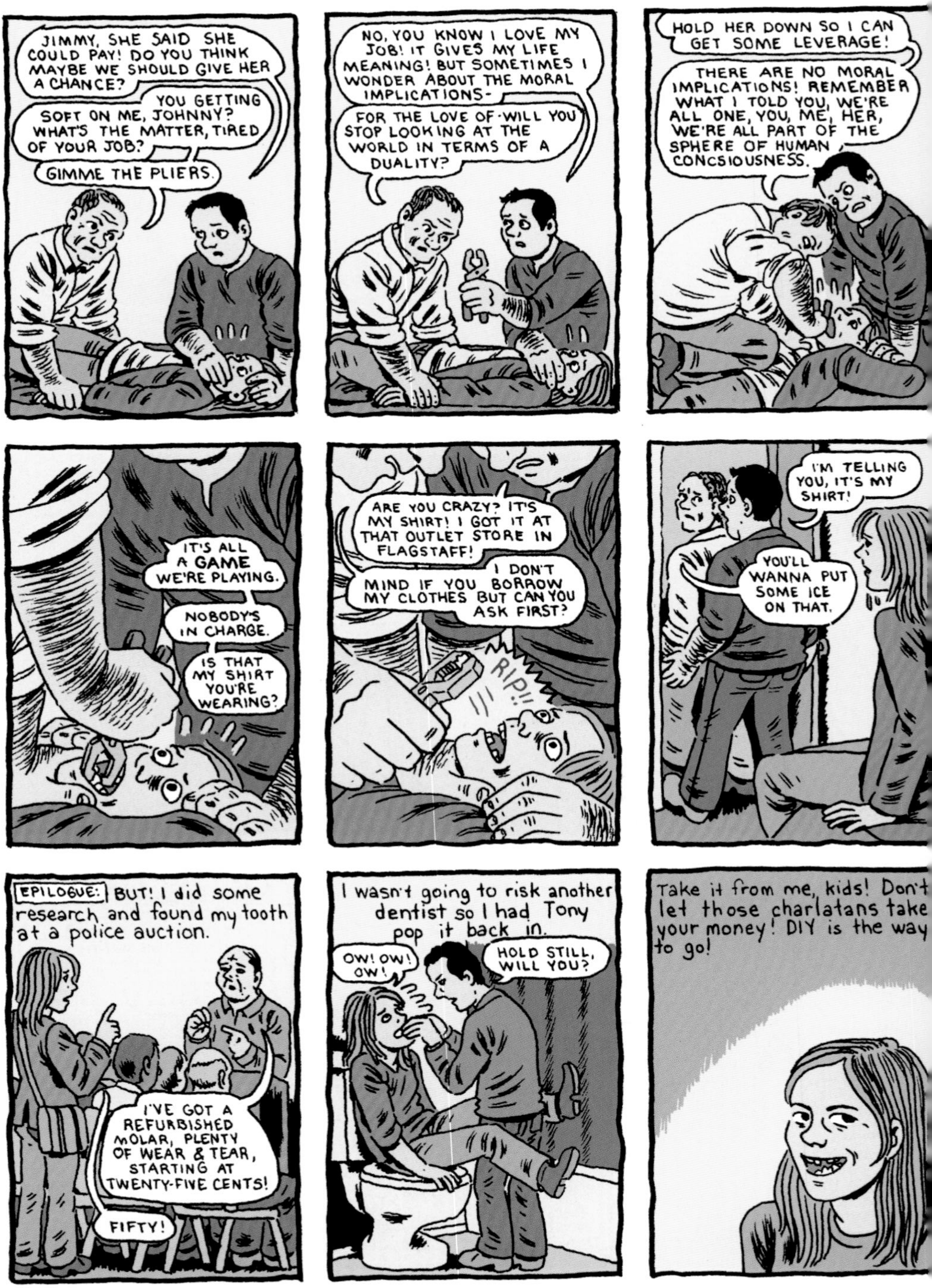
JIMMY, SHE SAID SHE COULD PAY! DO YOU THINK MAYBE WE SHOULD GIVE HER A CHANCE?
YOU GETTING SOFT ON ME, JOHNNY? WHAT'S THE MATTER, TIRED OF YOUR JOB?
GIMME THE PLIERS.
NO, YOU KNOW I LOVE MY JOB! IT GIVES MY LIFE MEANING! BUT SOMETIMES I WONDER ABOUT THE MORAL IMPLICATIONS-
FOR THE LOVE OF-WILL YOU STOP LOOKING AT THE WORLD IN TERMS OF A DUALITY?
HOLD HER DOWN SO I CAN GET SOME LEVERAGE!
THERE ARE NO MORAL IMPLICATIONS! REMEMBER WHAT I TOLD YOU, WE'RE ALL ONE, YOU, ME, HER, WE'RE ALL PART OF THE SPHERE OF HUMAN CONCSIOUSNESS.
IT'S ALL A GAME WE'RE PLAYING.
NOBODY'S IN CHARGE.
IS THAT MY SHIRT YOU'RE WEARING?
ARE YOU CRAZY? IT'S MY SHIRT! I GOT IT AT THAT OUTLET STORE IN FLAGSTAFF!
I DON'T MIND IF YOU BORROW MY CLOTHES BUT CAN YOU ASK FIRST?
RIP!!
I'M TELLING YOU, IT'S MY SHIRT!
YOU'LL WANNA PUT SOME ICE ON THAT.
EPILOGUE: BUT! I did some research and found my tooth at a police auction.
I'VE GOT A REFURBISHED MOLAR, PLENTY OF WEAR & TEAR, STARTING AT TWENTY-FIVE CENTS!
FIFTY!
I wasn't going to risk another dentist so I had Tony pop it back in.
OW! OW! OW!
HOLD STILL, WILL YOU?
Take it from me, kids! Don't let those charlatans take your money! DIY is the way to go!

NOCTURNAL GUESTS

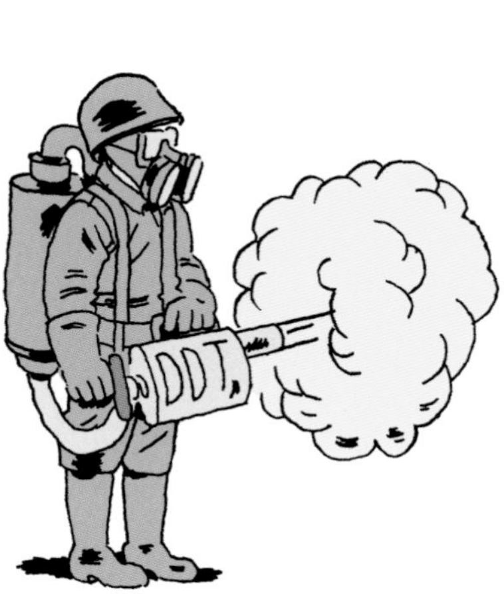
DDT.

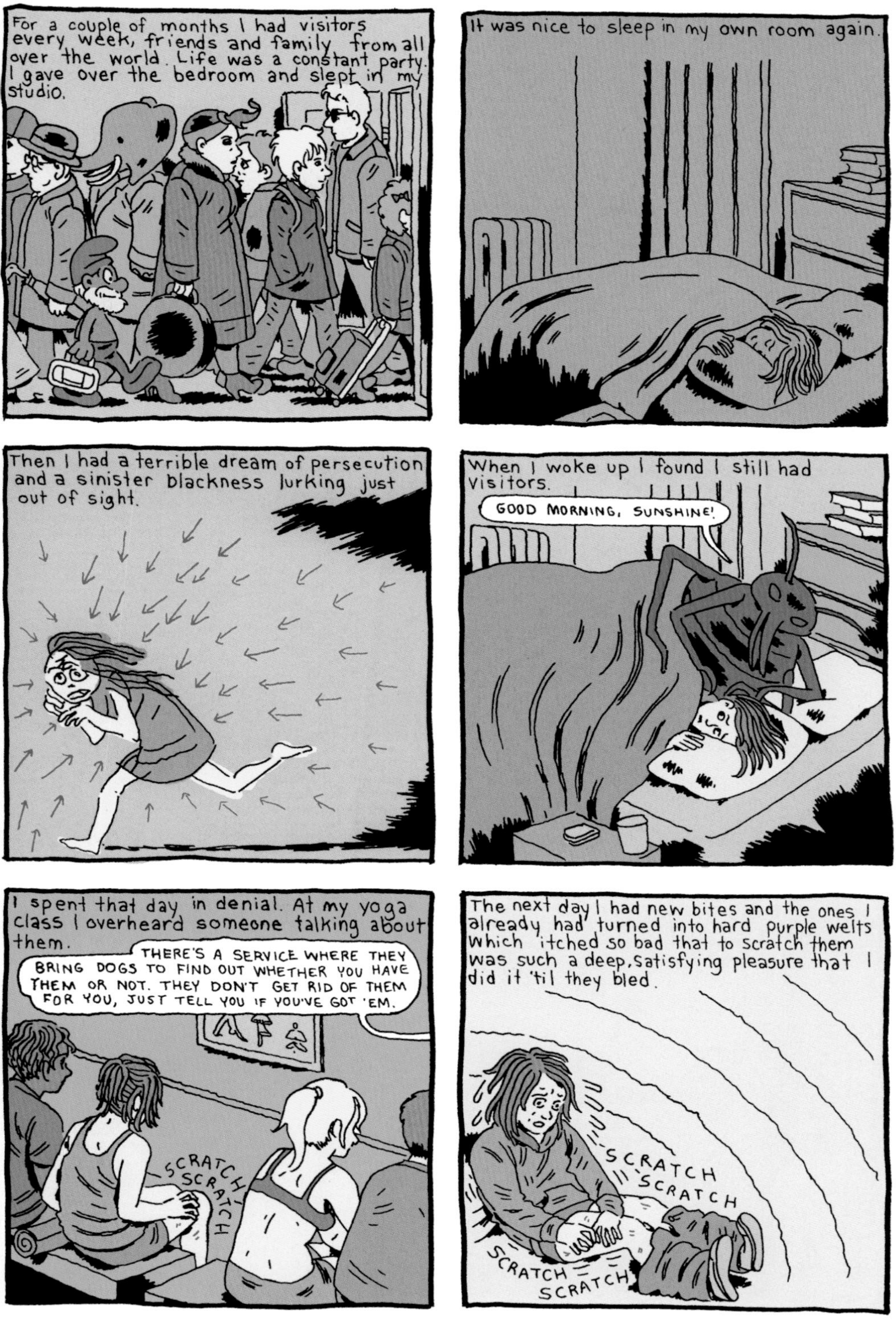
For a couple of months I had visitors every week, friends and family from all over the world. Life was a constant party. I gave over the bedroom and slept in my studio.
It was nice to sleep in my own room again.
Then I had a terrible dream of persecution and a sinister blackness lurking just out of sight.
When I woke up I found I still had visitors.
GOOD MORNING, SUNSHINE!
I spent that day in denial. At my yoga class I overheard someone talking about them.
THERE'S A SERVICE WHERE THEY BRING DOGS TO FIND OUT WHETHER YOU HAVE THEM OR NOT. THEY DON'T GET RID OF THEM FOR YOU, JUST TELL YOU IF YOU'VE GOT 'EM.
SCRATCH SCRATCH SCRATCH
The next day I had new bites and the ones I already had turned into hard purple welts which itched so bad that to scratch them was such a deep, satisfying pleasure that I did it 'til they bled.
SCRATCH SCRATCH
SCRATCH SCRATCH

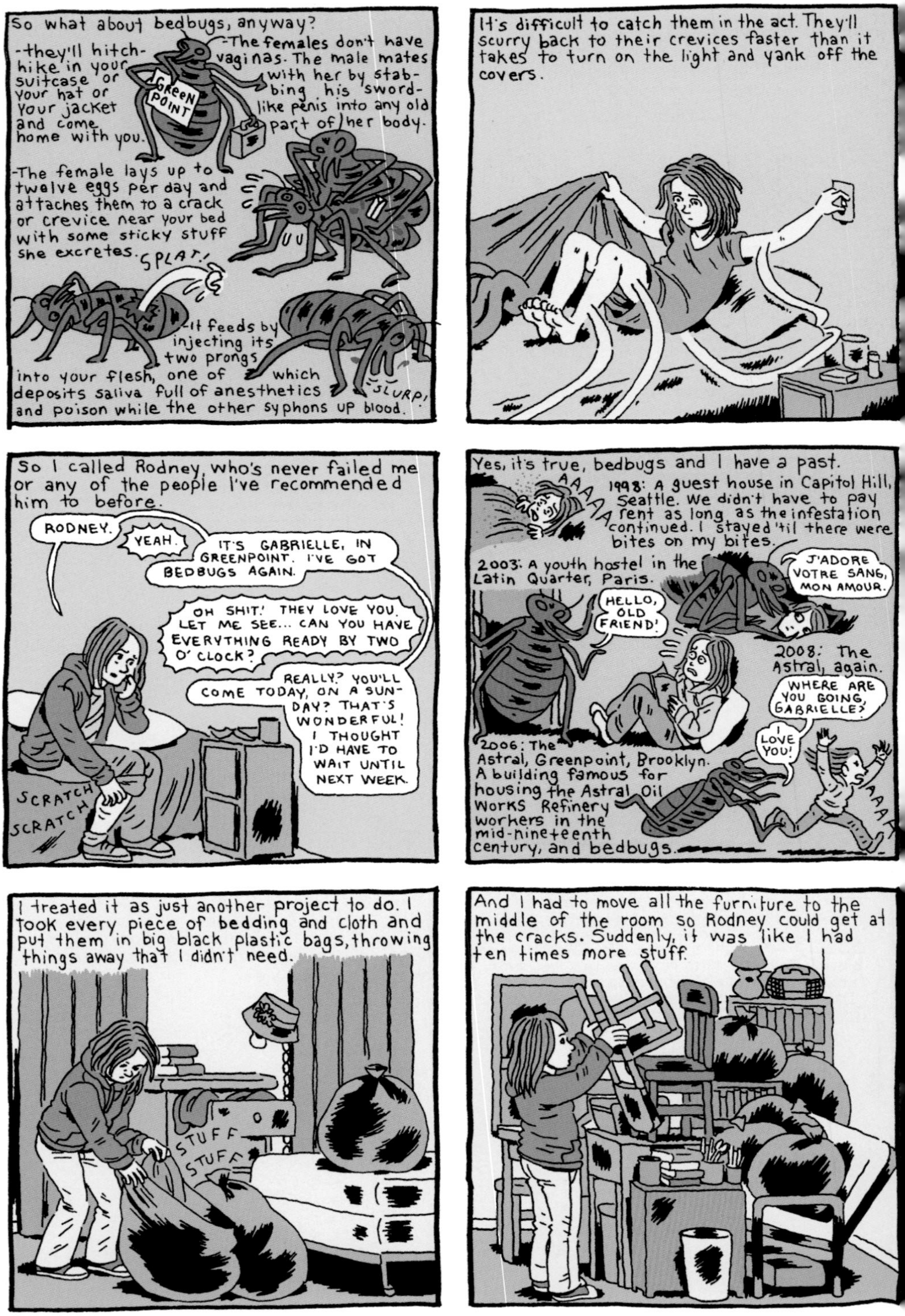
So what about bedbugs, anyway?
-they'll hitch-hike in your suitcase or your hat or your jacket and come home with you.
GREEN POINT
-The females don't have vaginas. The male mates with her by stabbing his sword-like penis into any old part of her body.
-The female lays up to twelve eggs per day and attaches them to a crack or crevice near your bed with some sticky stuff she excretes.
SPLAT!
-It feeds by injecting its two prongs into your flesh, one of which deposits saliva full of anesthetics and poison while the other syphons up blood.
SLURP!
It's difficult to catch them in the act. They'll scurry back to their crevices faster than it takes to turn on the light and yank off the covers.
So I called Rodney, who's never failed me or any of the people I've recommended him to before.
RODNEY.
YEAH.
IT'S GABRIELLE, IN GREENPOINT. I'VE GOT BEDBUGS AGAIN.
OH SHIT! THEY LOVE YOU. LET ME SEE... CAN YOU HAVE EVERYTHING READY BY TWO O'CLOCK?
REALLY? YOU'LL COME TODAY, ON A SUNDAY? THAT'S WONDERFUL! I THOUGHT I'D HAVE TO WAIT UNTIL NEXT WEEK.
SCRATCH
SCRATCH
Yes, it's true, bedbugs and I have a past.
AAAAA
1998: A guest house in Capitol Hill, Seattle. We didn't have to pay rent as long as the infestation continued. I stayed 'til there were bites on my bites.
2003: A youth hostel in the Latin Quarter, Paris.
J'ADORE VOTRE SANG, MON AMOUR.
HELLO, OLD FRIEND!
2006: The Astral, Greenpoint, Brooklyn. A building famous for housing the Astral Oil Works Refinery workers in the mid-nineteenth century, and bedbugs.
2008: The Astral, again.
WHERE ARE YOU GOING, GABRIELLE?
I LOVE YOU!
AAA
I treated it as just another project to do. I took every piece of bedding and cloth and put them in big black plastic bags, throwing things away that I didn't need.
STUFF
STUFF
And I had to move all the furniture to the middle of the room so Rodney could get at the cracks. Suddenly, it was like I had ten times more stuff.

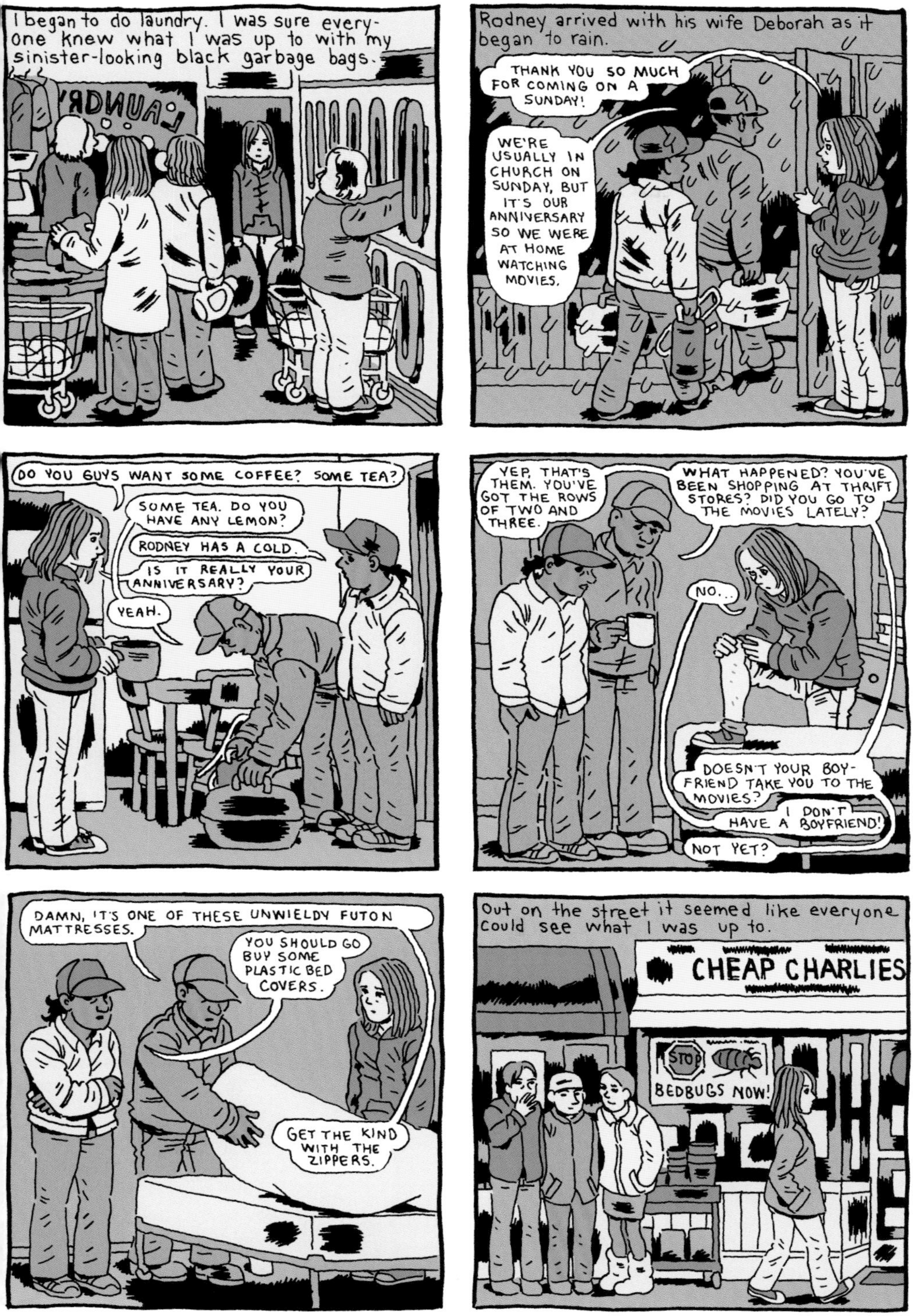
I began to do laundry. I was sure everyone knew what I was up to with my sinister-looking black garbage bags.
LAUNDRY
Rodney arrived with his wife Deborah as it began to rain.
THANK YOU SO MUCH FOR COMING ON A SUNDAY!
WE'RE USUALLY IN CHURCH ON SUNDAY, BUT IT'S OUR ANNIVERSARY SO WE WERE AT HOME WATCHING MOVIES.
DO YOU GUYS WANT SOME COFFEE? SOME TEA?
SOME TEA. DO YOU HAVE ANY LEMON?
RODNEY HAS A COLD.
IS IT REALLY YOUR ANNIVERSARY?
YEAH.
YEP, THAT'S THEM. YOU'VE GOT THE ROWS OF TWO AND THREE.
WHAT HAPPENED? YOU'VE BEEN SHOPPING AT THRIFT STORES? DID YOU GO TO THE MOVIES LATELY?
NO...
DOESN'T YOUR BOYFRIEND TAKE YOU TO THE MOVIES?
I DON'T HAVE A BOYFRIEND!
NOT YET?
DAMN, IT'S ONE OF THESE UNWIELDY FUTON MATTRESSES.
YOU SHOULD GO BUY SOME PLASTIC BED COVERS.
GET THE KIND WITH THE ZIPPERS.
Out on the street it seemed like everyone could see what I was up to.
CHEAP CHARLIES
STOP
BEDBUGS NOW!

DO YOU HAVE PLASTIC BED COVERS? QUEEN SIZED, WITH THE ZIPPERS?

CHARLIE, CAN YOU CHECK IF WE HAVE QUEEN-SIZED PLASTIC BED COVERS?

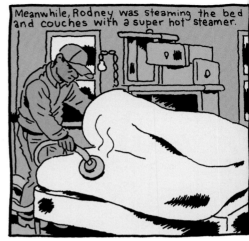

Meanwhile, Rodney was steaming the bed and couches with a super hot steamer.

Then, after filling the outlets and cracks with poison, he saturated the room with a toxic cocktail of chemicals; one to keep any eggs from hatching, one to confuse them and keep them from running away and one to kill them.

I stayed out of the way in the laundromat while Deborah read in the van.

I sat in the van with them to pay.

HOW LONG SHOULD I STAY OUT OF MY APARTMENT?

GIVE IT AT LEAST FOUR HOURS.

I'M SORRY I RUINED YOUR ANNIVERSARY.

I thought I should splurge on a nice meal but all I felt like was Subway.

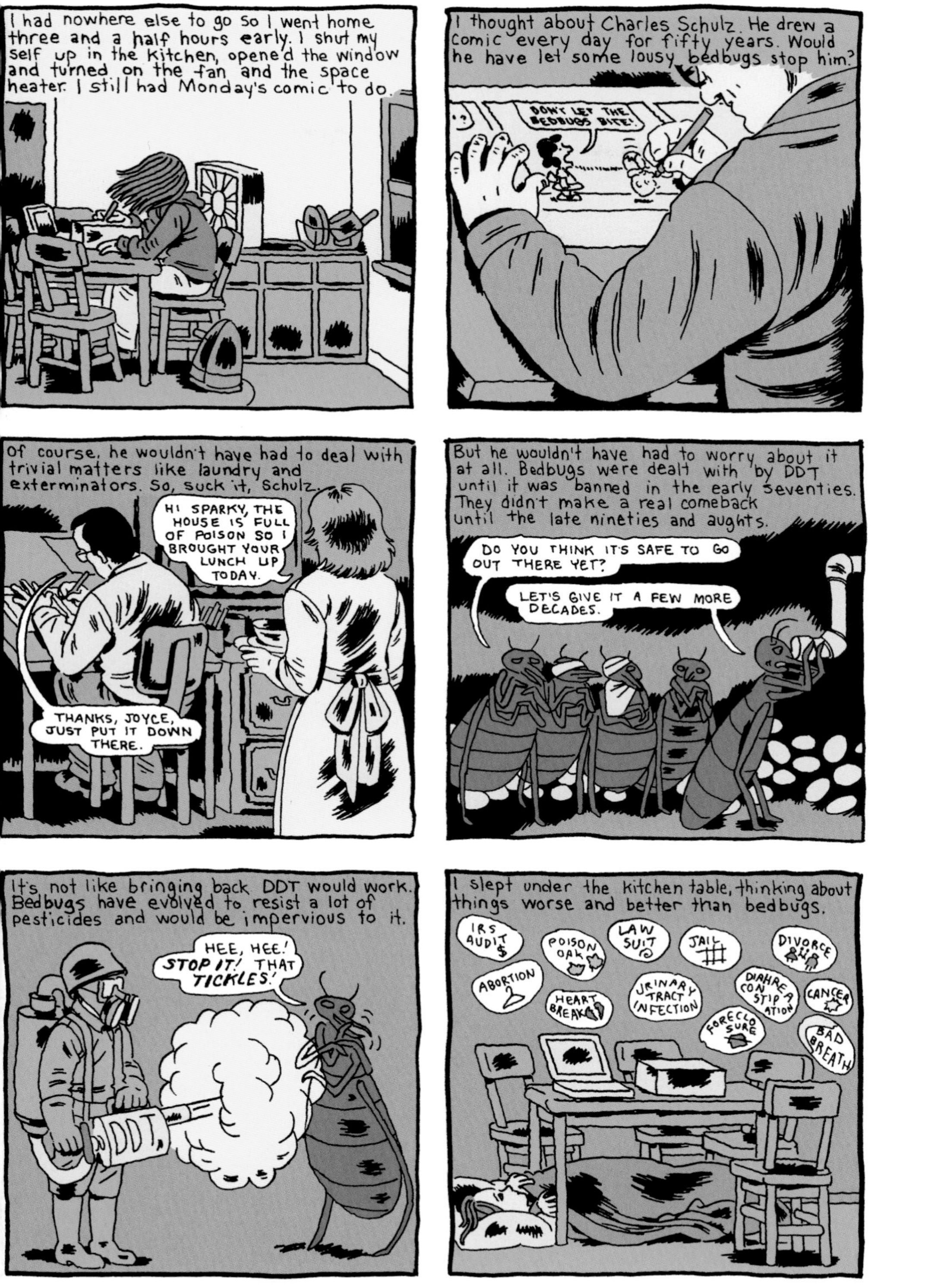
I had nowhere else to go so I went home three and a half hours early. I shut myself up in the kitchen, opene'd the window and turned on the fan and the space heater. I still had Monday's comic to do.
I thought about Charles Schulz. He drew a comic every day for fifty years. Would he have let some lousy bedbugs stop him?
DON'T LET THE BEDBUGS BITE!
Of course, he wouldn't have had to deal with trivial matters like laundry and exterminators. So, suck it, Schulz.
HI SPARKY, THE HOUSE IS FULL OF POISON SO I BROUGHT YOUR LUNCH UP TODAY.
THANKS, JOYCE, JUST PUT IT DOWN THERE.
But he wouldn't have had to worry about it at all. Bedbugs were dealt with by DDT until it was banned in the early seventies. They didn't make a real comeback until the late nineties and aughts.
DO YOU THINK IT'S SAFE TO GO OUT THERE YET?
LET'S GIVE IT A FEW MORE DECADES.
It's not like bringing back DDT would work. Bedbugs have evolved to resist a lot of pesticides and would be impervious to it.
HEE, HEE! STOP IT! THAT TICKLES!
DDT
I slept under the kitchen table, thinking about things worse and better than bedbugs.
IRS AUDIT $
POISON OAK
LAW SUIT
JAIL
DIVORCE
ABORTION
HEART BREAK
URINARY TRACT INFECTION
DIAHREA CON STIP ATION
CANCER
FORECLO SURE
BAD BREATH

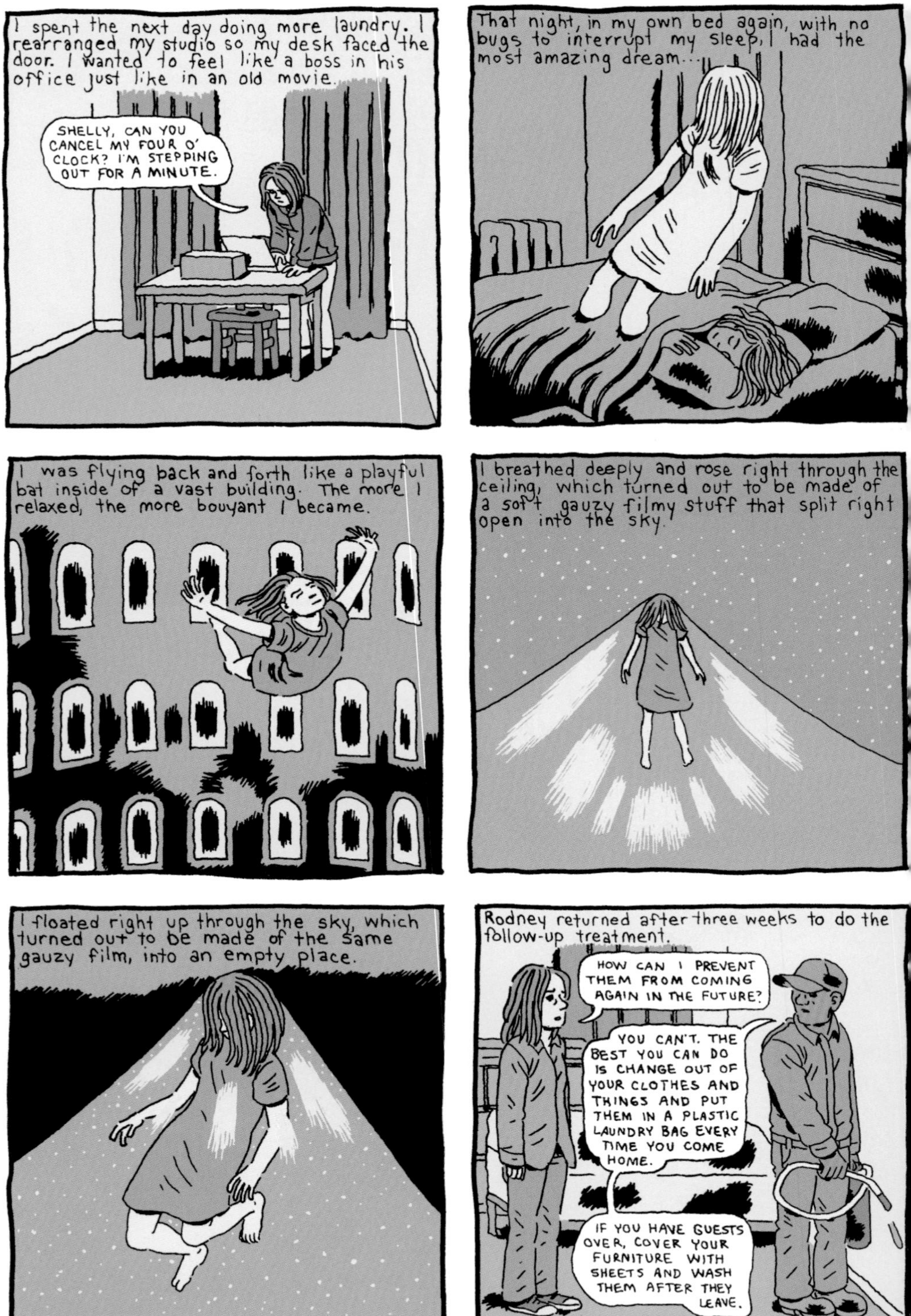
I spent the next day doing more laundry. I rearranged my studio so my desk faced the door. I wanted to feel like a boss in his office just like in an old movie.
SHELLY, CAN YOU CANCEL MY FOUR O'CLOCK? I'M STEPPING OUT FOR A MINUTE.
That night, in my own bed again, with no bugs to interrupt my sleep, I had the most amazing dream...
I was flying back and forth like a playful bat inside of a vast building. The more I relaxed, the more bouyant I became.
I breathed deeply and rose right through the ceiling, which turned out to be made of a soft gauzy filmy stuff that split right open into the sky.
I floated right up through the sky, which turned out to be made of the same gauzy film, into an empty place.
Rodney returned after three weeks to do the follow-up treatment.
HOW CAN I PREVENT THEM FROM COMING AGAIN IN THE FUTURE?
YOU CAN'T. THE BEST YOU CAN DO IS CHANGE OUT OF YOUR CLOTHES AND THINGS AND PUT THEM IN A PLASTIC LAUNDRY BAG EVERY TIME YOU COME HOME.
IF YOU HAVE GUESTS OVER, COVER YOUR FURNITURE WITH SHEETS AND WASH THEM AFTER THEY LEAVE.

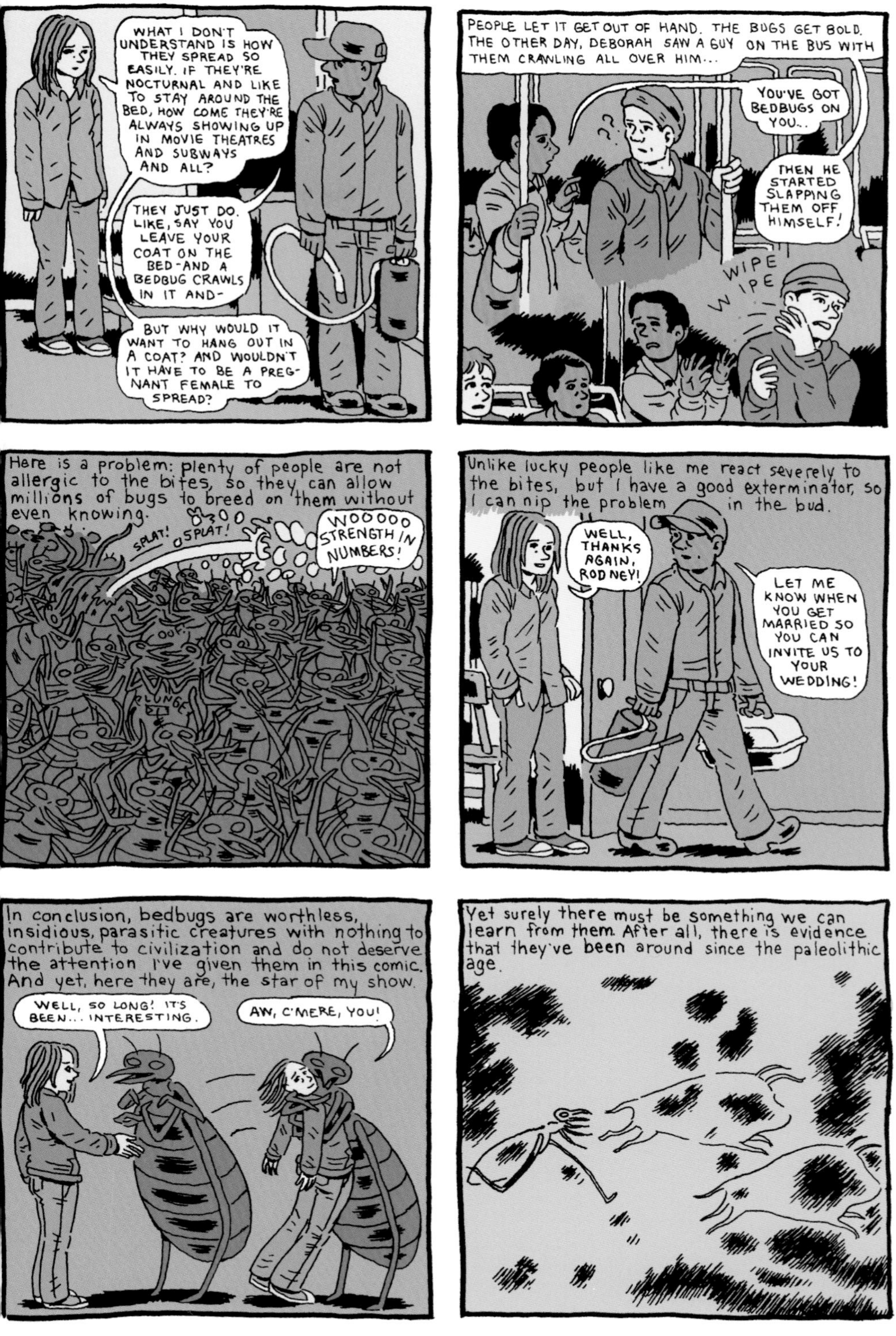
WHAT I DON'T UNDERSTAND IS HOW THEY SPREAD SO EASILY. IF THEY'RE NOCTURNAL AND LIKE TO STAY AROUND THE BED, HOW COME THEY'RE ALWAYS SHOWING UP IN MOVIE THEATRES AND SUBWAYS AND ALL?
THEY JUST DO. LIKE, SAY YOU LEAVE YOUR COAT ON THE BED - AND A BEDBUG CRAWLS IN IT AND-
BUT WHY WOULD IT WANT TO HANG OUT IN A COAT? AND WOULDN'T IT HAVE TO BE A PREGNANT FEMALE TO SPREAD?
PEOPLE LET IT GET OUT OF HAND. THE BUGS GET BOLD. THE OTHER DAY, DEBORAH SAW A GUY ON THE BUS WITH THEM CRAWLING ALL OVER HIM...
YOU'VE GOT BEDBUGS ON YOU...
THEN HE STARTED SLAPPING THEM OFF HIMSELF!
WIPE
WIPE
Here is a problem: plenty of people are not allergic to the bites, so they can allow millions of bugs to breed on them without even knowing.
SPLAT!
SPLAT!
WOOOOO STRENGTH IN NUMBERS!
OOF!
Unlike lucky people like me react severely to the bites, but I have a good exterminator, so I can nip the problem in the bud.
WELL, THANKS AGAIN, RODNEY!
LET ME KNOW WHEN YOU GET MARRIED SO YOU CAN INVITE US TO YOUR WEDDING!
In conclusion, bedbugs are worthless, insidious, parasitic creatures with nothing to contribute to civilization and do not deserve the attention I've given them in this comic. And yet, here they are, the star of my show.
WELL, SO LONG! IT'S BEEN... INTERESTING.
AW, C'MERE, YOU!
Yet surely there must be something we can learn from them. After all, there is evidence that they've been around since the paleolithic age.

Or, at the very least, how to keep them out of your bed. You can quarantine it, move it to the center of the room and cover the legs with vaseline so they can't climb up.

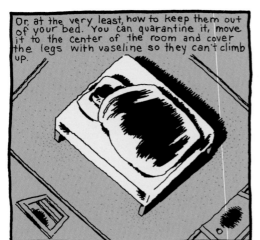

But they are known to climb up the walls and onto the ceiling...

...And drop down on you.

GEE-RONIMO!!!

JOHN PORCELLINO

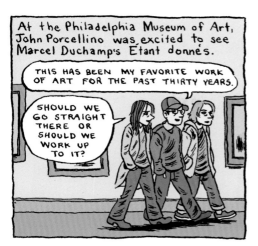

At the Philadelphia Museum of Art, John Porcellino was excited to see Marcel Duchamp's Étant donnés.

THIS HAS BEEN MY FAVORITE WORK OF ART FOR THE PAST THIRTY YEARS.

SHOULD WE GO STRAIGHT THERE OR SHOULD WE WORK UP TO IT?

John told Jen & me that Duchamp retired from art and became a chess champion, but secretly worked on Étant donnés for twenty years.

I'M GETTING READY TO RETIRE, MYSELF. I'M GOING TO SHUT DOWN THE DISTRO COMPANY, STOP TRAVELING AND STAY HOME WITH STEPHANIE AND THE DOGS AND CATS.

Duchamp had the work installed at the museum with the stipulation that they only display it after his death.

ALL I'LL DO IS DRAW COMICS AND MEDITATE...

WE WILL ALL HAVE TO MAKE PILGRIMAGES TO YOU.

WHOA, LOOK AT THAT!

THIS CÉZANNE CHANGED MY LIFE!

SEE HOW THE LINE OF THE TABLE DOESN'T MATCH UP BEHIND THE PITCHER?

WHEN I SAW THAT IN ART SCHOOL I REALIZED THAT THE COMPOSITION OF THE SCENE WAS MORE IMPORTANT THAN RENDERING IT ACCURATELY.

I'M JUST REALIZING THAT NOW!

HERE IT IS!

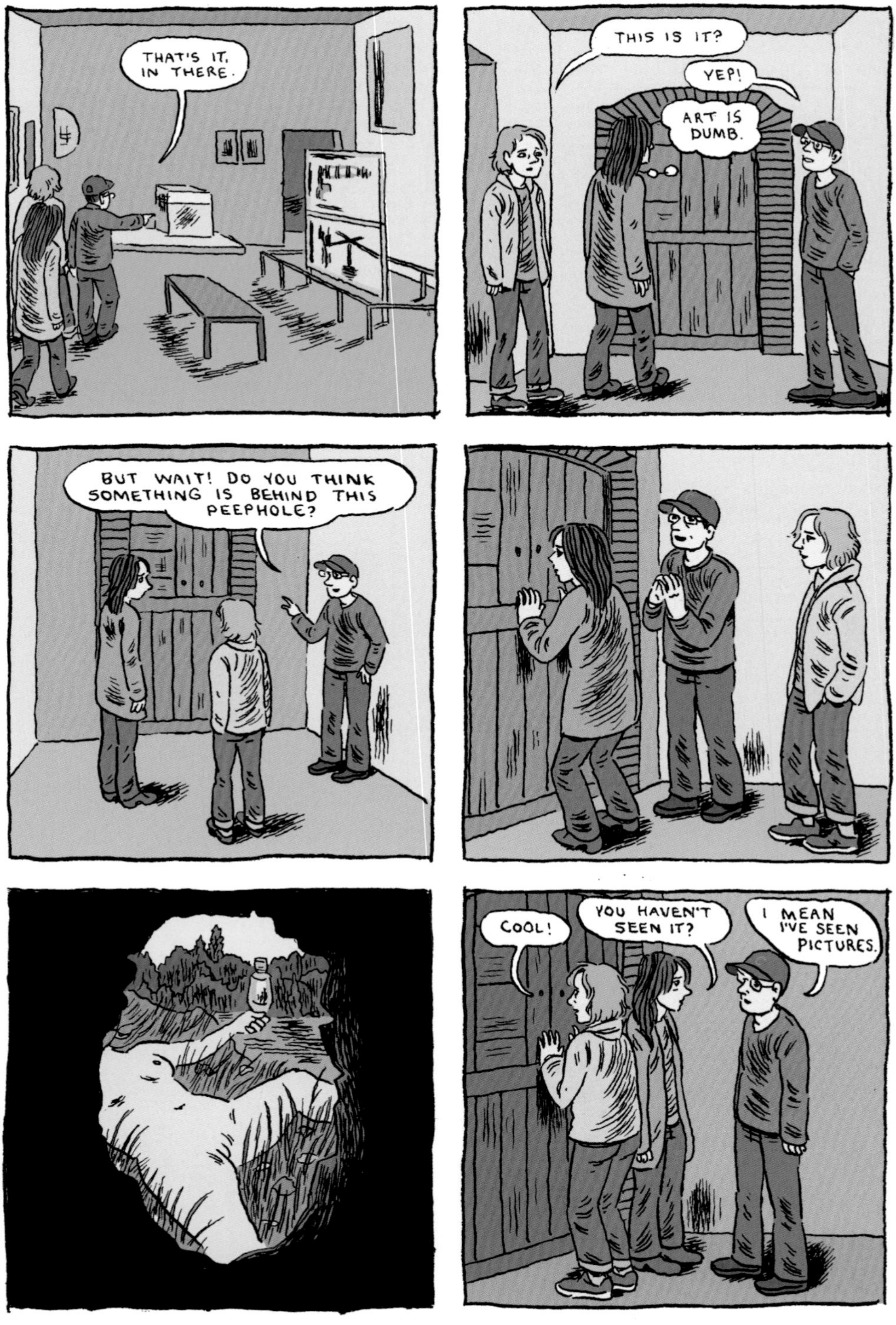
THAT'S IT, IN THERE.
THIS IS IT?
YEP!
ART IS DUMB.
BUT WAIT! DO YOU THINK SOMETHING IS BEHIND THIS PEEPHOLE?
COOL!
YOU HAVEN'T SEEN IT?
I MEAN I'VE SEEN PICTURES.

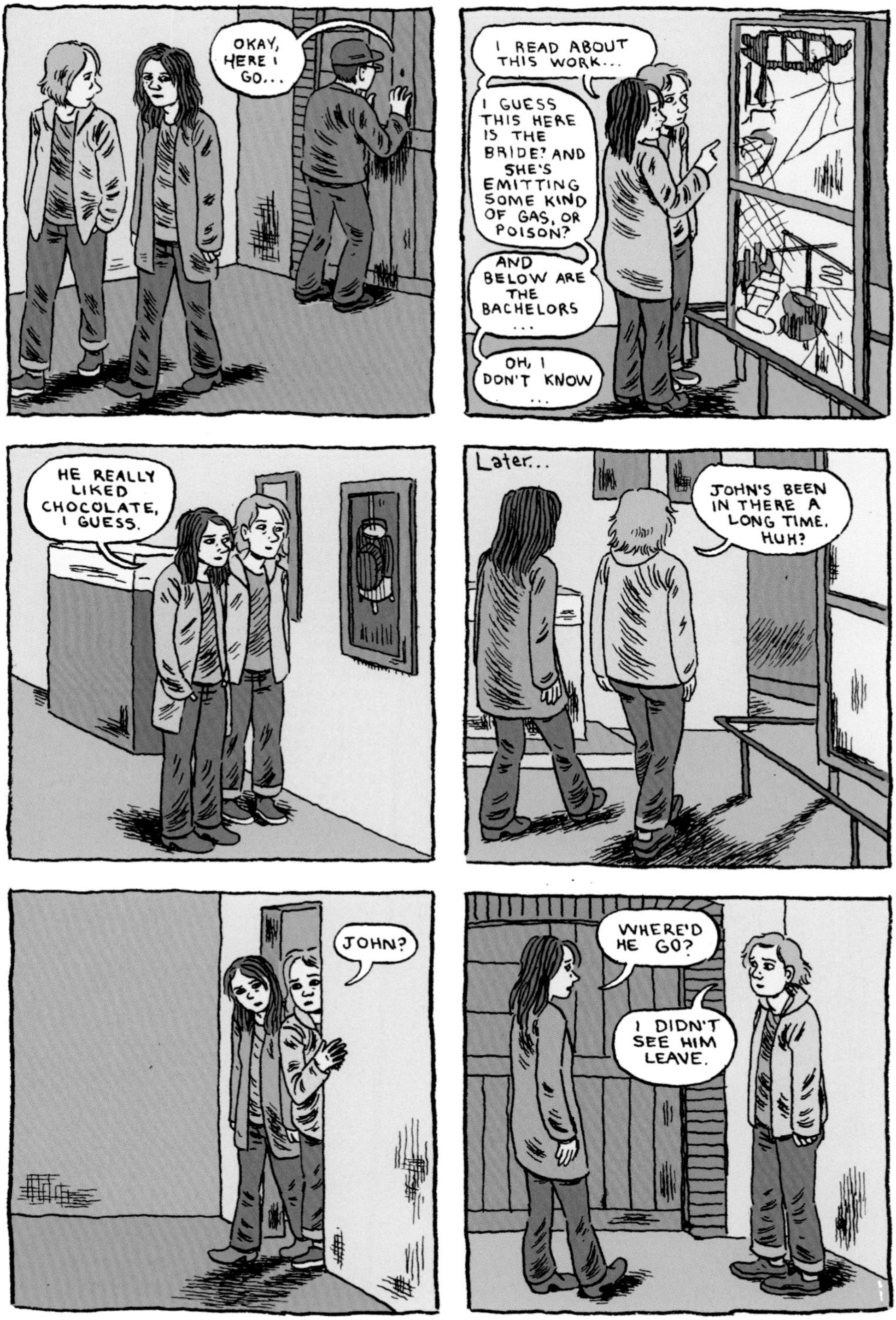
OKAY, HERE I GO...
I READ ABOUT THIS WORK...
I GUESS THIS HERE IS THE BRIDE? AND SHE'S EMITTING SOME KIND OF GAS, OR POISON?
AND BELOW ARE THE BACHELORS ...
OH, I DON'T KNOW ...
HE REALLY LIKED CHOCOLATE, I GUESS.
Later...
JOHN'S BEEN IN THERE A LONG TIME, HUH?
JOHN?
WHERE'D HE GO?
I DIDN'T SEE HIM LEAVE.

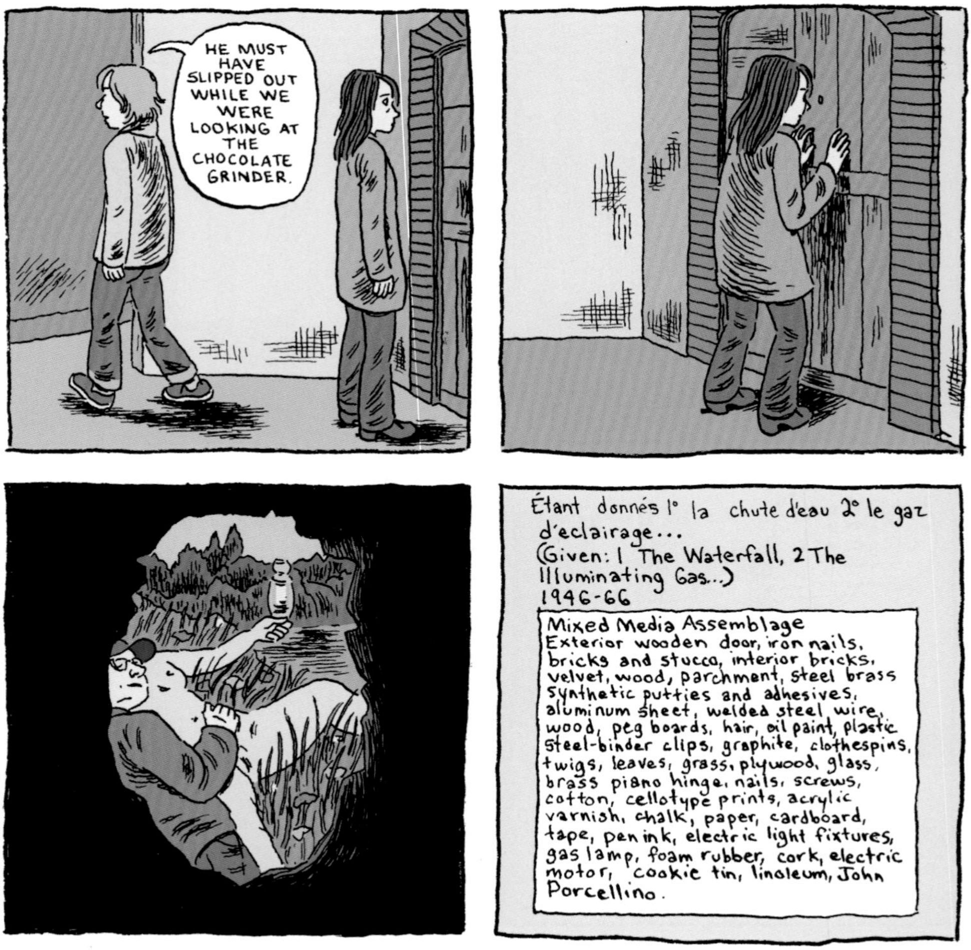
HE MUST HAVE SLIPPED OUT WHILE WE WERE LOOKING AT THE CHOCOLATE GRINDER.
Étant donnés 1° la chute d'eau 2° le gaz d'eclairage...
(Given: 1 The Waterfall, 2 The Illuminating Gas...)
1946-66
Mixed Media Assemblage
Exterior wooden door, iron nails, bricks and stucco, interior bricks, velvet, wood, parchment, steel brass synthetic putties and adhesives, aluminum sheet, welded steel wire, wood, peg boards, hair, oil paint, plastic steel-binder clips, graphite, clothespins, twigs, leaves, grass, plywood, glass, brass piano hinge, nails, screws, cotton, cellotype prints, acrylic varnish, chalk, paper, cardboard, tape, pen ink, electric light fixtures, gas lamp, foam rubber, cork, electric motor, cookie tin, linoleum, John Porcellino.

DOCTOR EMMANUEL

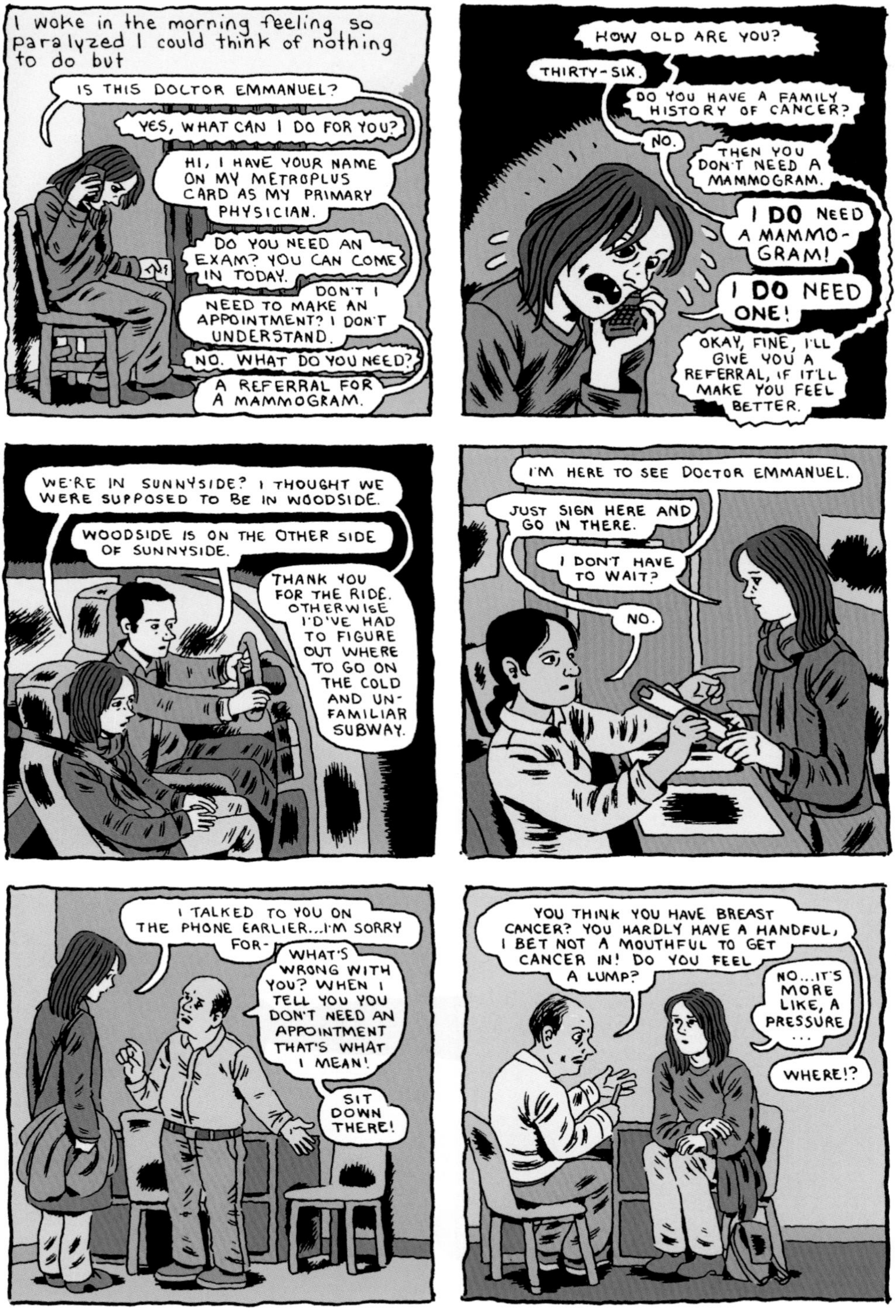
I woke in the morning feeling so paralyzed I could think of nothing to do but
IS THIS DOCTOR EMMANUEL?
YES, WHAT CAN I DO FOR YOU?
HI, I HAVE YOUR NAME ON MY METROPLUS CARD AS MY PRIMARY PHYSICIAN.
DO YOU NEED AN EXAM? YOU CAN COME IN TODAY.
DON'T I NEED TO MAKE AN APPOINTMENT? I DON'T UNDERSTAND.
NO. WHAT DO YOU NEED?
A REFERRAL FOR A MAMMOGRAM.
HOW OLD ARE YOU?
THIRTY-SIX.
DO YOU HAVE A FAMILY HISTORY OF CANCER?
NO.
THEN YOU DON'T NEED A MAMMOGRAM.
I DO NEED A MAMMO-GRAM!
I DO NEED ONE!
OKAY, FINE, I'LL GIVE YOU A REFERRAL, IF IT'LL MAKE YOU FEEL BETTER.
WE'RE IN SUNNYSIDE? I THOUGHT WE WERE SUPPOSED TO BE IN WOODSIDE.
WOODSIDE IS ON THE OTHER SIDE OF SUNNYSIDE.
THANK YOU FOR THE RIDE. OTHERWISE I'D'VE HAD TO FIGURE OUT WHERE TO GO ON THE COLD AND UN-FAMILIAR SUBWAY.
I'M HERE TO SEE DOCTOR EMMANUEL.
JUST SIGN HERE AND GO IN THERE.
I DON'T HAVE TO WAIT?
NO.
I TALKED TO YOU ON THE PHONE EARLIER...I'M SORRY FOR-
WHAT'S WRONG WITH YOU? WHEN I TELL YOU YOU DON'T NEED AN APPOINTMENT THAT'S WHAT I MEAN!
SIT DOWN THERE!
YOU THINK YOU HAVE BREAST CANCER? YOU HARDLY HAVE A HANDFUL, I BET NOT A MOUTHFUL TO GET CANCER IN! DO YOU FEEL A LUMP?
NO...IT'S MORE LIKE, A PRESSURE ...
WHERE!?

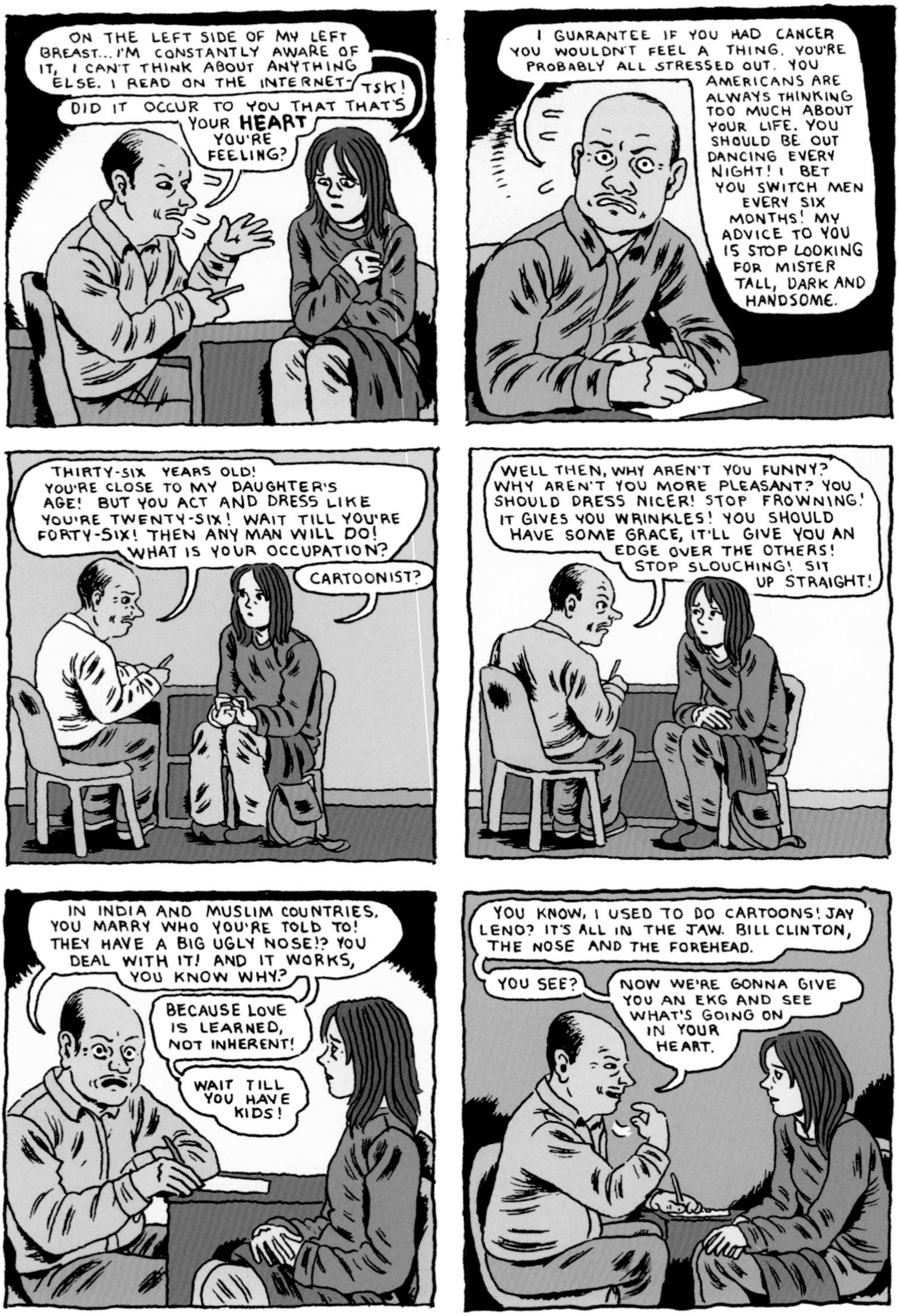
ON THE LEFT SIDE OF MY LEFT BREAST... I'M CONSTANTLY AWARE OF IT, I CAN'T THINK ABOUT ANYTHING ELSE. I READ ON THE INTERNET-
TSK!
DID IT OCCUR TO YOU THAT THAT'S YOUR **HEART** YOU'RE FEELING?
I GUARANTEE IF YOU HAD CANCER YOU WOULDN'T FEEL A THING. YOU'RE PROBABLY ALL STRESSED OUT. YOU AMERICANS ARE ALWAYS THINKING TOO MUCH ABOUT YOUR LIFE. YOU SHOULD BE OUT DANCING EVERY NIGHT! I BET YOU SWITCH MEN EVERY SIX MONTHS! MY ADVICE TO YOU IS STOP LOOKING FOR MISTER TALL, DARK AND HANDSOME.
THIRTY-SIX YEARS OLD! YOU'RE CLOSE TO MY DAUGHTER'S AGE! BUT YOU ACT AND DRESS LIKE YOU'RE TWENTY-SIX! WAIT TILL YOU'RE FORTY-SIX! THEN ANY MAN WILL DO! WHAT IS YOUR OCCUPATION?
CARTOONIST?
WELL THEN, WHY AREN'T YOU FUNNY? WHY AREN'T YOU MORE PLEASANT? YOU SHOULD DRESS NICER! STOP FROWNING! IT GIVES YOU WRINKLES! YOU SHOULD HAVE SOME GRACE, IT'LL GIVE YOU AN EDGE OVER THE OTHERS! STOP SLOUCHING! SIT UP STRAIGHT!
IN INDIA AND MUSLIM COUNTRIES, YOU MARRY WHO YOU'RE TOLD TO! THEY HAVE A BIG UGLY NOSE!? YOU DEAL WITH IT! AND IT WORKS, YOU KNOW WHY?
BECAUSE LOVE IS LEARNED, NOT INHERENT!
WAIT TILL YOU HAVE KIDS!
YOU KNOW, I USED TO DO CARTOONS! JAY LENO? IT'S ALL IN THE JAW. BILL CLINTON, THE NOSE AND THE FOREHEAD.
YOU SEE?
NOW WE'RE GONNA GIVE YOU AN EKG AND SEE WHAT'S GOING ON IN YOUR HEART.

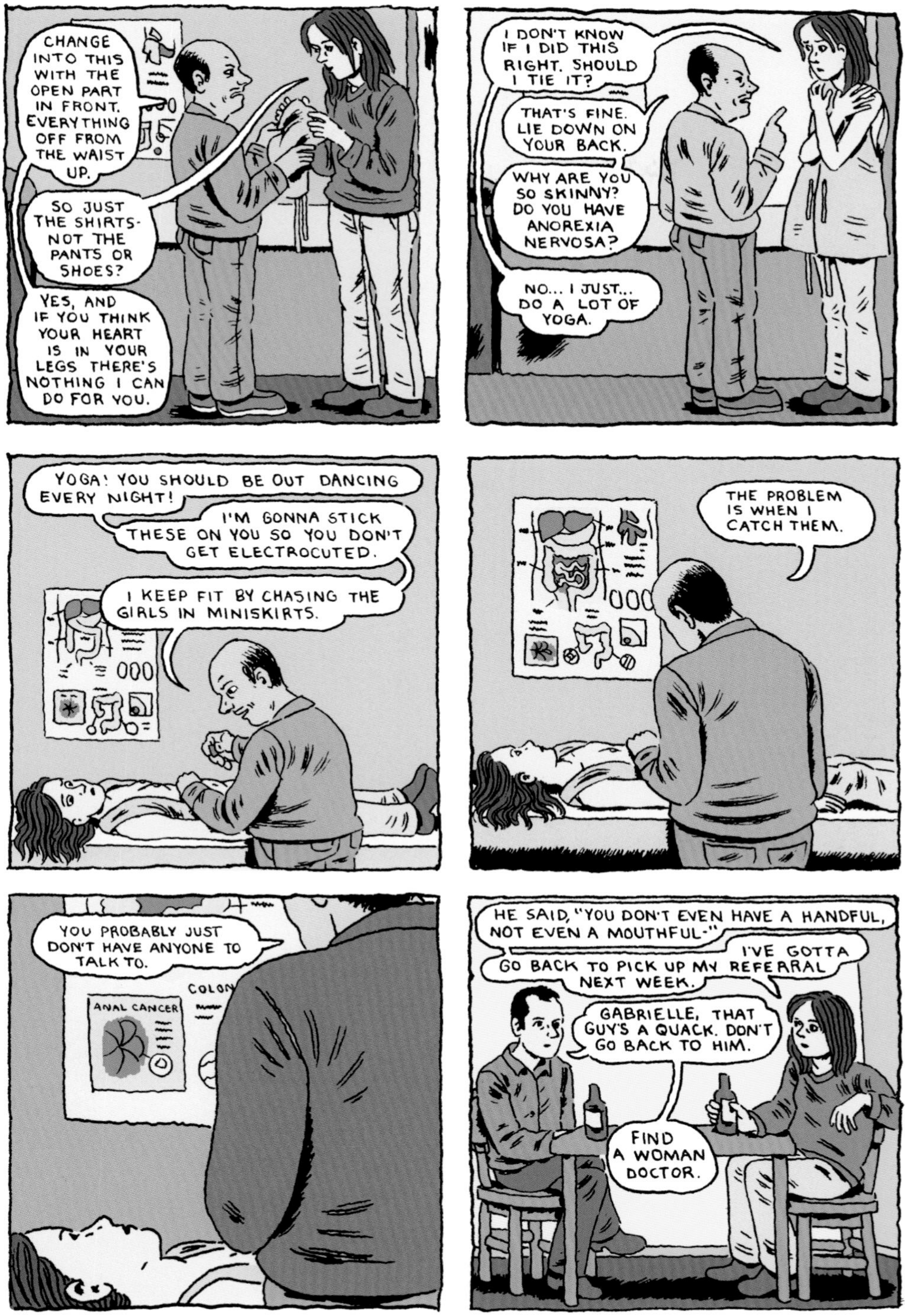
CHANGE INTO THIS WITH THE OPEN PART IN FRONT. EVERYTHING OFF FROM THE WAIST UP.
SO JUST THE SHIRTS- NOT THE PANTS OR SHOES?
YES, AND IF YOU THINK YOUR HEART IS IN YOUR LEGS THERE'S NOTHING I CAN DO FOR YOU.
I DON'T KNOW IF I DID THIS RIGHT. SHOULD I TIE IT?
THAT'S FINE. LIE DOWN ON YOUR BACK.
WHY ARE YOU SO SKINNY? DO YOU HAVE ANOREXIA NERVOSA?
NO... I JUST... DO A LOT OF YOGA.
YOGA! YOU SHOULD BE OUT DANCING EVERY NIGHT!
I'M GONNA STICK THESE ON YOU SO YOU DON'T GET ELECTROCUTED.
I KEEP FIT BY CHASING THE GIRLS IN MINISKIRTS.
THE PROBLEM IS WHEN I CATCH THEM.
YOU PROBABLY JUST DON'T HAVE ANYONE TO TALK TO.
ANAL CANCER
COLON
HE SAID, "YOU DON'T EVEN HAVE A HANDFUL, NOT EVEN A MOUTHFUL-"
I'VE GOTTA GO BACK TO PICK UP MY REFERRAL NEXT WEEK.
GABRIELLE, THAT GUY'S A QUACK. DON'T GO BACK TO HIM.
FIND A WOMAN DOCTOR.

CAROLINE

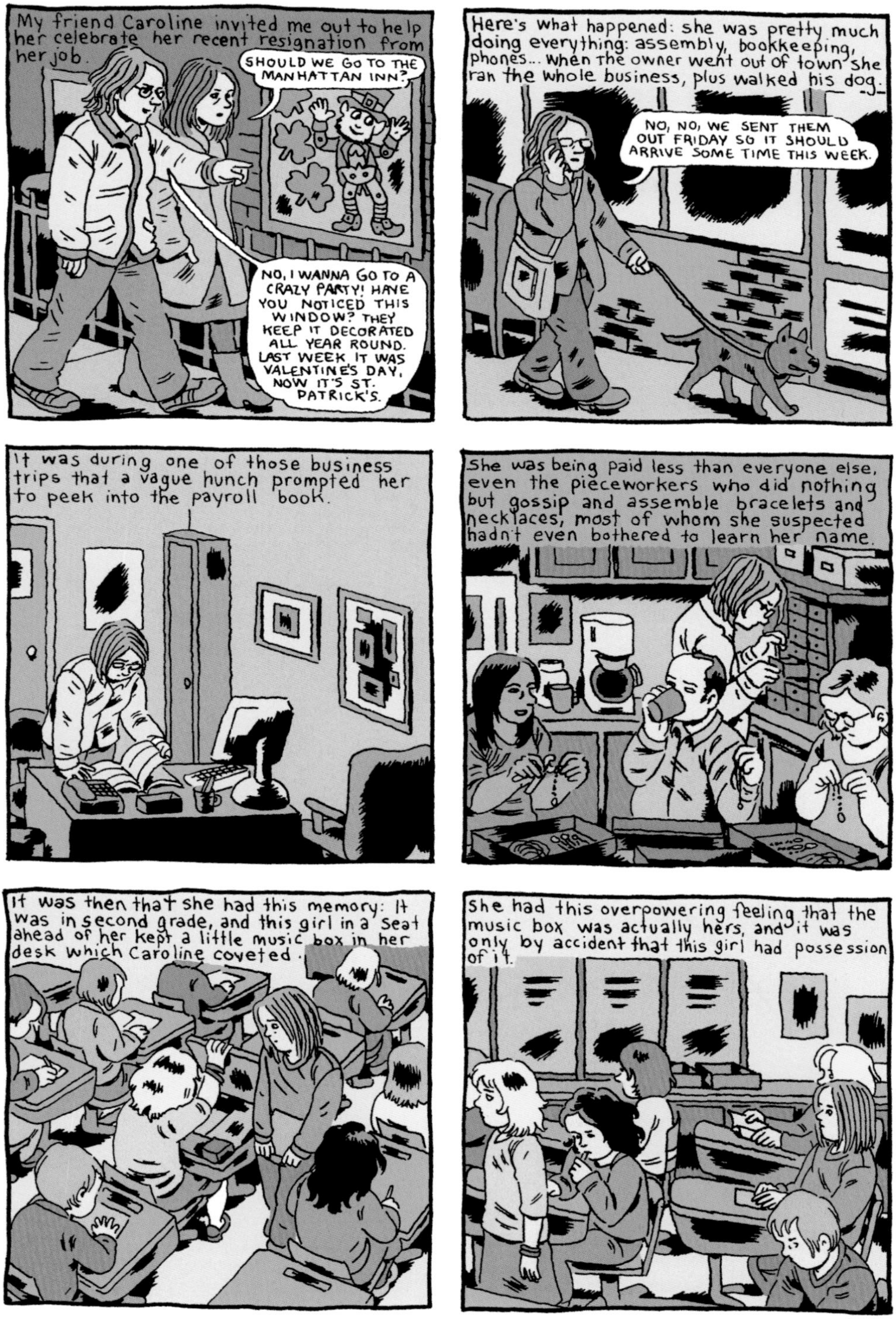

My friend Caroline invited me out to help her celebrate her recent resignation from her job.
SHOULD WE GO TO THE MANHATTAN INN?
NO, I WANNA GO TO A CRAZY PARTY! HAVE YOU NOTICED THIS WINDOW? THEY KEEP IT DECORATED ALL YEAR ROUND. LAST WEEK IT WAS VALENTINE'S DAY, NOW IT'S ST. PATRICK'S.
Here's what happened: she was pretty much doing everything: assembly, bookkeeping, phones... when the owner went out of town she ran the whole business, plus walked his dog.
NO, NO, WE SENT THEM OUT FRIDAY SO IT SHOULD ARRIVE SOME TIME THIS WEEK.
It was during one of those business trips that a vague hunch prompted her to peek into the payroll book.
She was being paid less than everyone else, even the pieceworkers who did nothing but gossip and assemble bracelets and necklaces, most of whom she suspected hadn't even bothered to learn her name.
It was then that she had this memory: It was in second grade, and this girl in a seat ahead of her kept a little music box in her desk which Caroline coveted.
She had this overpowering feeling that the music box was actually hers, and it was only by accident that this girl had possession of it.

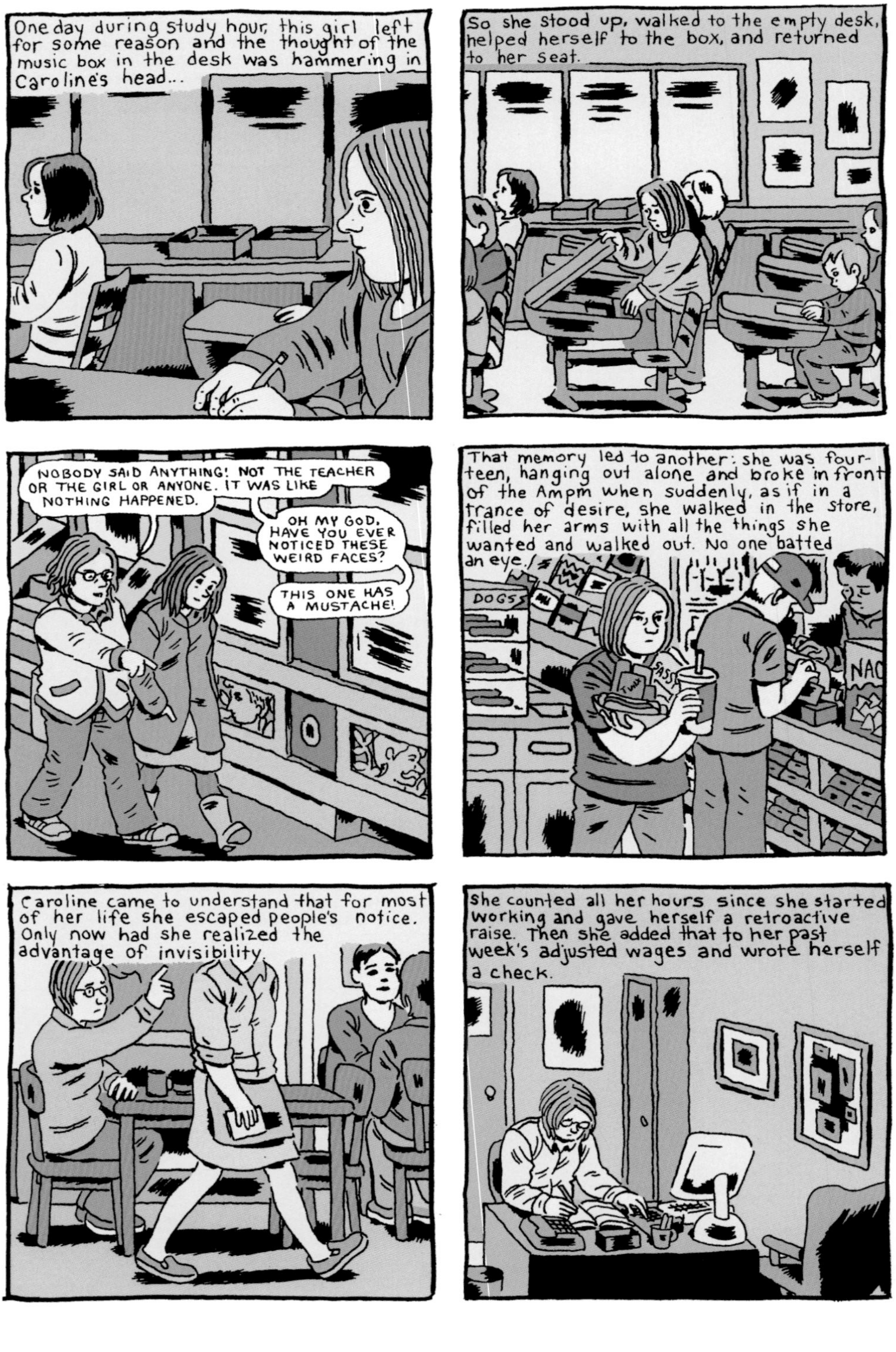
One day during study hour, this girl left for some reason and the thought of the music box in the desk was hammering in Caroline's head...
So she stood up, walked to the empty desk, helped herself to the box, and returned to her seat.
NOBODY SAID ANYTHING! NOT THE TEACHER OR THE GIRL OR ANYONE. IT WAS LIKE NOTHING HAPPENED.
OH MY GOD, HAVE YOU EVER NOTICED THESE WEIRD FACES?
THIS ONE HAS A MUSTACHE!
That memory led to another: she was fourteen, hanging out alone and broke in front of the Ampm when suddenly, as if in a trance of desire, she walked in the store, filled her arms with all the things she wanted and walked out. No one batted an eye.
DOGS
Caroline came to understand that for most of her life she escaped people's notice. Only now had she realized the advantage of invisibility.
She counted all her hours since she started working and gave herself a retroactive raise. Then she added that to her past week's adjusted wages and wrote herself a check.

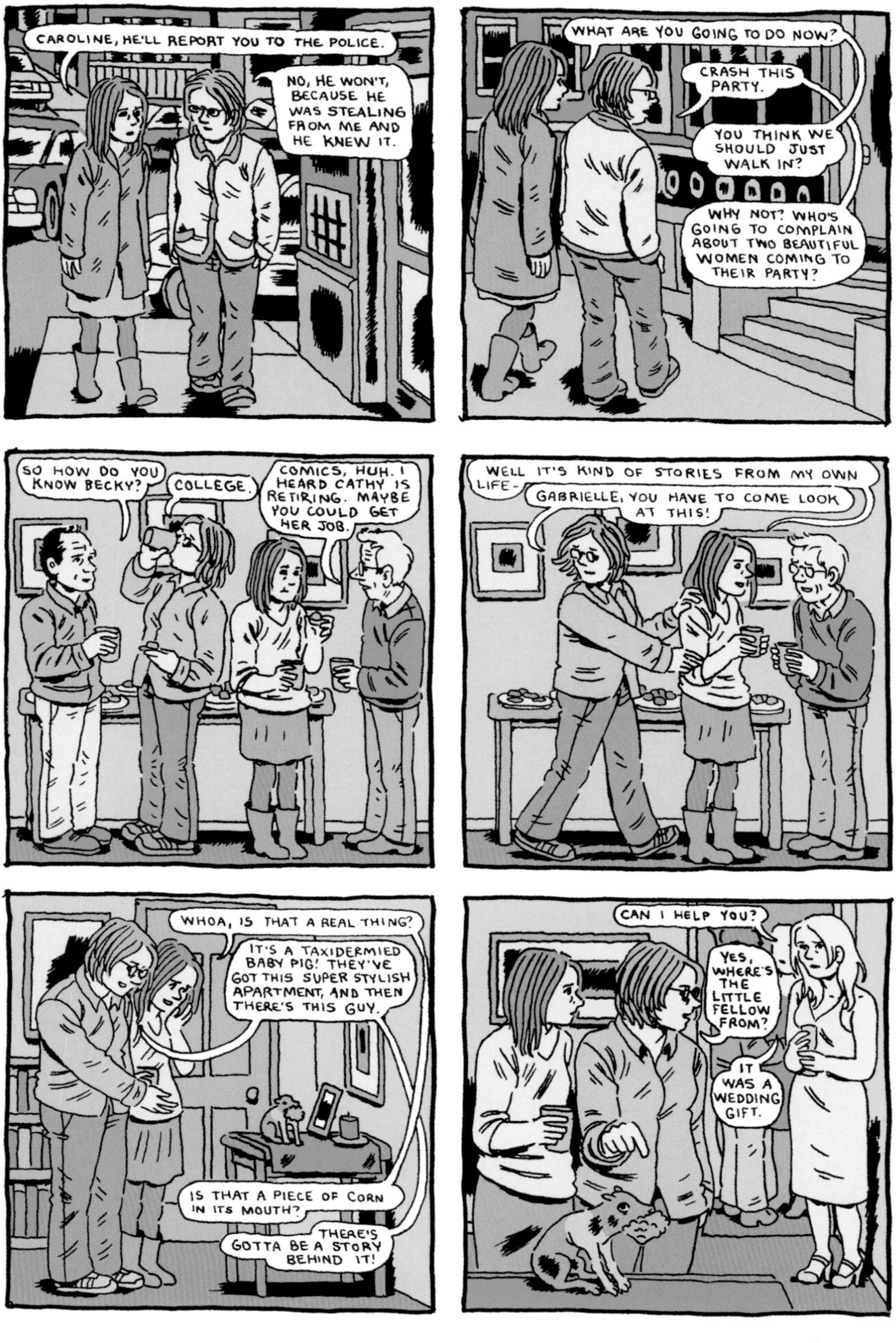
CAROLINE, HE'LL REPORT YOU TO THE POLICE.
NO, HE WON'T, BECAUSE HE WAS STEALING FROM ME AND HE KNEW IT.
WHAT ARE YOU GOING TO DO NOW?
CRASH THIS PARTY.
YOU THINK WE SHOULD JUST WALK IN?
WHY NOT? WHO'S GOING TO COMPLAIN ABOUT TWO BEAUTIFUL WOMEN COMING TO THEIR PARTY?
SO HOW DO YOU KNOW BECKY?
COLLEGE.
COMICS, HUH. I HEARD CATHY IS RETIRING. MAYBE YOU COULD GET HER JOB.
WELL IT'S KIND OF STORIES FROM MY OWN LIFE-
GABRIELLE, YOU HAVE TO COME LOOK AT THIS!
WHOA, IS THAT A REAL THING?
IT'S A TAXIDERMIED BABY PIG! THEY'VE GOT THIS SUPER STYLISH APARTMENT, AND THEN THERE'S THIS GUY.
IS THAT A PIECE OF CORN IN ITS MOUTH?
THERE'S GOTTA BE A STORY BEHIND IT!
CAN I HELP YOU?
YES, WHERE'S THE LITTLE FELLOW FROM?
IT WAS A WEDDING GIFT.

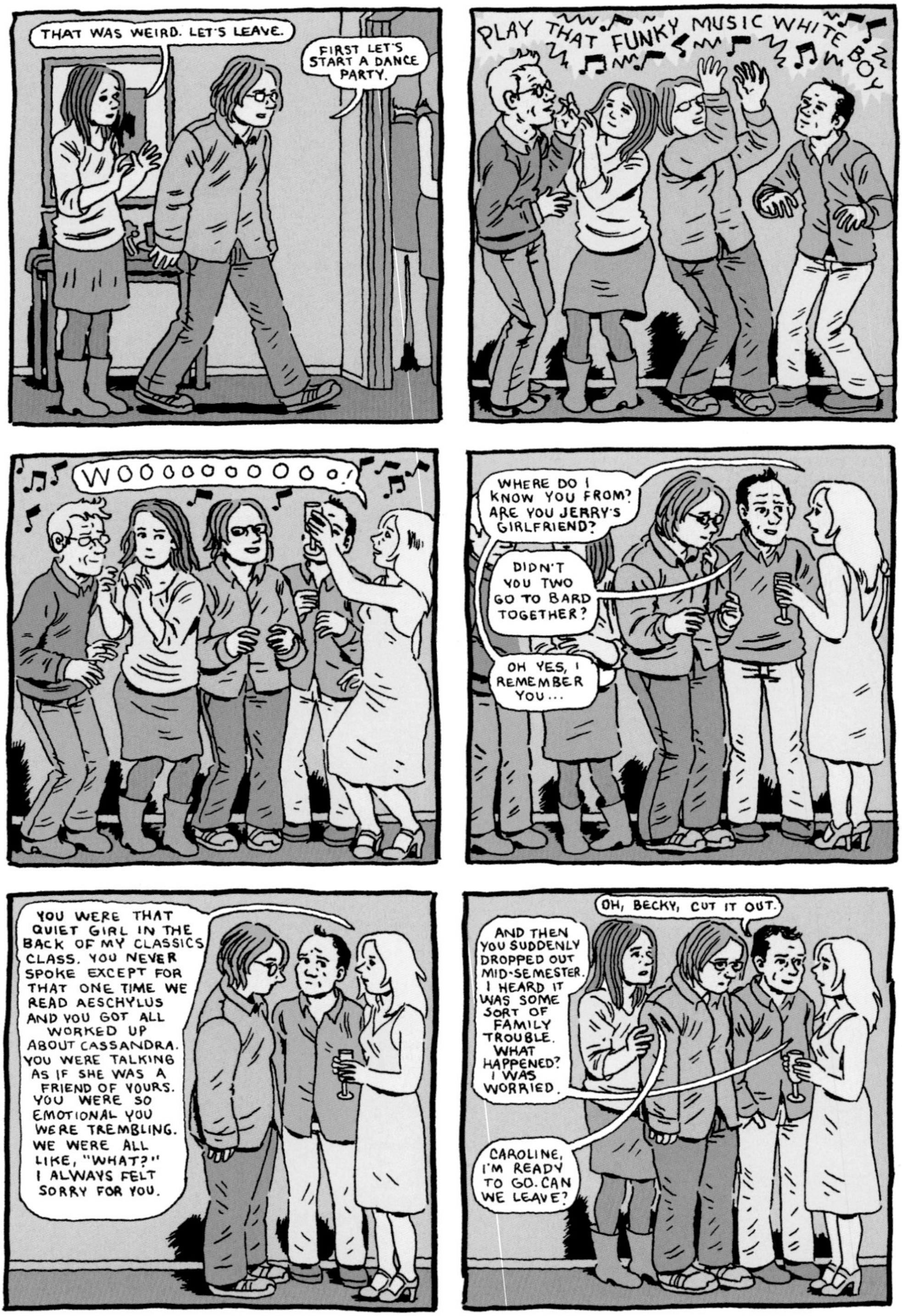
THAT WAS WEIRD. LET'S LEAVE.
FIRST LET'S START A DANCE PARTY.
PLAY THAT FUNKY MUSIC WHITE BOY
WOOOOOOOOOOo!
WHERE DO I KNOW YOU FROM? ARE YOU JERRY'S GIRLFRIEND?
DIDN'T YOU TWO GO TO BARD TOGETHER?
OH YES, I REMEMBER YOU...
YOU WERE THAT QUIET GIRL IN THE BACK OF MY CLASSICS CLASS. YOU NEVER SPOKE EXCEPT FOR THAT ONE TIME WE READ AESCHYLUS AND YOU GOT ALL WORKED UP ABOUT CASSANDRA. YOU WERE TALKING AS IF SHE WAS A FRIEND OF YOURS. YOU WERE SO EMOTIONAL YOU WERE TREMBLING. WE WERE ALL LIKE, "WHAT?" I ALWAYS FELT SORRY FOR YOU.
OH, BECKY, CUT IT OUT.
AND THEN YOU SUDDENLY DROPPED OUT MID-SEMESTER. I HEARD IT WAS SOME SORT OF FAMILY TROUBLE. WHAT HAPPENED? I WAS WORRIED.
CAROLINE, I'M READY TO GO. CAN WE LEAVE?

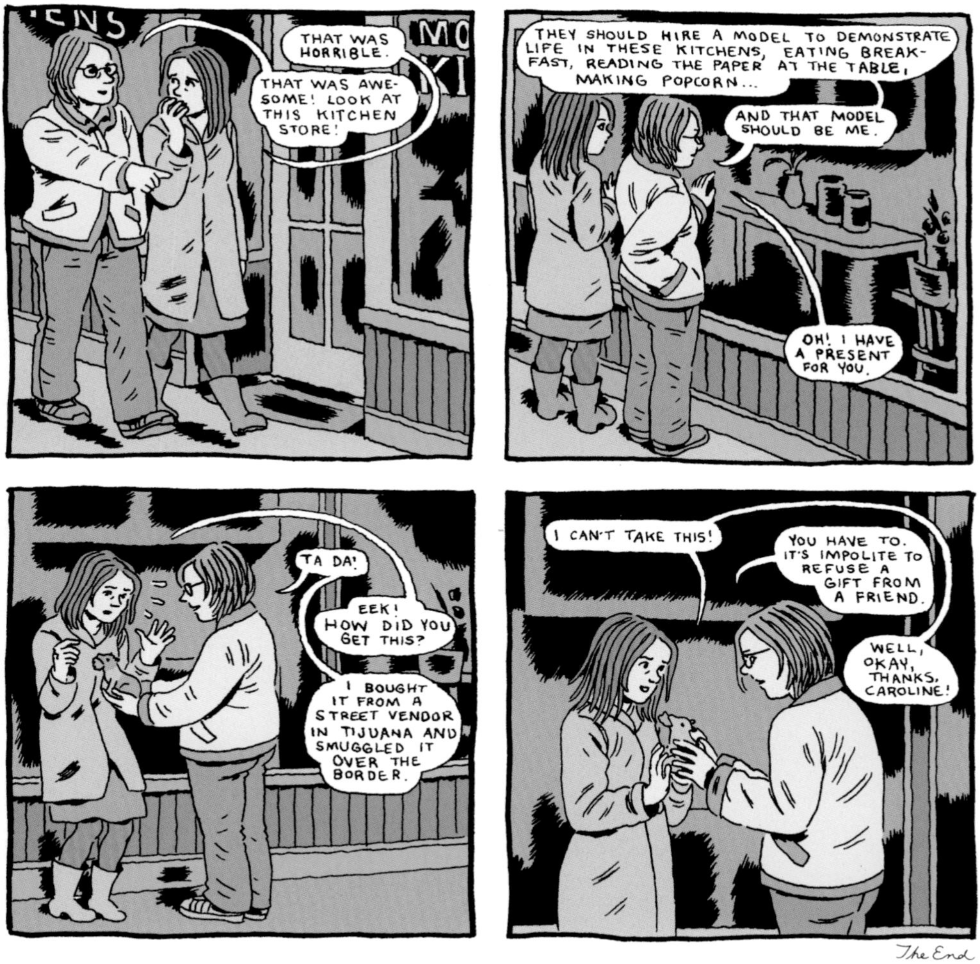
THAT WAS HORRIBLE.
THAT WAS AWESOME! LOOK AT THIS KITCHEN STORE!
THEY SHOULD HIRE A MODEL TO DEMONSTRATE LIFE IN THESE KITCHENS, EATING BREAKFAST, READING THE PAPER AT THE TABLE, MAKING POPCORN...
AND THAT MODEL SHOULD BE ME.
OH! I HAVE A PRESENT FOR YOU.
TA DA!
EEK! HOW DID YOU GET THIS?
I BOUGHT IT FROM A STREET VENDOR IN TIJUANA AND SMUGGLED IT OVER THE BORDER.
I CAN'T TAKE THIS!
YOU HAVE TO. IT'S IMPOLITE TO REFUSE A GIFT FROM A FRIEND.
WELL, OKAY, THANKS, CAROLINE!
The End

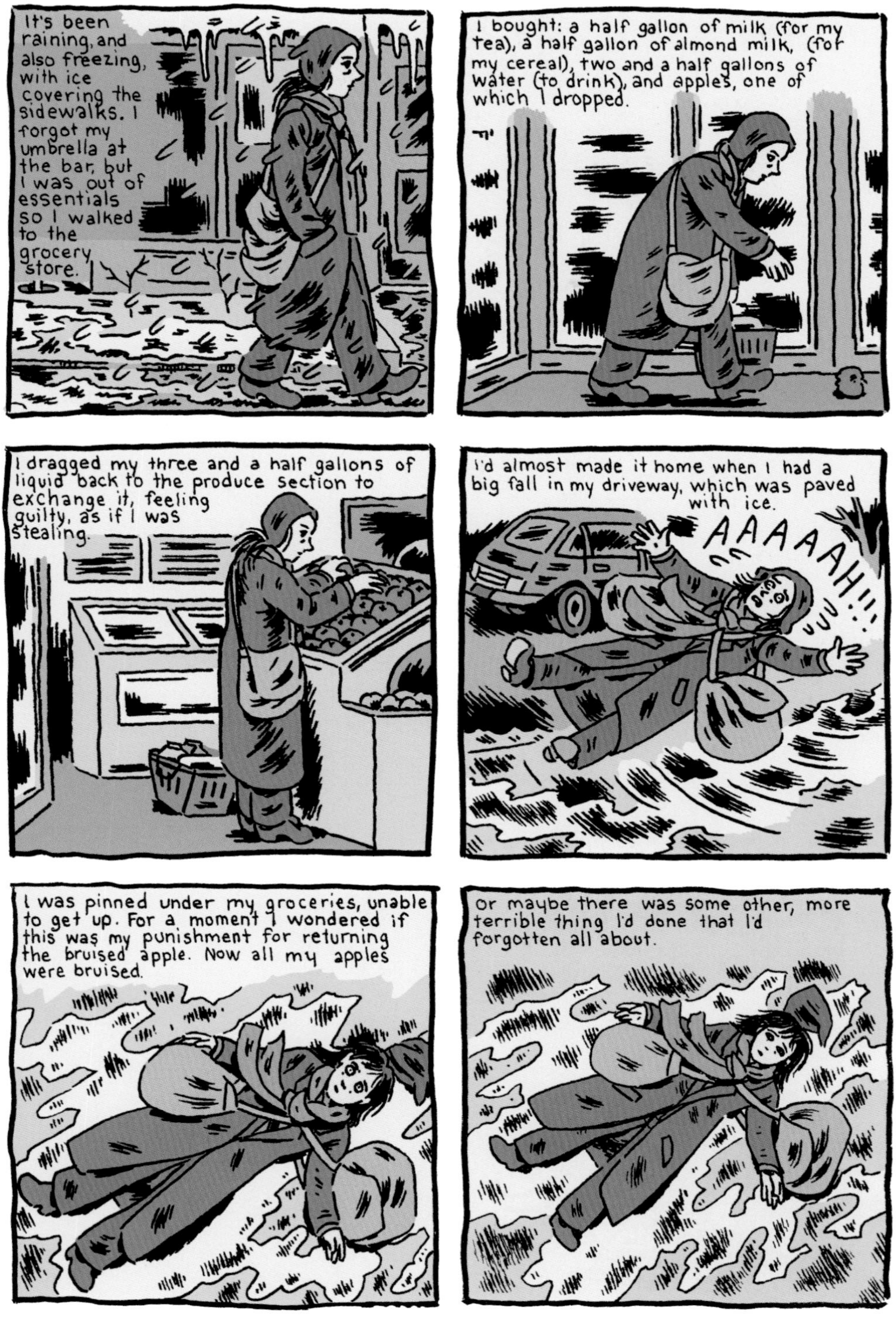
It's been raining, and also freezing, with ice covering the sidewalks. I forgot my umbrella at the bar, but I was out of essentials so I walked to the grocery store.
I bought: a half gallon of milk (for my tea), a half gallon of almond milk, (for my cereal), two and a half gallons of water (to drink), and apples, one of which I dropped.
I dragged my three and a half gallons of liquid back to the produce section to exchange it, feeling guilty, as if I was stealing.
I'd almost made it home when I had a big fall in my driveway, which was paved with ice.
AAAAAH!!!
I was pinned under my groceries, unable to get up. For a moment I wondered if this was my punishment for returning the bruised apple. Now all my apples were bruised.
Or maybe there was some other, more terrible thing I'd done that I'd forgotten all about.

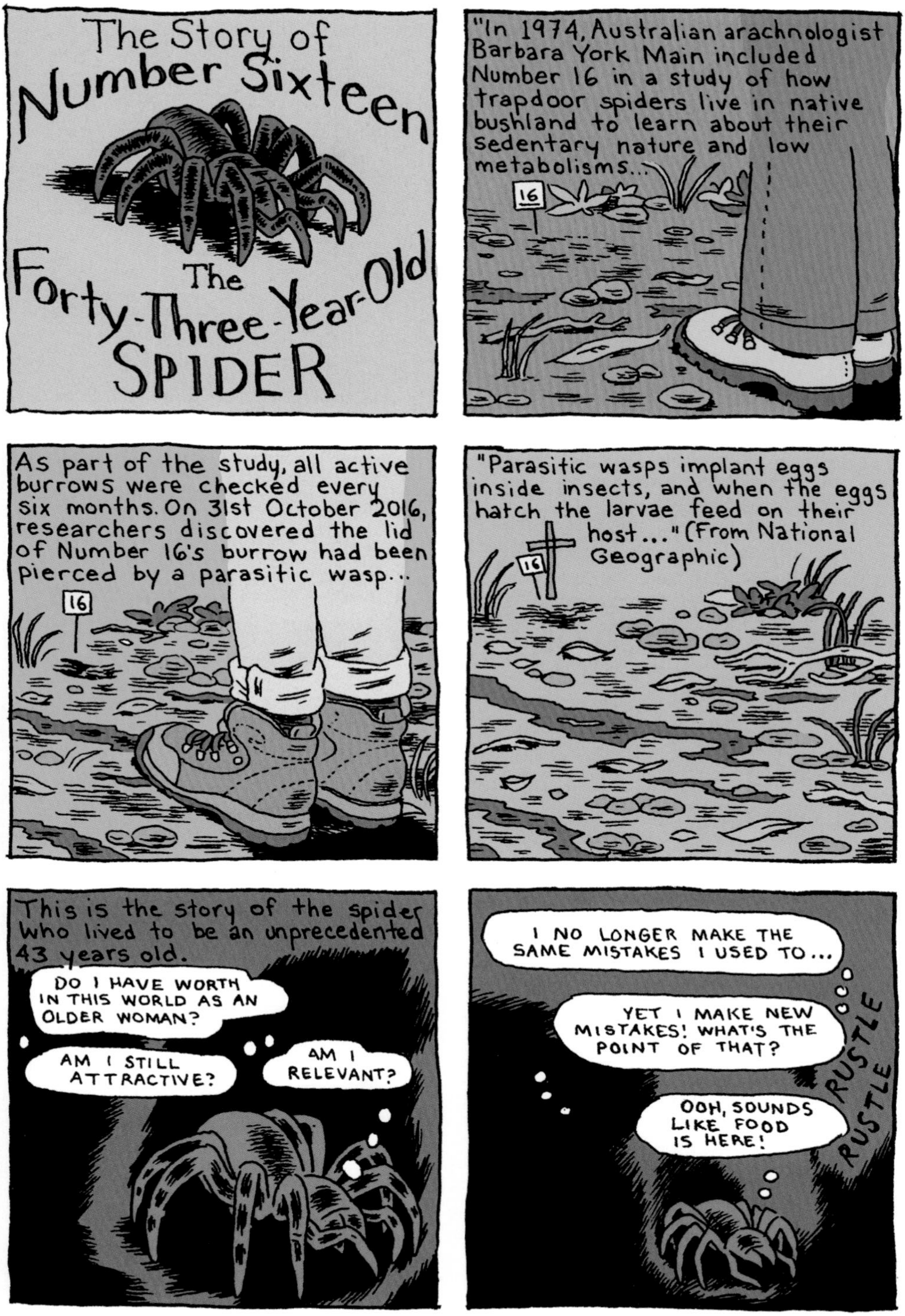
The Story of
Number Sixteen
The
Forty-Three-Year-Old
SPIDER
"In 1974, Australian arachnologist Barbara York Main included Number 16 in a study of how trapdoor spiders live in native bushland to learn about their sedentary nature and low metabolisms...
16
As part of the study, all active burrows were checked every six months. On 31st October 2016, researchers discovered the lid of Number 16's burrow had been pierced by a parasitic wasp...
16
"Parasitic wasps implant eggs inside insects, and when the eggs hatch the larvae feed on their host..." (From National Geographic)
16
This is the story of the spider who lived to be an unprecedented 43 years old.
DO I HAVE WORTH IN THIS WORLD AS AN OLDER WOMAN?
AM I STILL ATTRACTIVE?
AM I RELEVANT?
I NO LONGER MAKE THE SAME MISTAKES I USED TO...
YET I MAKE NEW MISTAKES! WHAT'S THE POINT OF THAT?
RUSTLE RUSTLE
OOH, SOUNDS LIKE FOOD IS HERE!

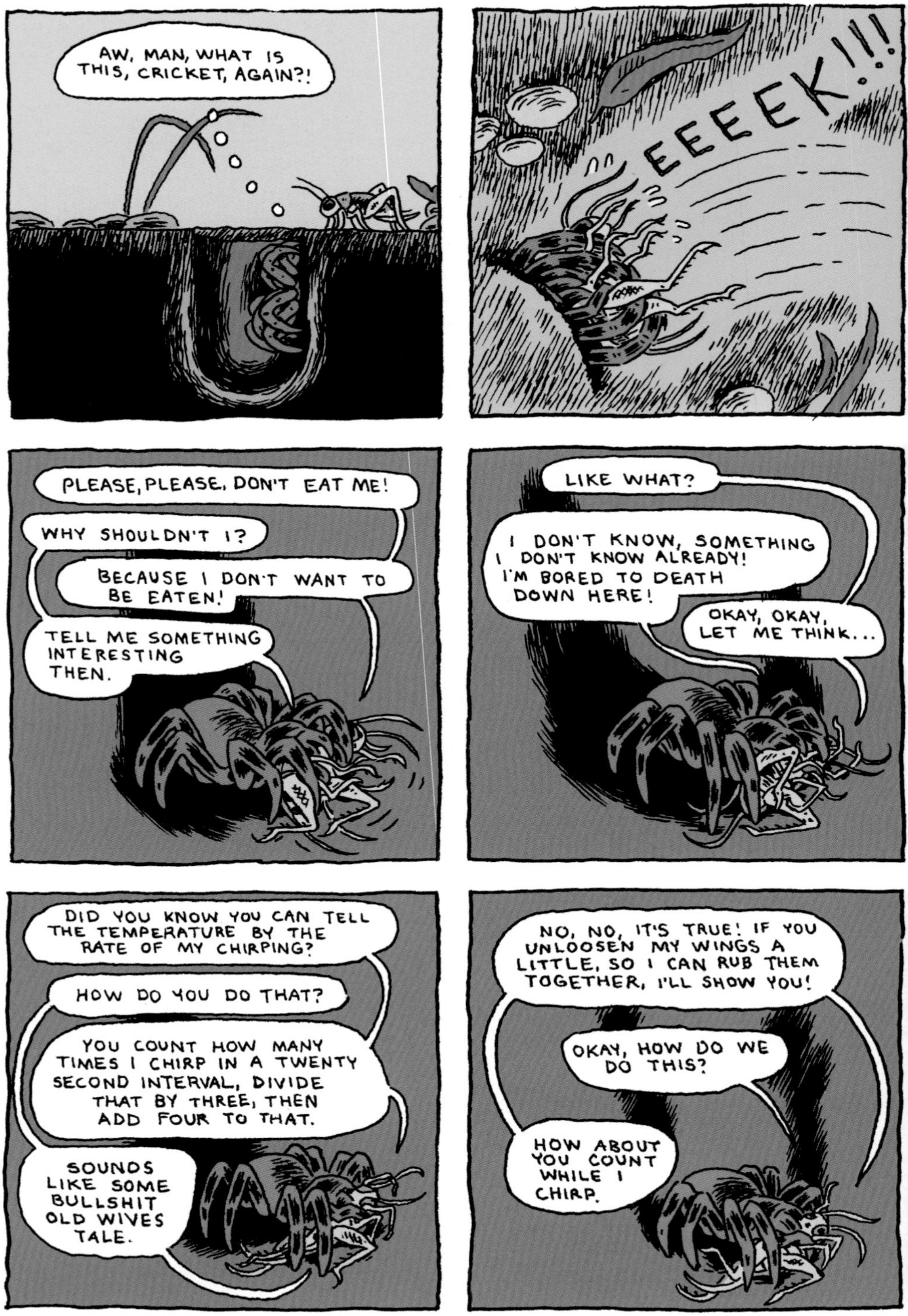

AW, MAN, WHAT IS THIS, CRICKET, AGAIN?!
EEEEK!!!
PLEASE, PLEASE, DON'T EAT ME!
WHY SHOULDN'T I?
BECAUSE I DON'T WANT TO BE EATEN!
TELL ME SOMETHING INTERESTING THEN.
LIKE WHAT?
I DON'T KNOW, SOMETHING I DON'T KNOW ALREADY! I'M BORED TO DEATH DOWN HERE!
OKAY, OKAY, LET ME THINK...
DID YOU KNOW YOU CAN TELL THE TEMPERATURE BY THE RATE OF MY CHIRPING?
HOW DO YOU DO THAT?
YOU COUNT HOW MANY TIMES I CHIRP IN A TWENTY SECOND INTERVAL, DIVIDE THAT BY THREE, THEN ADD FOUR TO THAT.
SOUNDS LIKE SOME BULLSHIT OLD WIVES TALE.
NO, NO, IT'S TRUE! IF YOU UNLOOSEN MY WINGS A LITTLE, SO I CAN RUB THEM TOGETHER, I'LL SHOW YOU!
OKAY, HOW DO WE DO THIS?
HOW ABOUT YOU COUNT WHILE I CHIRP.

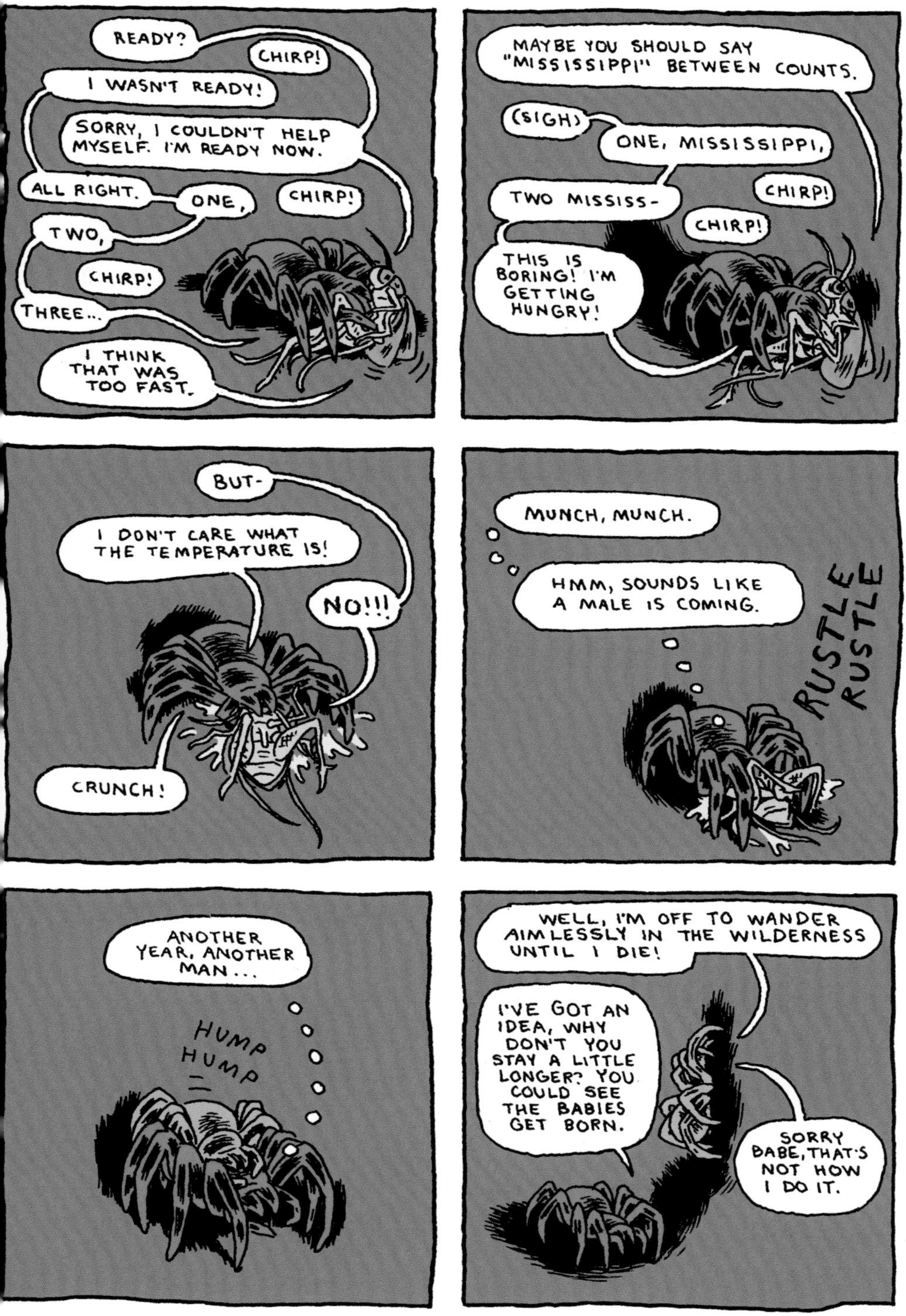
READY?
CHIRP!
I WASN'T READY!
SORRY, I COULDN'T HELP MYSELF. I'M READY NOW.
ALL RIGHT.
ONE,
CHIRP!
TWO,
CHIRP!
THREE...
I THINK THAT WAS TOO FAST.
MAYBE YOU SHOULD SAY "MISSISSIPPI" BETWEEN COUNTS.
(SIGH)
ONE, MISSISSIPPI,
TWO MISSISS-
CHIRP!
CHIRP!
THIS IS BORING! I'M GETTING HUNGRY!
BUT-
I DON'T CARE WHAT THE TEMPERATURE IS!
NO!!!
CRUNCH!
MUNCH, MUNCH.
HMM, SOUNDS LIKE A MALE IS COMING.
RUSTLE RUSTLE
ANOTHER YEAR, ANOTHER MAN...
HUMP HUMP
WELL, I'M OFF TO WANDER AIMLESSLY IN THE WILDERNESS UNTIL I DIE!
I'VE GOT AN IDEA, WHY DON'T YOU STAY A LITTLE LONGER? YOU COULD SEE THE BABIES GET BORN.
SORRY BABE, THAT'S NOT HOW I DO IT.

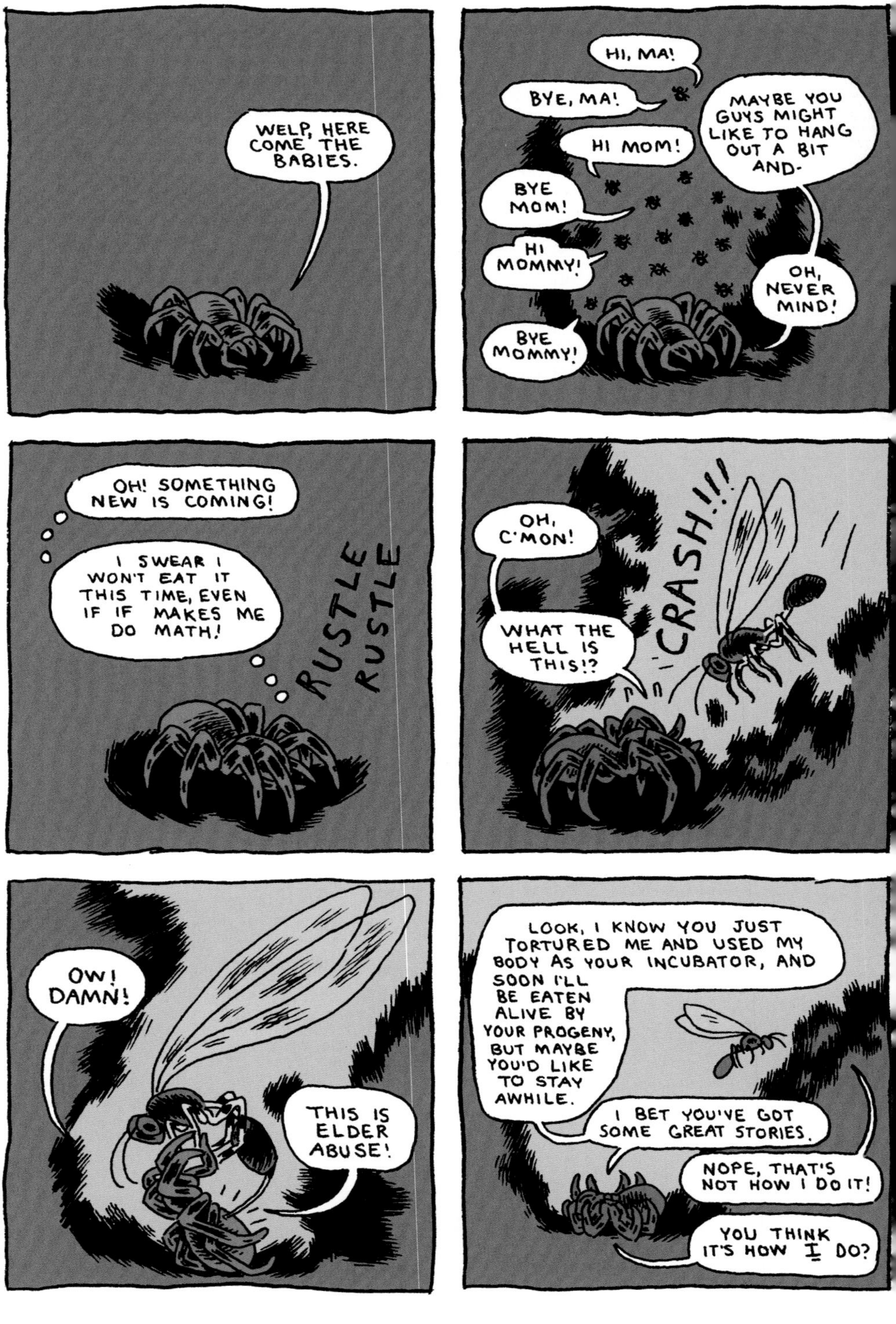
WELP, HERE COME THE BABIES.
HI, MA!
BYE, MA!
HI MOM!
BYE MOM!
HI MOMMY!
BYE MOMMY!
MAYBE YOU GUYS MIGHT LIKE TO HANG OUT A BIT AND-
OH, NEVER MIND!
OH! SOMETHING NEW IS COMING!
I SWEAR I WON'T EAT IT THIS TIME, EVEN IF IF MAKES ME DO MATH!
RUSTLE RUSTLE
OH, C'MON!
WHAT THE HELL IS THIS!?
CRASH!!!
OW! DAMN!
THIS IS ELDER ABUSE!
LOOK, I KNOW YOU JUST TORTURED ME AND USED MY BODY AS YOUR INCUBATOR, AND SOON I'LL BE EATEN ALIVE BY YOUR PROGENY, BUT MAYBE YOU'D LIKE TO STAY AWHILE.
I BET YOU'VE GOT SOME GREAT STORIES.
NOPE, THAT'S NOT HOW I DO IT!
YOU THINK IT'S HOW I DO?

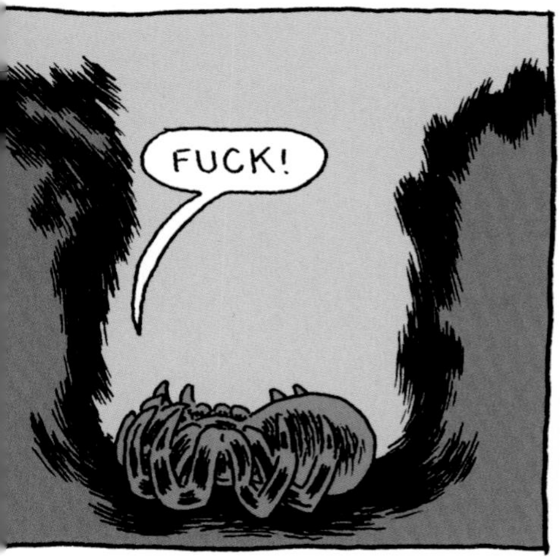
FUCK!

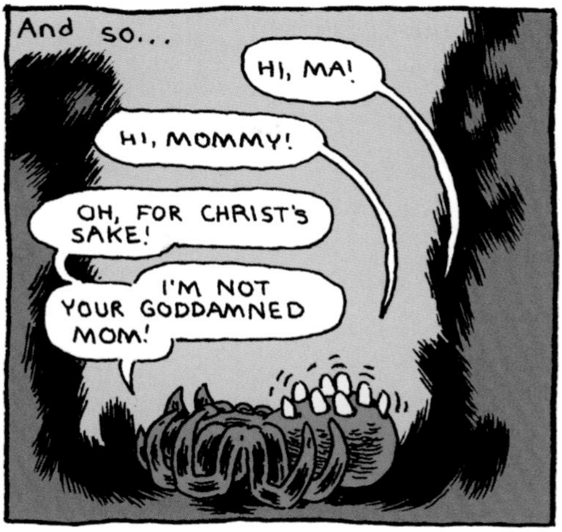
And so...
HI, MA!
HI, MOMMY!
OH, FOR CHRIST'S SAKE!
I'M NOT YOUR GODDAMNED MOM!

Talking Rats

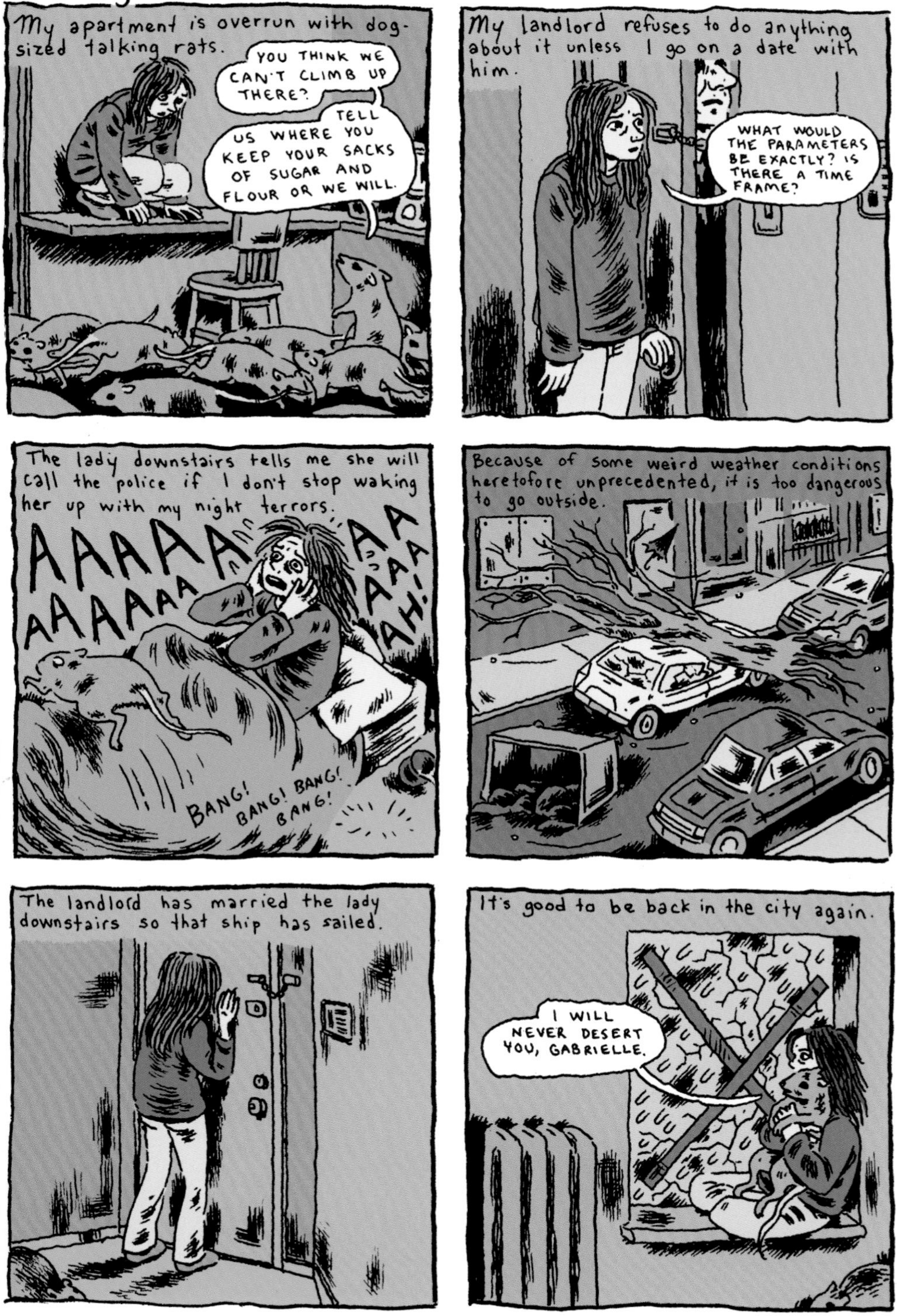

My apartment is overrun with dog-sized talking rats.
YOU THINK WE CAN'T CLIMB UP THERE?
TELL US WHERE YOU KEEP YOUR SACKS OF SUGAR AND FLOUR OR WE WILL.
My landlord refuses to do anything about it unless I go on a date with him.
WHAT WOULD THE PARAMETERS BE EXACTLY? IS THERE A TIME FRAME?
The lady downstairs tells me she will call the police if I don't stop waking her up with my night terrors.
AAAAA AAAAAA AAAAAH!
BANG! BANG! BANG! BANG!
Because of some weird weather conditions heretofore unprecedented, it is too dangerous to go outside.
The landlord has married the lady downstairs so that ship has sailed.
It's good to be back in the city again.
I WILL NEVER DESERT YOU, GABRIELLE.

CODY

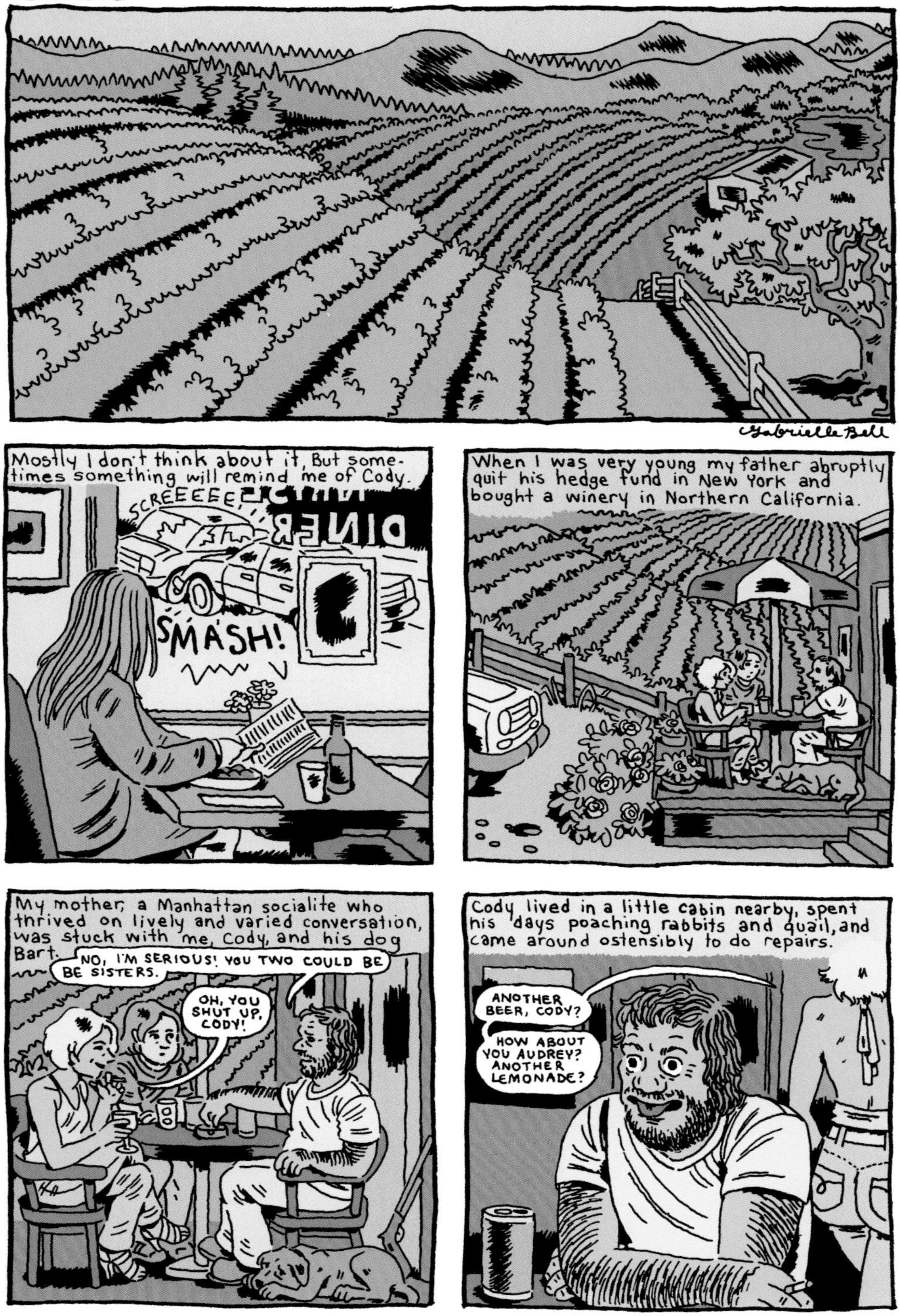
Gabrielle Bell
Mostly I don't think about it, But sometimes something will remind me of Cody.
SCREEEEE!
SMASH!
When I was very young my father abruptly quit his hedge fund in New York and bought a winery in Northern California.
My mother, a Manhattan socialite who thrived on lively and varied conversation, was stuck with me, Cody, and his dog Bart.
NO, I'M SERIOUS! YOU TWO COULD BE BE SISTERS.
OH, YOU SHUT UP, CODY!
Cody lived in a little cabin nearby, spent his days poaching rabbits and quail, and came around ostensibly to do repairs.
ANOTHER BEER, CODY?
HOW ABOUT YOU AUDREY? ANOTHER LEMONADE?

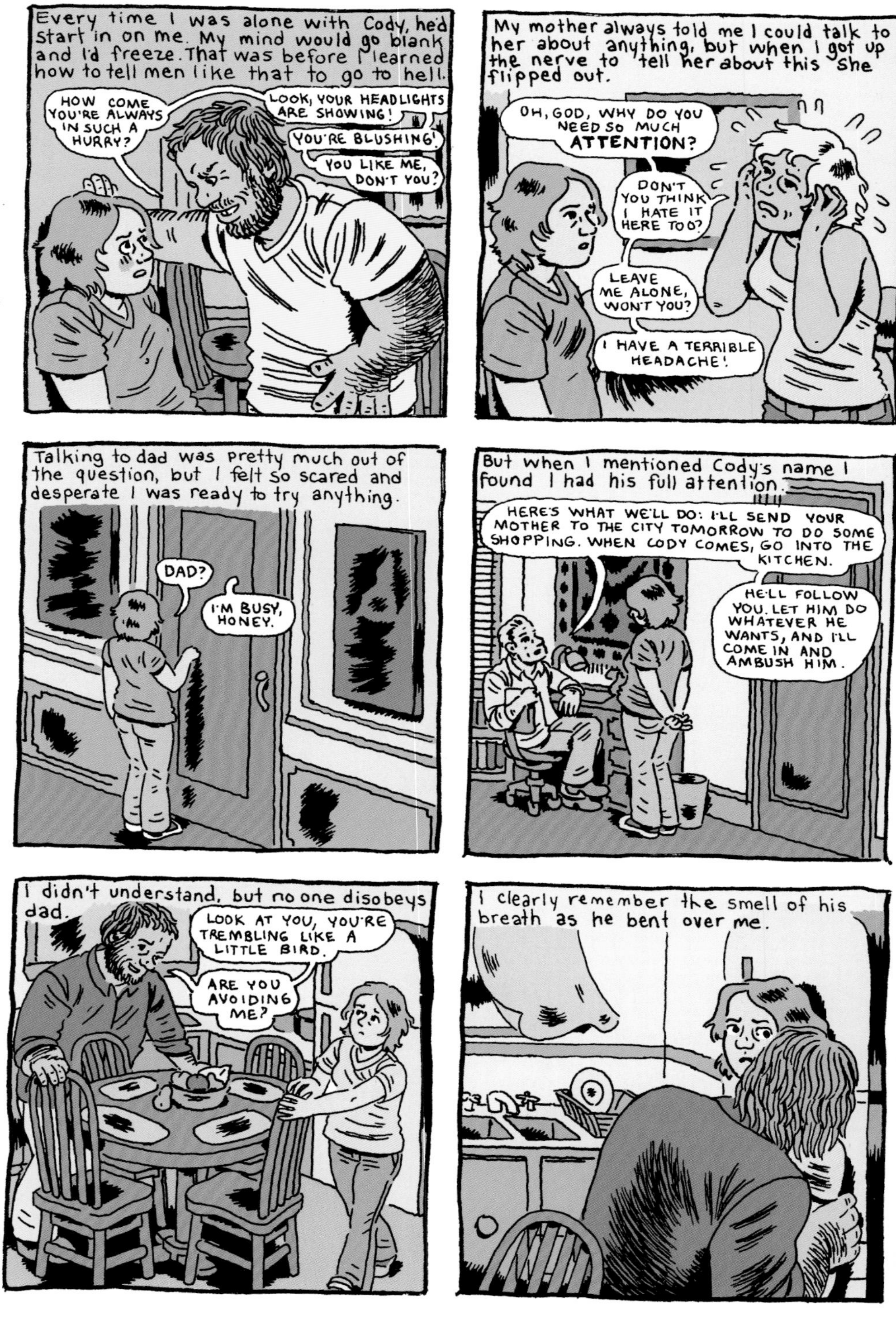
Every time I was alone with Cody, he'd start in on me. My mind would go blank and I'd freeze. That was before I learned how to tell men like that to go to hell.
HOW COME YOU'RE ALWAYS IN SUCH A HURRY?
LOOK, YOUR HEADLIGHTS ARE SHOWING!
YOU'RE BLUSHING!
YOU LIKE ME, DON'T YOU?
My mother always told me I could talk to her about anything, but when I got up the nerve to tell her about this she flipped out.
OH, GOD, WHY DO YOU NEED SO MUCH ATTENTION?
DON'T YOU THINK I HATE IT HERE TOO?
LEAVE ME ALONE, WON'T YOU?
I HAVE A TERRIBLE HEADACHE!
Talking to dad was pretty much out of the question, but I felt so scared and desperate I was ready to try anything.
DAD?
I'M BUSY, HONEY.
But when I mentioned Cody's name I found I had his full attention.
HERE'S WHAT WE'LL DO: I'LL SEND YOUR MOTHER TO THE CITY TOMORROW TO DO SOME SHOPPING. WHEN CODY COMES, GO INTO THE KITCHEN.
HE'LL FOLLOW YOU. LET HIM DO WHATEVER HE WANTS, AND I'LL COME IN AND AMBUSH HIM.
I didn't understand, but no one disobeys dad.
LOOK AT YOU, YOU'RE TREMBLING LIKE A LITTLE BIRD.
ARE YOU AVOIDING ME?
I clearly remember the smell of his breath as he bent over me.

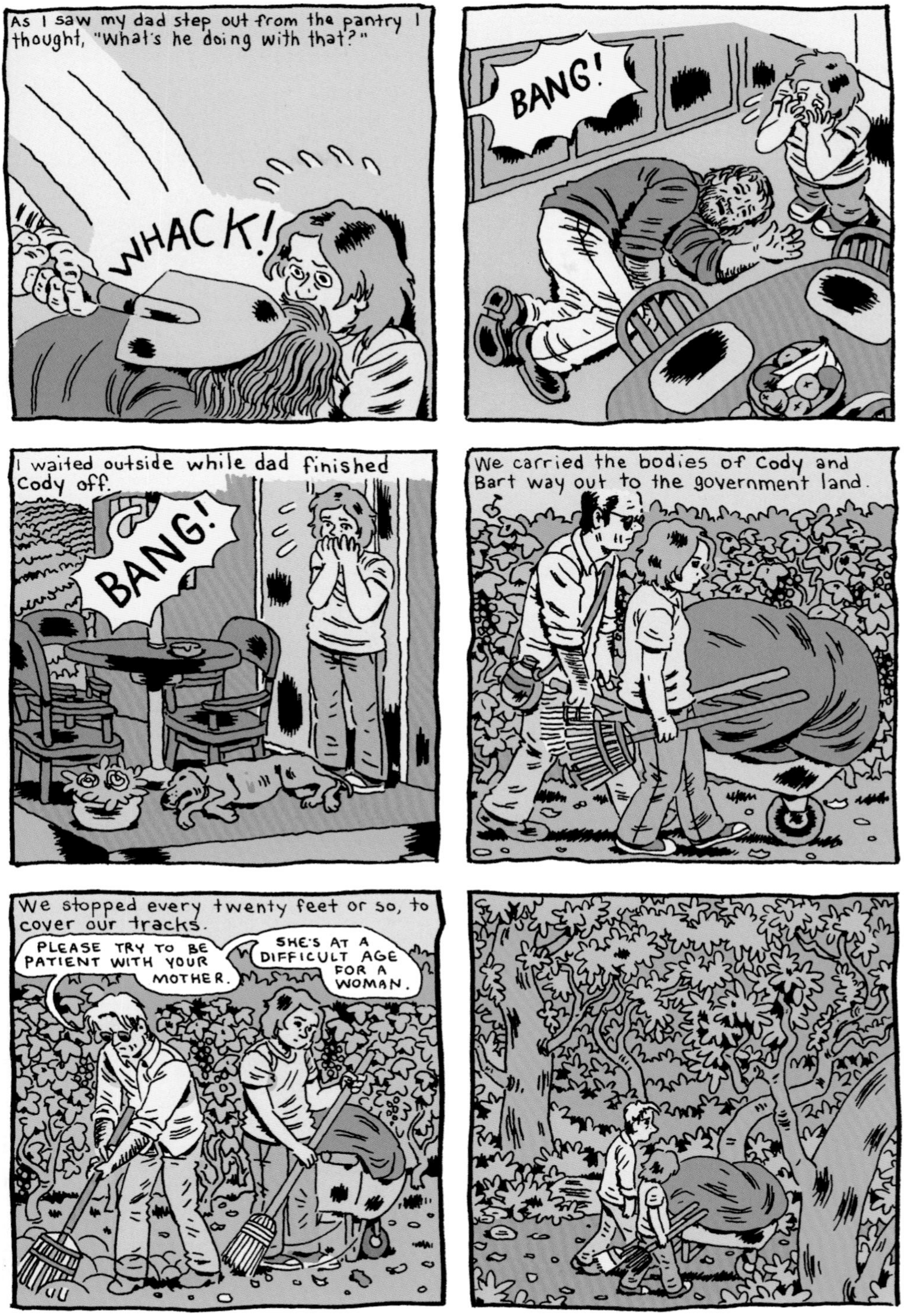

As I saw my dad step out from the pantry I thought, "What's he doing with that?"
WHACK!
BANG!
I waited outside while dad finished Cody off.
BANG!
We carried the bodies of Cody and Bart way out to the government land.
We stopped every twenty feet or so, to cover our tracks.
PLEASE TRY TO BE PATIENT WITH YOUR MOTHER.
SHE'S AT A DIFFICULT AGE FOR A WOMAN.

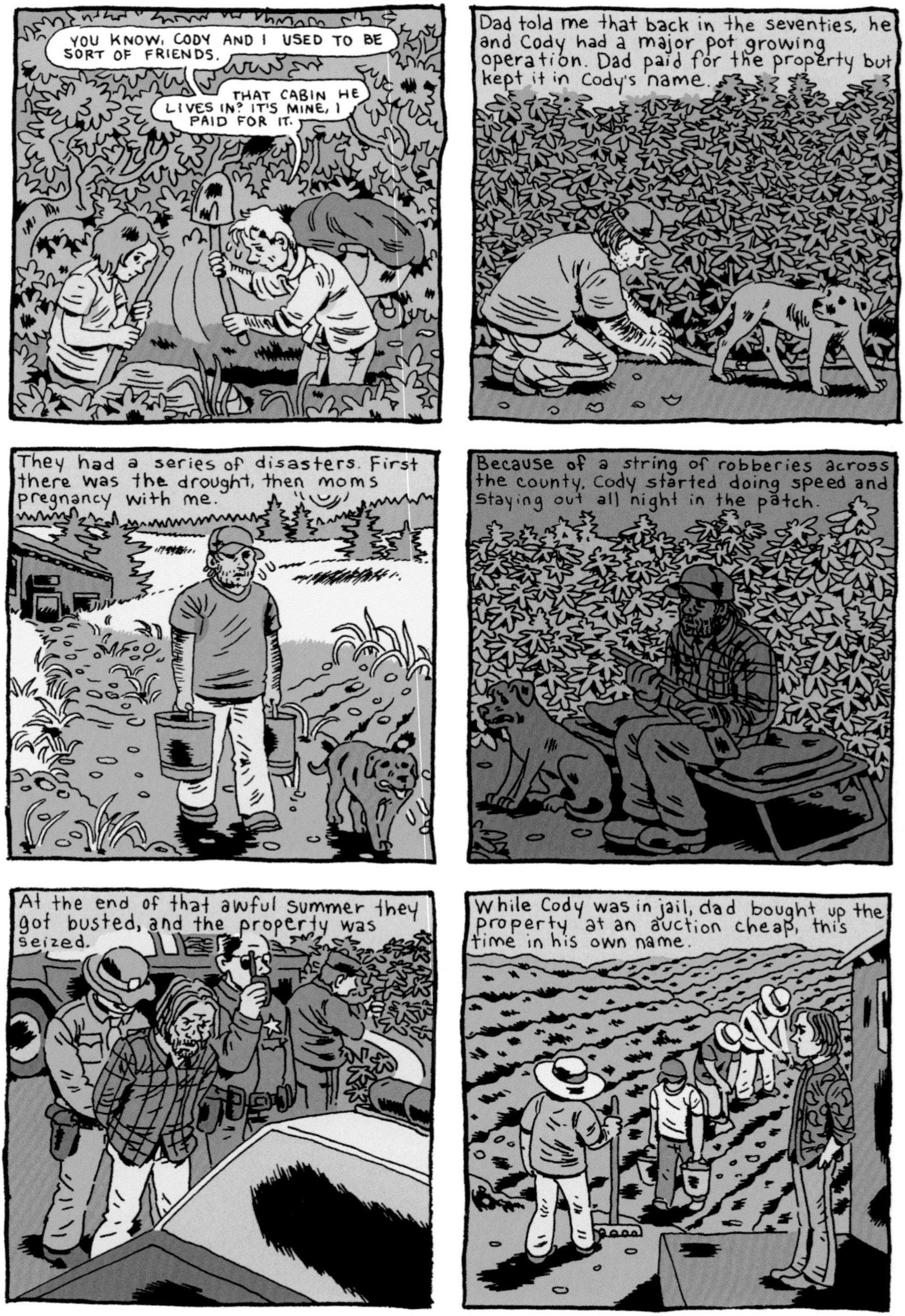
YOU KNOW, CODY AND I USED TO BE SORT OF FRIENDS.
THAT CABIN HE LIVES IN? IT'S MINE, I PAID FOR IT.
Dad told me that back in the seventies, he and Cody had a major pot growing operation. Dad paid for the property but kept it in Cody's name.
They had a series of disasters. First there was the drought, then moms pregnancy with me.
Because of a string of robberies across the county, Cody started doing speed and staying out all night in the patch.
At the end of that awful summer they got busted, and the property was seized.
While Cody was in jail, dad bought up the property at an auction cheap, this time in his own name.

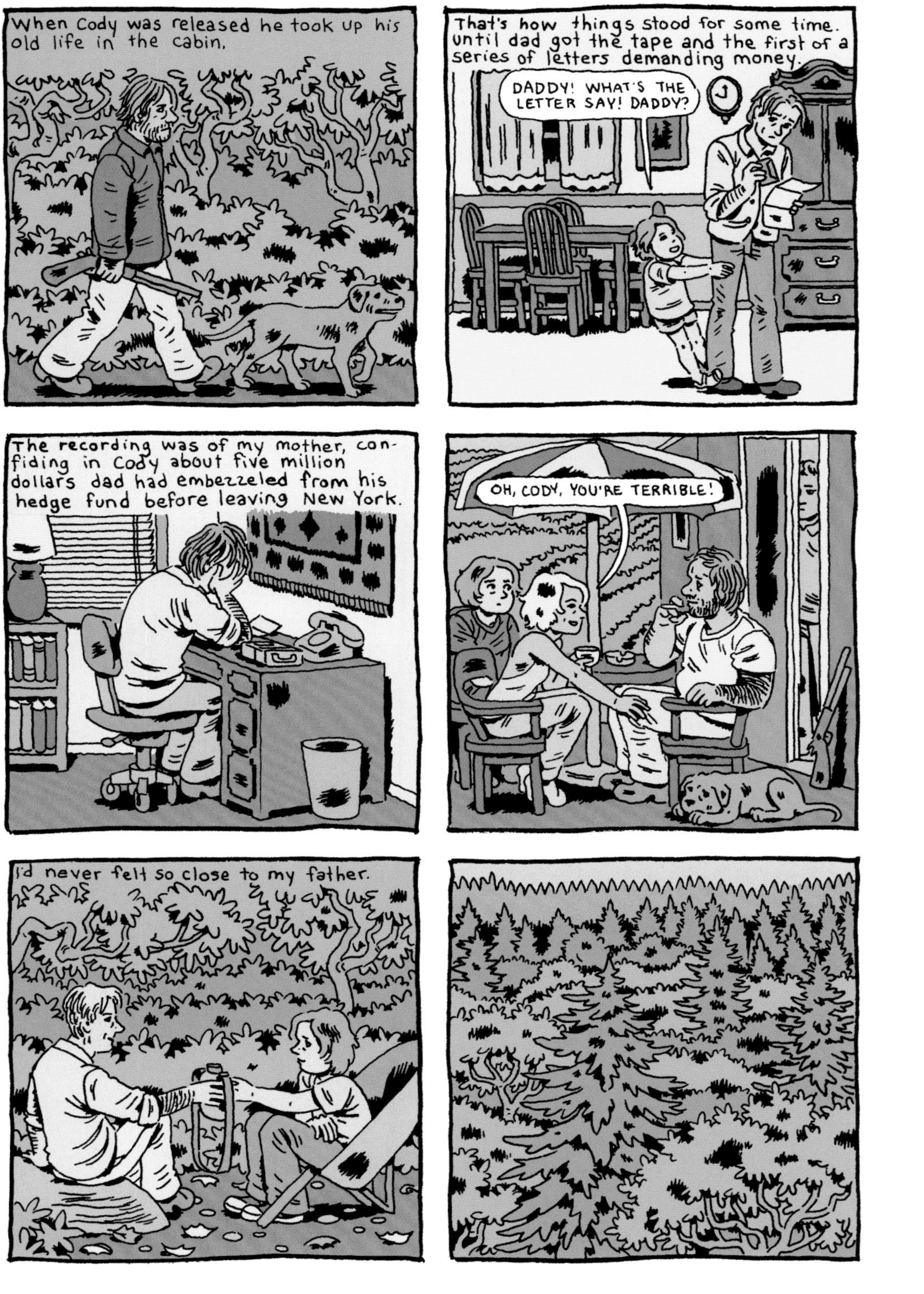
When Cody was released he took up his old life in the cabin.
That's how things stood for some time. Until dad got the tape and the first of a series of letters demanding money.
DADDY! WHAT'S THE LETTER SAY! DADDY?
The recording was of my mother, confiding in Cody about five million dollars dad had embezzeled from his hedge fund before leaving New York.
OH, CODY, YOU'RE TERRIBLE!
I'd never felt so close to my father.

How Do You Do Things

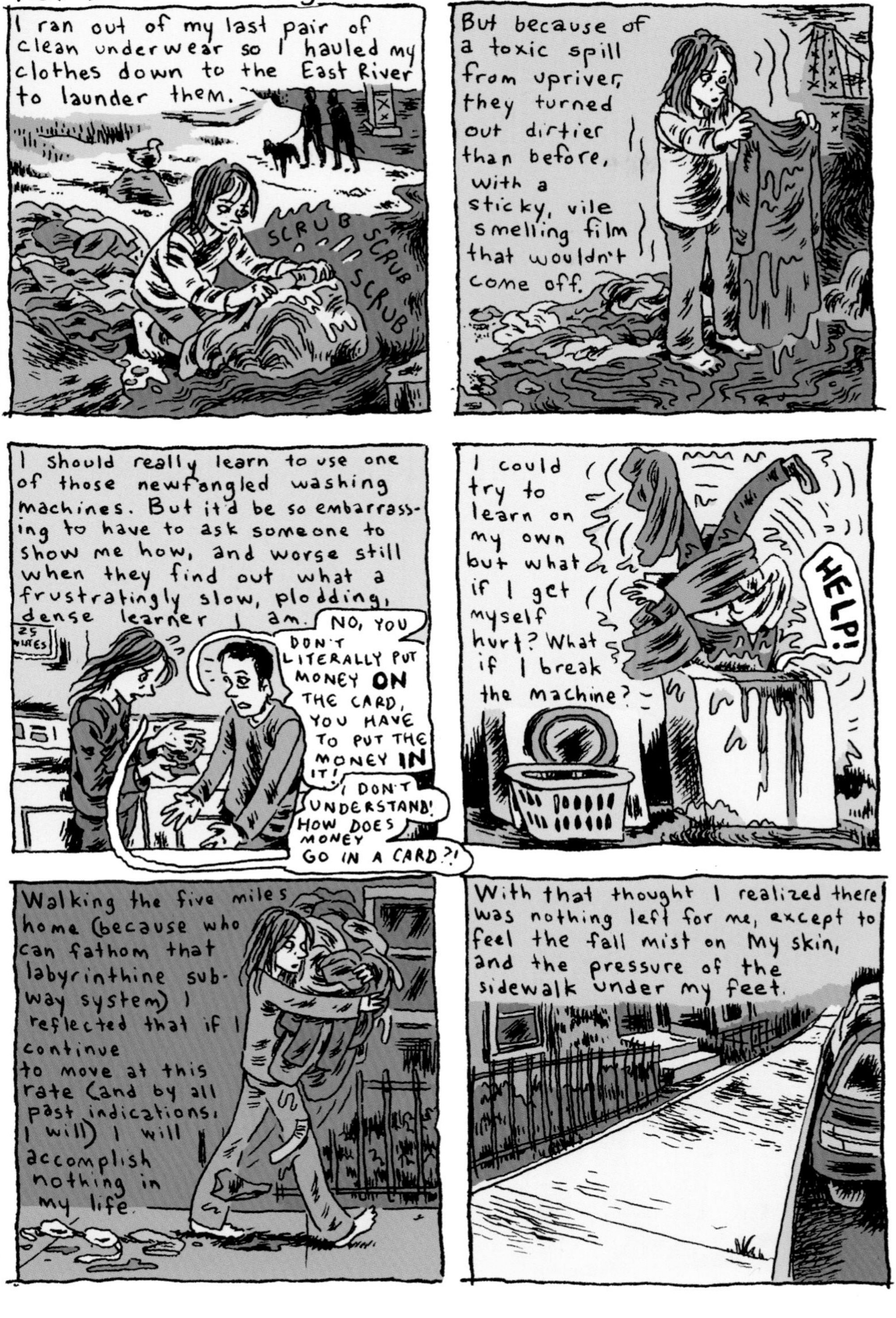
I ran out of my last pair of clean underwear so I hauled my clothes down to the East River to launder them.
SCRUB
SCRUB
SCRUB
But because of a toxic spill from upriver, they turned out dirtier than before, with a sticky, vile smelling film that wouldn't come off.
I should really learn to use one of those newfangled washing machines. But it'd be so embarrassing to have to ask someone to show me how, and worse still when they find out what a frustratingly slow, plodding, dense learner I am.
NO, YOU DON'T LITERALLY PUT MONEY ON THE CARD, YOU HAVE TO PUT THE MONEY IN IT!
I DON'T UNDERSTAND! HOW DOES MONEY GO IN A CARD?!
I could try to learn on my own but what if I get myself hurt? What if I break the machine?
HELP!
Walking the five miles home (because who can fathom that labyrinthine subway system) I reflected that if I continue to move at this rate (and by all past indications, I will) I will accomplish nothing in my life.
With that thought I realized there was nothing left for me, except to feel the fall mist on my skin, and the pressure of the sidewalk under my feet.

LATE MARCH

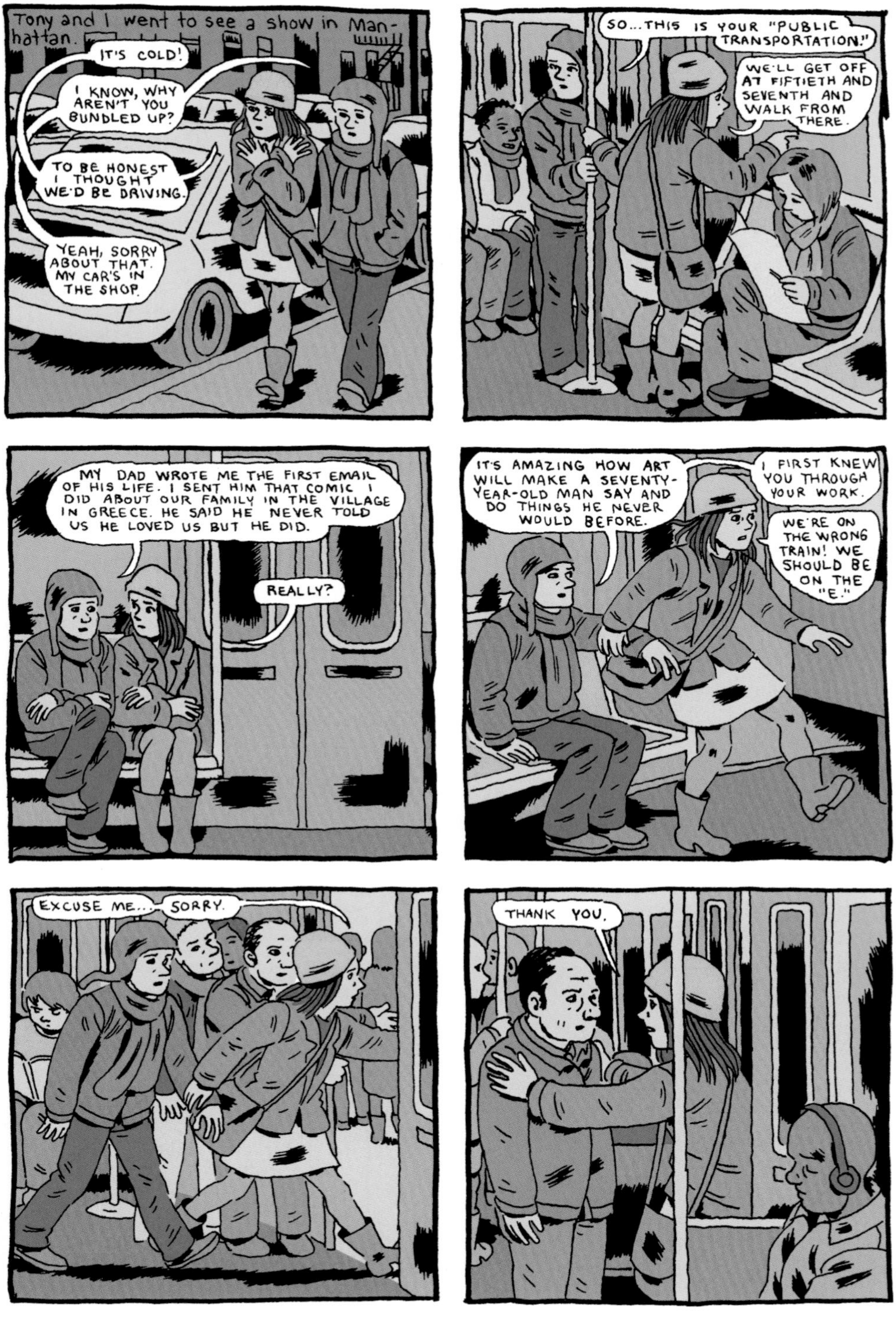
Tony and I went to see a show in Manhattan.
IT'S COLD!
I KNOW, WHY AREN'T YOU BUNDLED UP?
TO BE HONEST I THOUGHT WE'D BE DRIVING.
YEAH, SORRY ABOUT THAT. MY CAR'S IN THE SHOP.
SO... THIS IS YOUR "PUBLIC TRANSPORTATION."
WE'LL GET OFF AT FIFTIETH AND SEVENTH AND WALK FROM THERE.
MY DAD WROTE ME THE FIRST EMAIL OF HIS LIFE. I SENT HIM THAT COMIC I DID ABOUT OUR FAMILY IN THE VILLAGE IN GREECE. HE SAID HE NEVER TOLD US HE LOVED US BUT HE DID.
REALLY?
IT'S AMAZING HOW ART WILL MAKE A SEVENTY-YEAR-OLD MAN SAY AND DO THINGS HE NEVER WOULD BEFORE.
I FIRST KNEW YOU THROUGH YOUR WORK.
WE'RE ON THE WRONG TRAIN! WE SHOULD BE ON THE "E."
EXCUSE ME... SORRY.
THANK YOU.

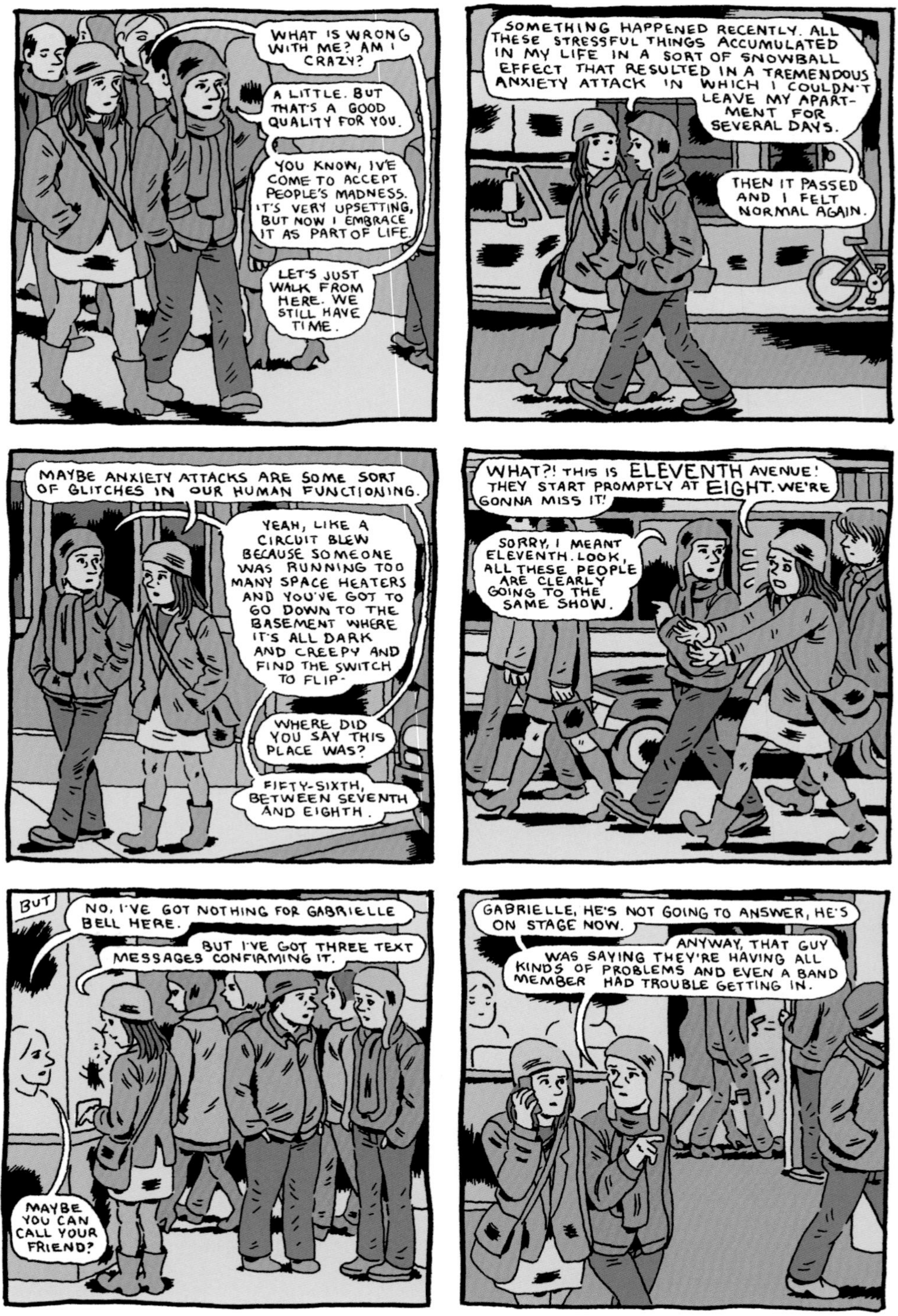
WHAT IS WRONG WITH ME? AM I CRAZY?
A LITTLE. BUT THAT'S A GOOD QUALITY FOR YOU.
YOU KNOW, I'VE COME TO ACCEPT PEOPLE'S MADNESS. IT'S VERY UPSETTING, BUT NOW I EMBRACE IT AS PART OF LIFE.
LET'S JUST WALK FROM HERE. WE STILL HAVE TIME.
SOMETHING HAPPENED RECENTLY. ALL THESE STRESSFUL THINGS ACCUMULATED IN MY LIFE IN A SORT OF SNOWBALL EFFECT THAT RESULTED IN A TREMENDOUS ANXIETY ATTACK IN WHICH I COULDN'T LEAVE MY APARTMENT FOR SEVERAL DAYS.
THEN IT PASSED AND I FELT NORMAL AGAIN.
MAYBE ANXIETY ATTACKS ARE SOME SORT OF GLITCHES IN OUR HUMAN FUNCTIONING.
YEAH, LIKE A CIRCUIT BLEW BECAUSE SOMEONE WAS RUNNING TOO MANY SPACE HEATERS AND YOU'VE GOT TO GO DOWN TO THE BASEMENT WHERE IT'S ALL DARK AND CREEPY AND FIND THE SWITCH TO FLIP-
WHERE DID YOU SAY THIS PLACE WAS?
FIFTY-SIXTH, BETWEEN SEVENTH AND EIGHTH.
WHAT?! THIS IS ELEVENTH AVENUE! THEY START PROMPTLY AT EIGHT. WE'RE GONNA MISS IT!
SORRY, I MEANT ELEVENTH. LOOK, ALL THESE PEOPLE ARE CLEARLY GOING TO THE SAME SHOW.
BUT
NO, I'VE GOT NOTHING FOR GABRIELLE BELL HERE.
BUT I'VE GOT THREE TEXT MESSAGES CONFIRMING IT.
MAYBE YOU CAN CALL YOUR FRIEND?
GABRIELLE, HE'S NOT GOING TO ANSWER, HE'S ON STAGE NOW.
ANYWAY, THAT GUY WAS SAYING THEY'RE HAVING ALL KINDS OF PROBLEMS AND EVEN A BAND MEMBER HAD TROUBLE GETTING IN.

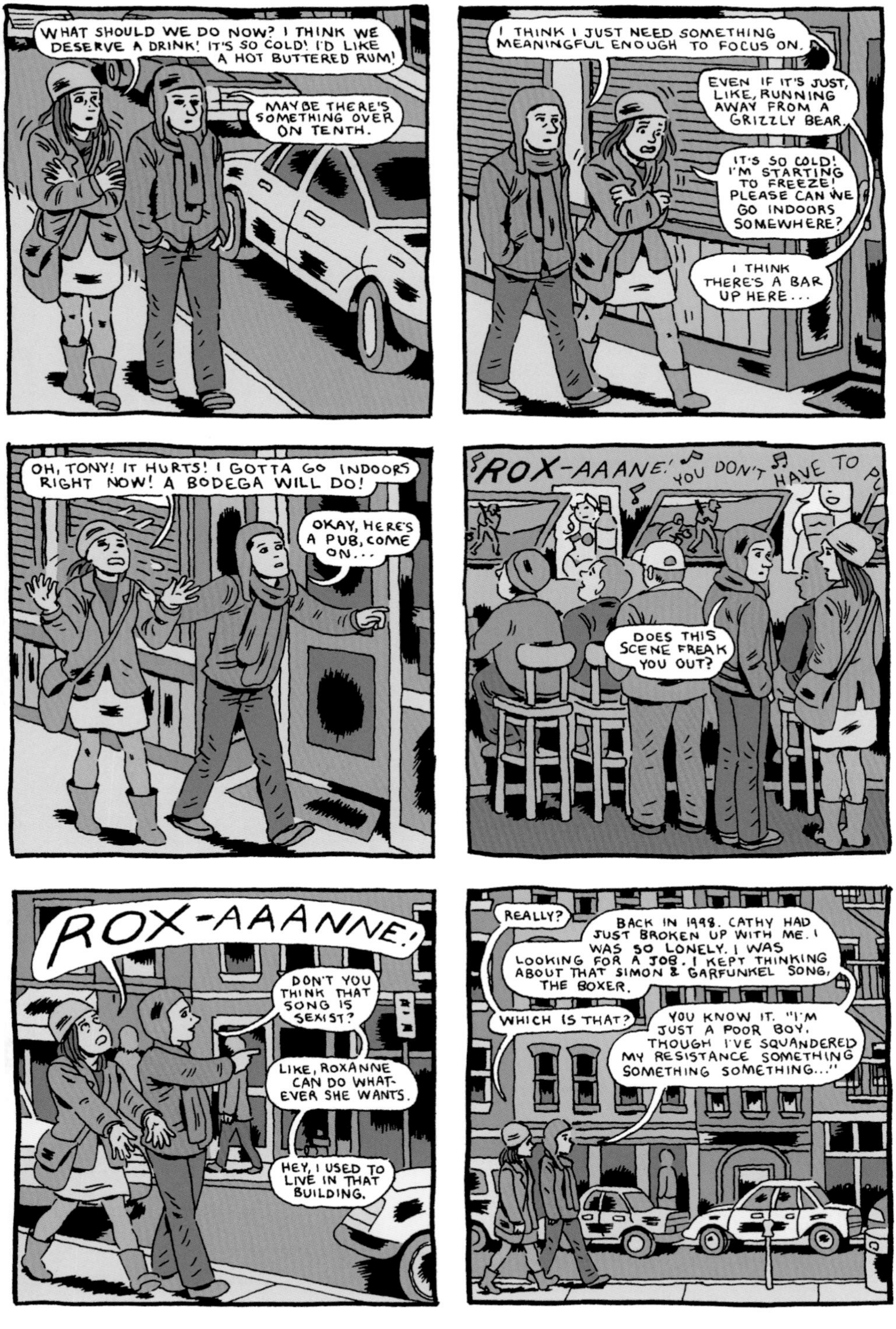
WHAT SHOULD WE DO NOW? I THINK WE DESERVE A DRINK! IT'S SO COLD! I'D LIKE A HOT BUTTERED RUM!
MAYBE THERE'S SOMETHING OVER ON TENTH.
I THINK I JUST NEED SOMETHING MEANINGFUL ENOUGH TO FOCUS ON.
EVEN IF IT'S JUST, LIKE, RUNNING AWAY FROM A GRIZZLY BEAR.
IT'S SO COLD! I'M STARTING TO FREEZE! PLEASE CAN WE GO INDOORS SOMEWHERE?
I THINK THERE'S A BAR UP HERE...
OH, TONY! IT HURTS! I GOTTA GO INDOORS RIGHT NOW! A BODEGA WILL DO!
OKAY, HERE'S A PUB, COME ON...
ROX-AAANE! YOU DON'T HAVE TO P
DOES THIS SCENE FREAK YOU OUT?
ROX-AAANNE!
DON'T YOU THINK THAT SONG IS SEXIST?
LIKE, ROXANNE CAN DO WHATEVER SHE WANTS.
HEY, I USED TO LIVE IN THAT BUILDING.
REALLY?
BACK IN 1998. CATHY HAD JUST BROKEN UP WITH ME. I WAS SO LONELY. I WAS LOOKING FOR A JOB. I KEPT THINKING ABOUT THAT SIMON & GARFUNKEL SONG, THE BOXER.
WHICH IS THAT?
YOU KNOW IT. "I'M JUST A POOR BOY, THOUGH I'VE SQUANDERED MY RESISTANCE SOMETHING SOMETHING SOMETHING..."

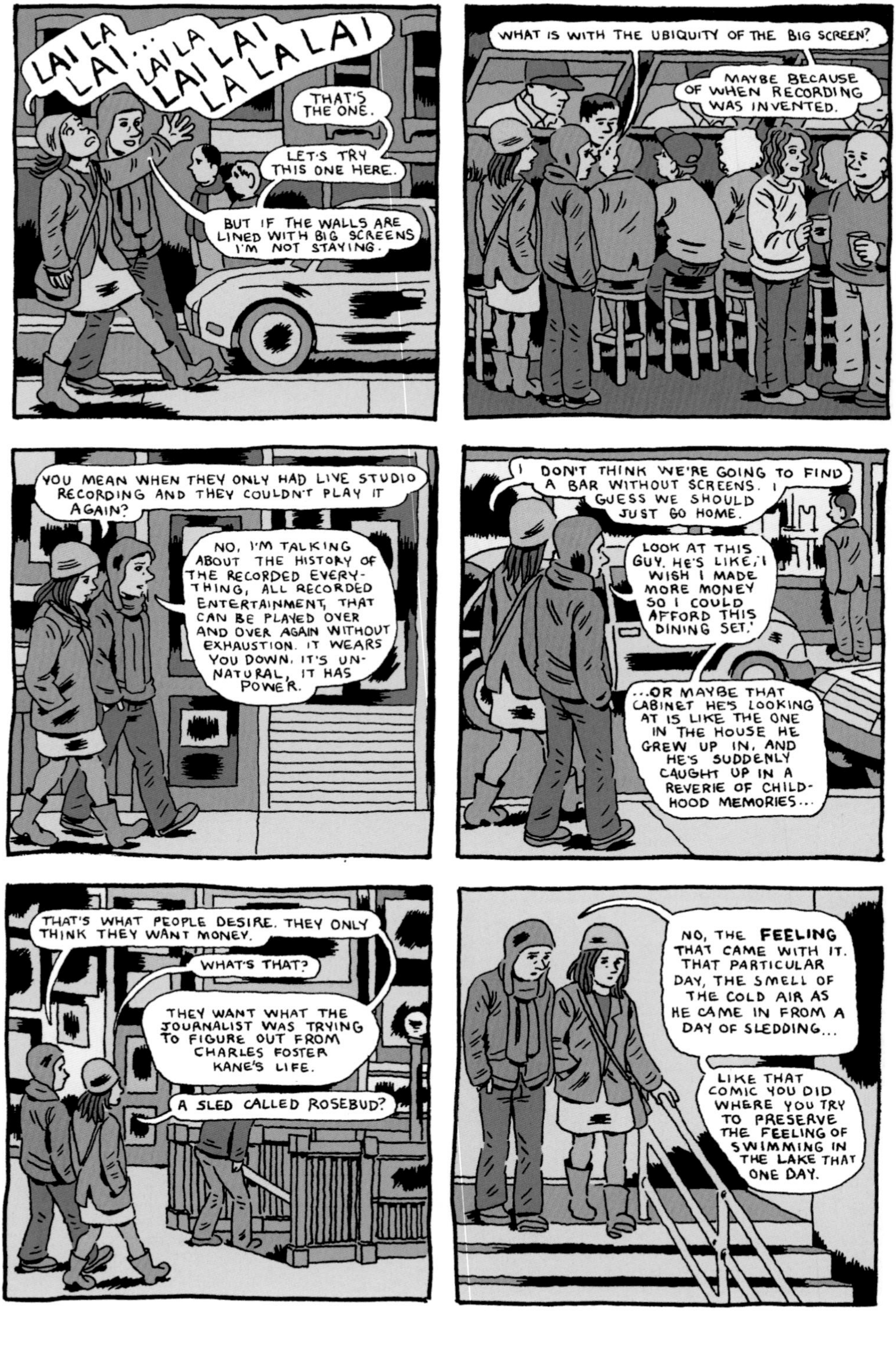
LAI LA LAI... LAI LA LAI LAI LA LA LAI
THAT'S THE ONE.
LET'S TRY THIS ONE HERE.
BUT IF THE WALLS ARE LINED WITH BIG SCREENS I'M NOT STAYING.
WHAT IS WITH THE UBIQUITY OF THE BIG SCREEN?
MAYBE BECAUSE OF WHEN RECORDING WAS INVENTED.
YOU MEAN WHEN THEY ONLY HAD LIVE STUDIO RECORDING AND THEY COULDN'T PLAY IT AGAIN?
NO, I'M TALKING ABOUT THE HISTORY OF THE RECORDED EVERY-THING, ALL RECORDED ENTERTAINMENT, THAT CAN BE PLAYED OVER AND OVER AGAIN WITHOUT EXHAUSTION. IT WEARS YOU DOWN. IT'S UN-NATURAL, IT HAS POWER.
I DON'T THINK WE'RE GOING TO FIND A BAR WITHOUT SCREENS. I GUESS WE SHOULD JUST GO HOME.
LOOK AT THIS GUY. HE'S LIKE, 'I WISH I MADE MORE MONEY SO I COULD AFFORD THIS DINING SET.'
...OR MAYBE THAT CABINET HE'S LOOKING AT IS LIKE THE ONE IN THE HOUSE HE GREW UP IN, AND HE'S SUDDENLY CAUGHT UP IN A REVERIE OF CHILD-HOOD MEMORIES...
THAT'S WHAT PEOPLE DESIRE. THEY ONLY THINK THEY WANT MONEY.
WHAT'S THAT?
THEY WANT WHAT THE JOURNALIST WAS TRYING TO FIGURE OUT FROM CHARLES FOSTER KANE'S LIFE.
A SLED CALLED ROSEBUD?
NO, THE FEELING THAT CAME WITH IT. THAT PARTICULAR DAY, THE SMELL OF THE COLD AIR AS HE CAME IN FROM A DAY OF SLEDDING...
LIKE THAT COMIC YOU DID WHERE YOU TRY TO PRESERVE THE FEELING OF SWIMMING IN THE LAKE THAT ONE DAY.

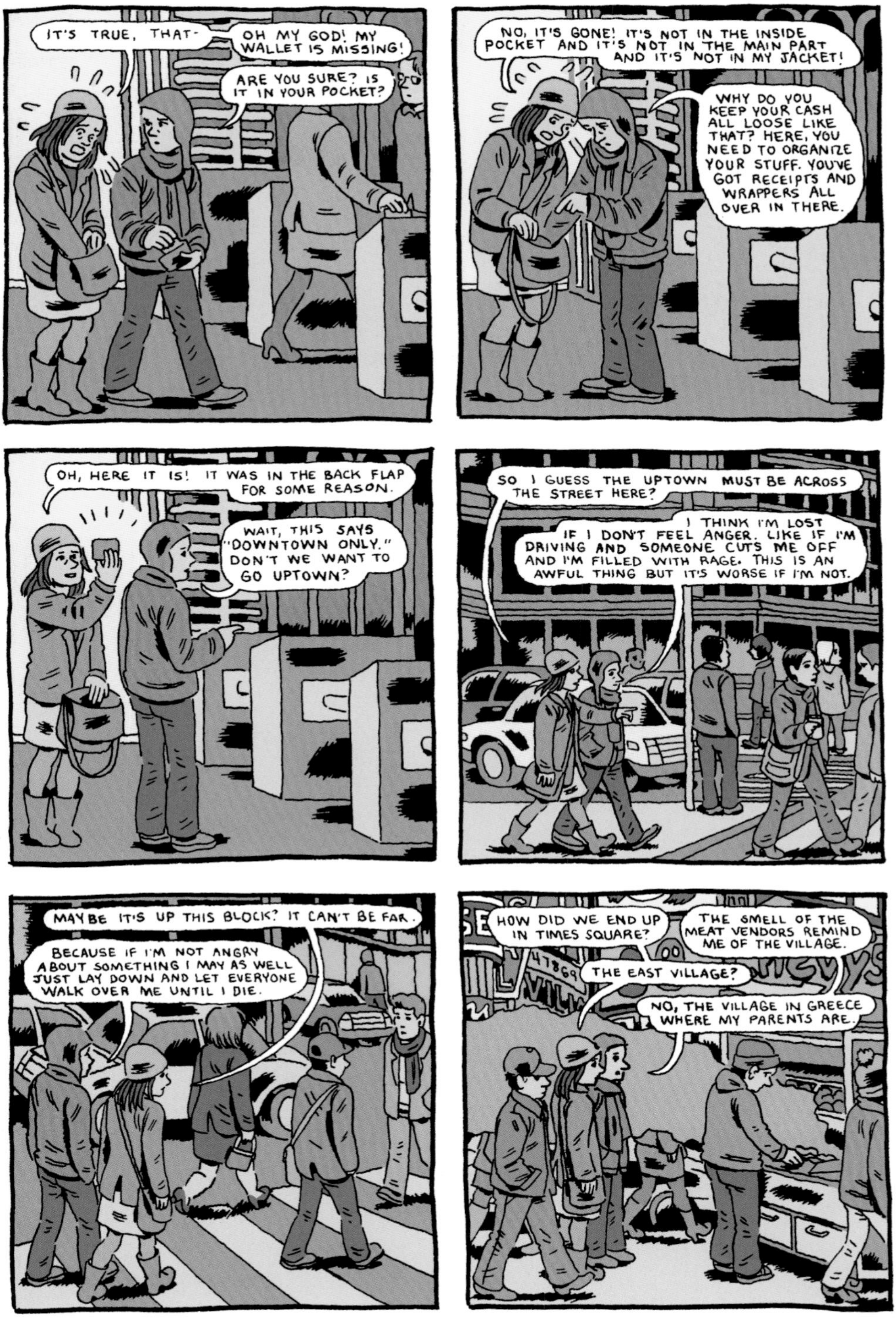
IT'S TRUE, THAT-
OH MY GOD! MY WALLET IS MISSING!
ARE YOU SURE? IS IT IN YOUR POCKET?
NO, IT'S GONE! IT'S NOT IN THE INSIDE POCKET AND IT'S NOT IN THE MAIN PART AND IT'S NOT IN MY JACKET!
WHY DO YOU KEEP YOUR CASH ALL LOOSE LIKE THAT? HERE, YOU NEED TO ORGANIZE YOUR STUFF. YOU'VE GOT RECEIPTS AND WRAPPERS ALL OVER IN THERE.
OH, HERE IT IS! IT WAS IN THE BACK FLAP FOR SOME REASON.
WAIT, THIS SAYS "DOWNTOWN ONLY." DON'T WE WANT TO GO UPTOWN?
SO I GUESS THE UPTOWN MUST BE ACROSS THE STREET HERE?
I THINK I'M LOST IF I DON'T FEEL ANGER. LIKE IF I'M DRIVING AND SOMEONE CUTS ME OFF AND I'M FILLED WITH RAGE. THIS IS AN AWFUL THING BUT IT'S WORSE IF I'M NOT.
MAYBE IT'S UP THIS BLOCK? IT CAN'T BE FAR.
BECAUSE IF I'M NOT ANGRY ABOUT SOMETHING I MAY AS WELL JUST LAY DOWN AND LET EVERYONE WALK OVER ME UNTIL I DIE.
HOW DID WE END UP IN TIMES SQUARE?
THE SMELL OF THE MEAT VENDORS REMIND ME OF THE VILLAGE.
THE EAST VILLAGE?
NO, THE VILLAGE IN GREECE WHERE MY PARENTS ARE.

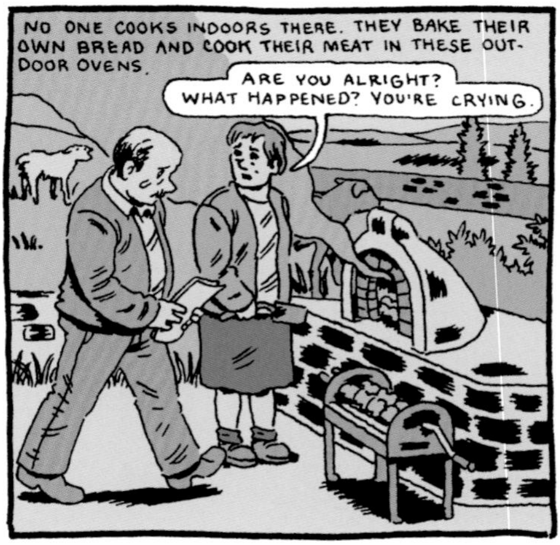
NO ONE COOKS INDOORS THERE. THEY BAKE THEIR OWN BREAD AND COOK THEIR MEAT IN THESE OUT-DOOR OVENS.
ARE YOU ALRIGHT? WHAT HAPPENED? YOU'RE CRYING.

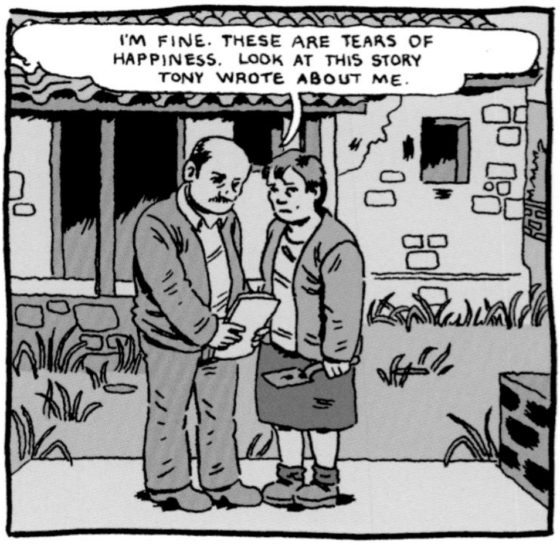
I'M FINE. THESE ARE TEARS OF HAPPINESS. LOOK AT THIS STORY TONY WROTE ABOUT ME.

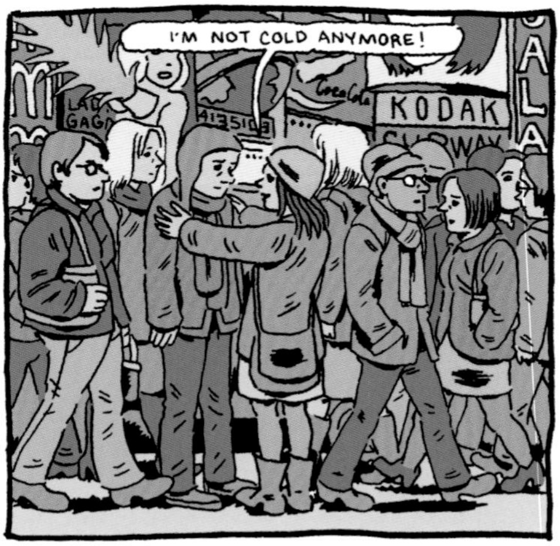
I'M NOT COLD ANYMORE!
KODAK

Don't Talk to Strangers

Hanging out on the pier at Coney Island while two scrubby fishermen spy on us.

LOOK, A CORMORANT!

WHERE? OH, HE WENT UNDER THE WATER.

IT WASN'T MORE THAN FIVE INCHES! NOT EVEN LEGAL!

I'LL BET YOU

TWO DOLLAAS!

FIVE!

As we leave they offer us a cookie.

HEY, YOU WANNA COOKIE?

TAKE A COOKIE!

YOU KNOW YOU WANNA!

THANK YOU.

GO ON, TAKE ANOTHER!

WAN'T SOME BEER WITH IT?

It's one of those dry, tasteless digestifs with the mouth feel of fiber board.

IT DOESN'T REALLY TASTE LIKE COOKIE.

YOU'RE EATING IT?!

ARE YOU CRAZY?!

GAK

REMEMBER, KIDS, DON'T TAKE CANDY FROM STRANGERS!

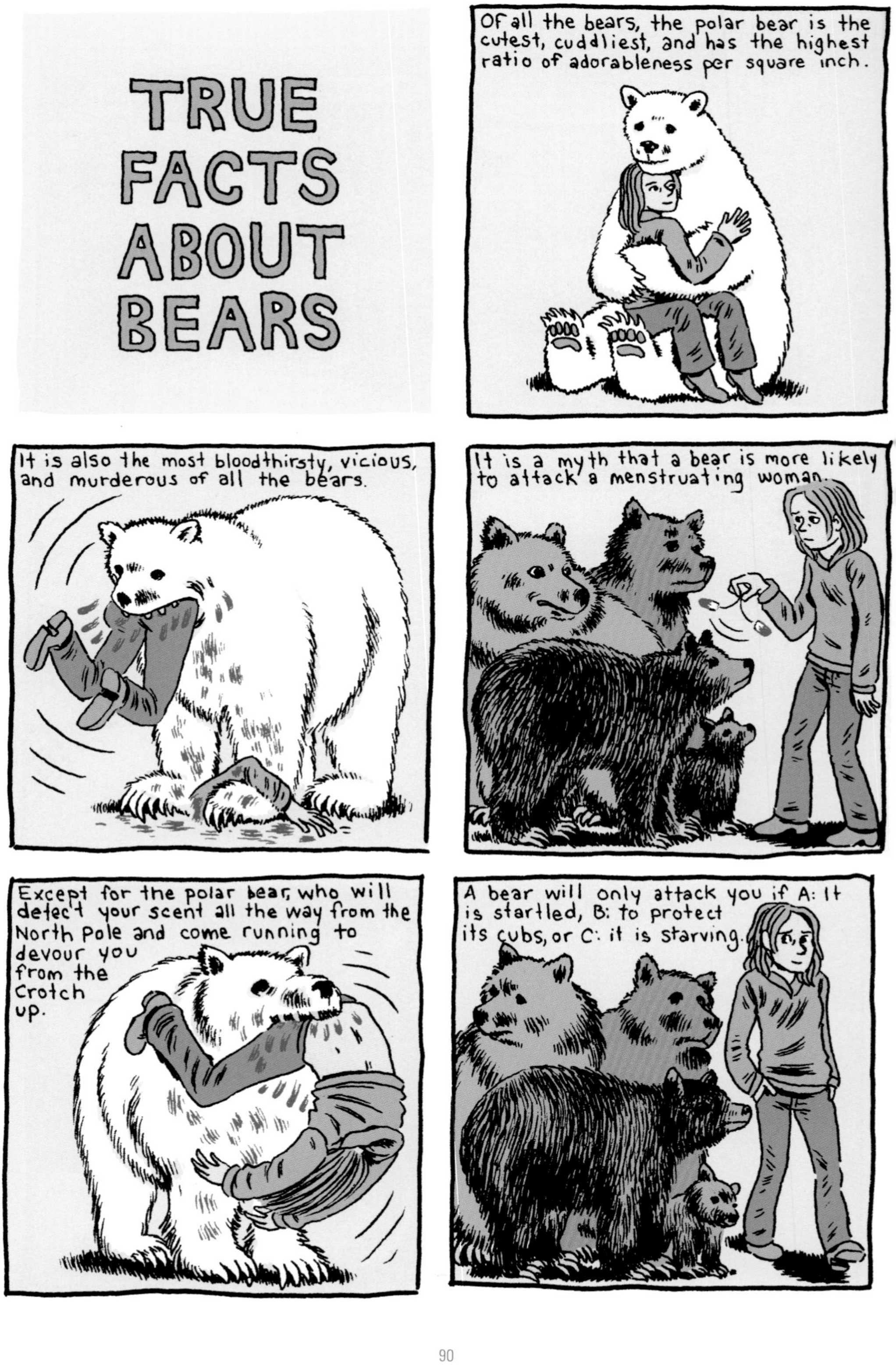
TRUE FACTS ABOUT BEARS
Of all the bears, the polar bear is the cutest, cuddliest, and has the highest ratio of adorableness per square inch.
It is also the most bloodthirsty, vicious, and murderous of all the bears.
It is a myth that a bear is more likely to attack a menstruating woman.
Except for the polar bear, who will detect your scent all the way from the North Pole and come running to devour you from the crotch up.
A bear will only attack you if A: It is startled, B: to protect its cubs, or C: it is starving.

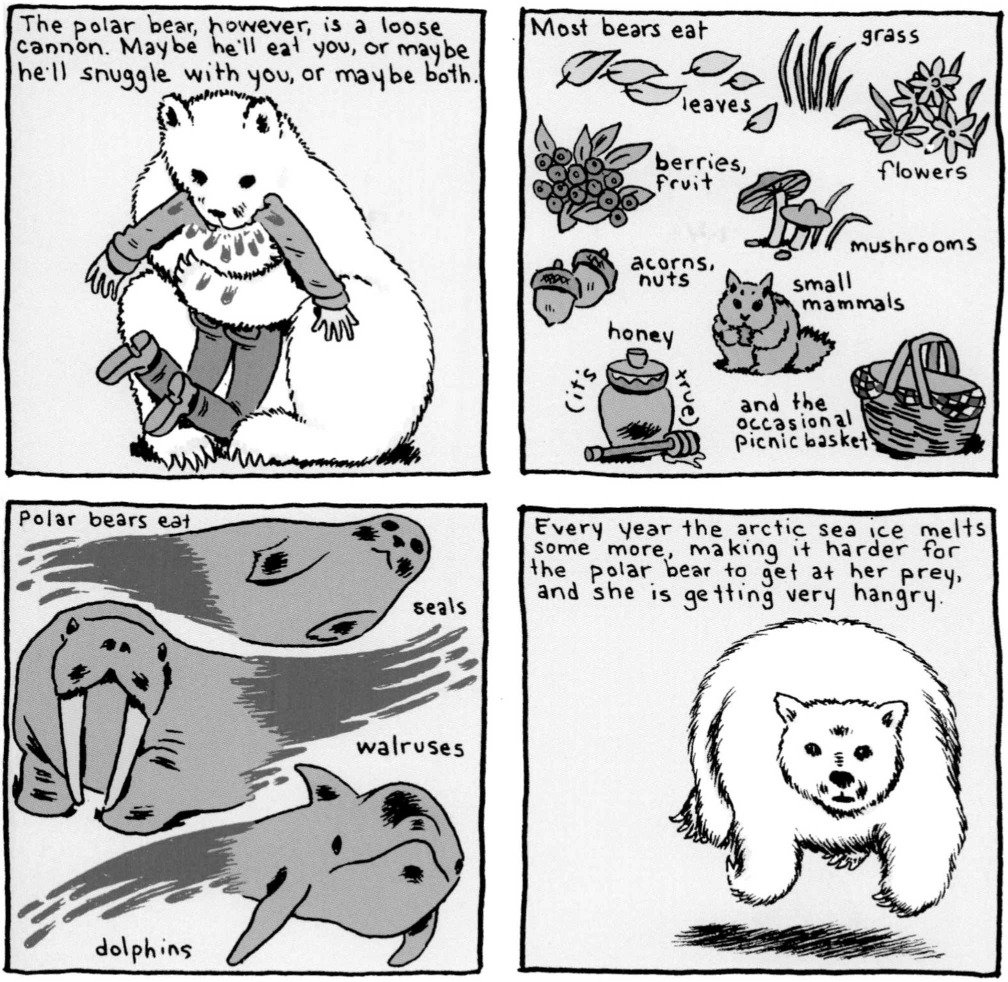
The polar bear, however, is a loose cannon. Maybe he'll eat you, or maybe he'll snuggle with you, or maybe both.
Most bears eat
grass
leaves
flowers
berries, fruit
mushrooms
acorns, nuts
small mammals
honey
(it's true)
and the occasional picnic basket
Polar bears eat
seals
walruses
dolphins
Every year the arctic sea ice melts some more, making it harder for the polar bear to get at her prey, and she is getting very hangry.

1-800-CATS

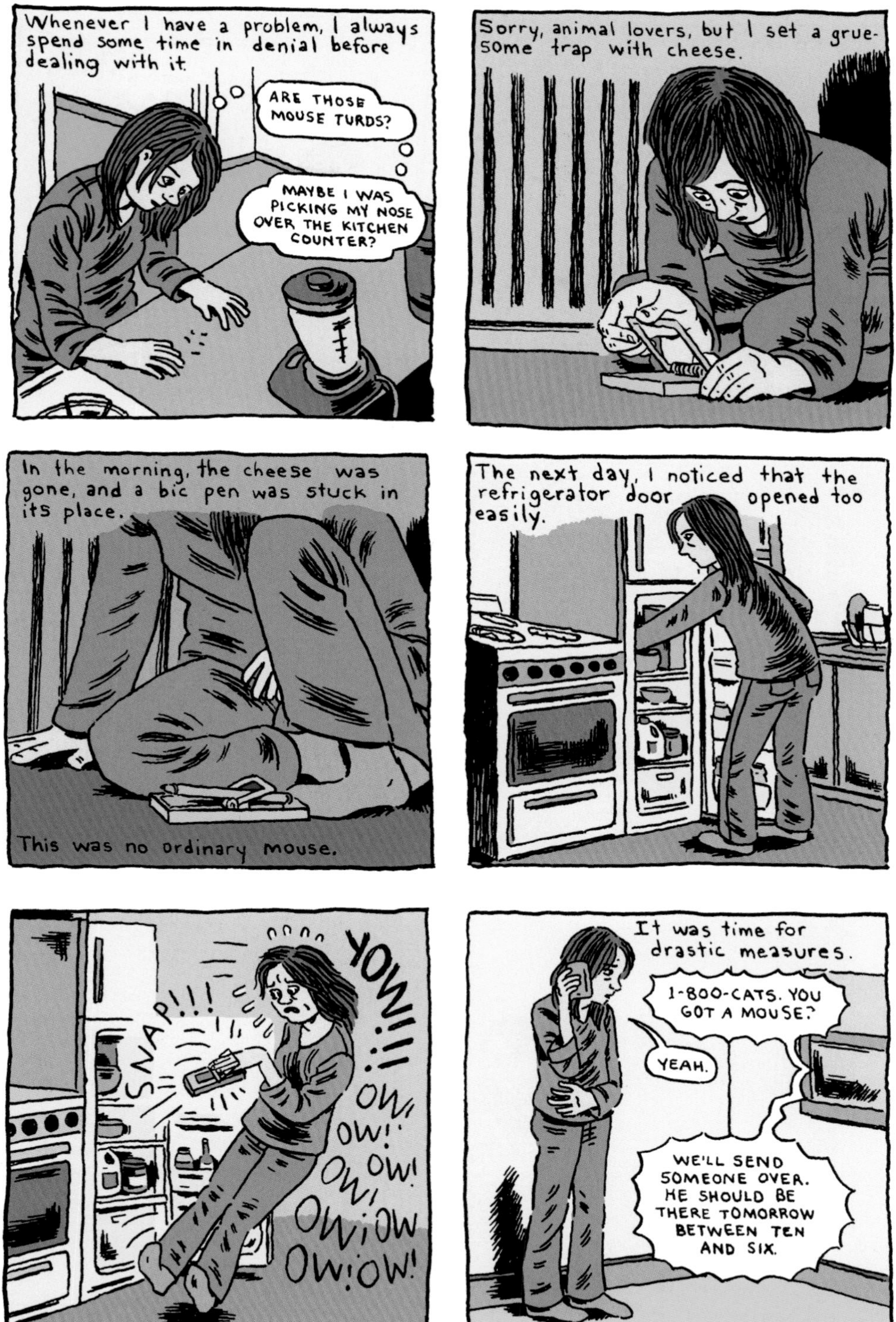
Whenever I have a problem, I always spend some time in denial before dealing with it.
ARE THOSE MOUSE TURDS?
MAYBE I WAS PICKING MY NOSE OVER THE KITCHEN COUNTER?
Sorry, animal lovers, but I set a gruesome trap with cheese.
In the morning, the cheese was gone, and a bic pen was stuck in its place.
This was no ordinary mouse.
The next day, I noticed that the refrigerator door opened too easily.
SNAP!!!
YOW!!!
OW! OW! OW! OW! OW!OW OW!OW!
It was time for drastic measures.
1-800-CATS. YOU GOT A MOUSE?
YEAH.
WE'LL SEND SOMEONE OVER. HE SHOULD BE THERE TOMORROW BETWEEN TEN AND SIX.

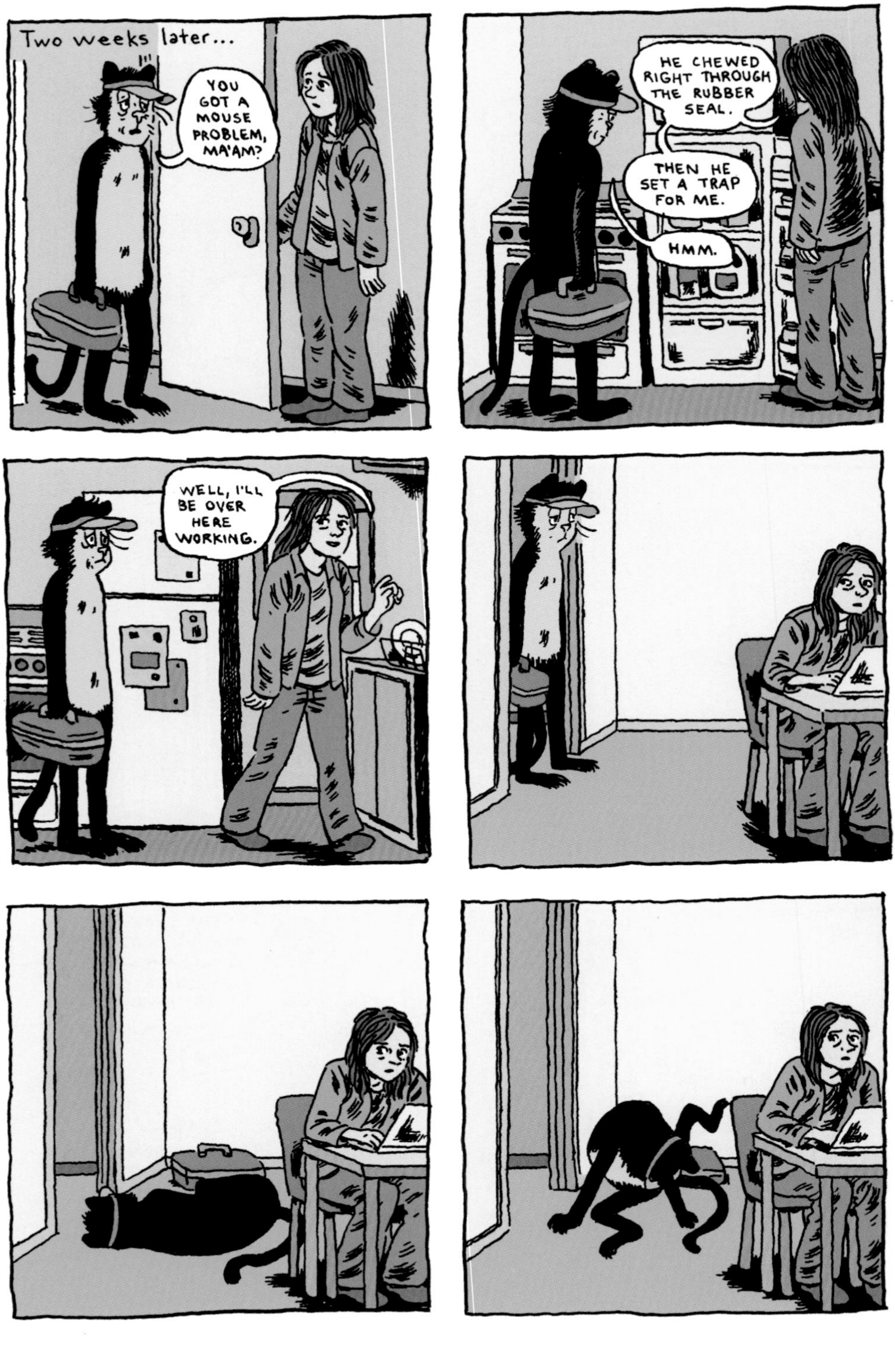
Two weeks later...
YOU GOT A MOUSE PROBLEM, MA'AM?
HE CHEWED RIGHT THROUGH THE RUBBER SEAL.
THEN HE SET A TRAP FOR ME.
HMM.
WELL, I'LL BE OVER HERE WORKING.

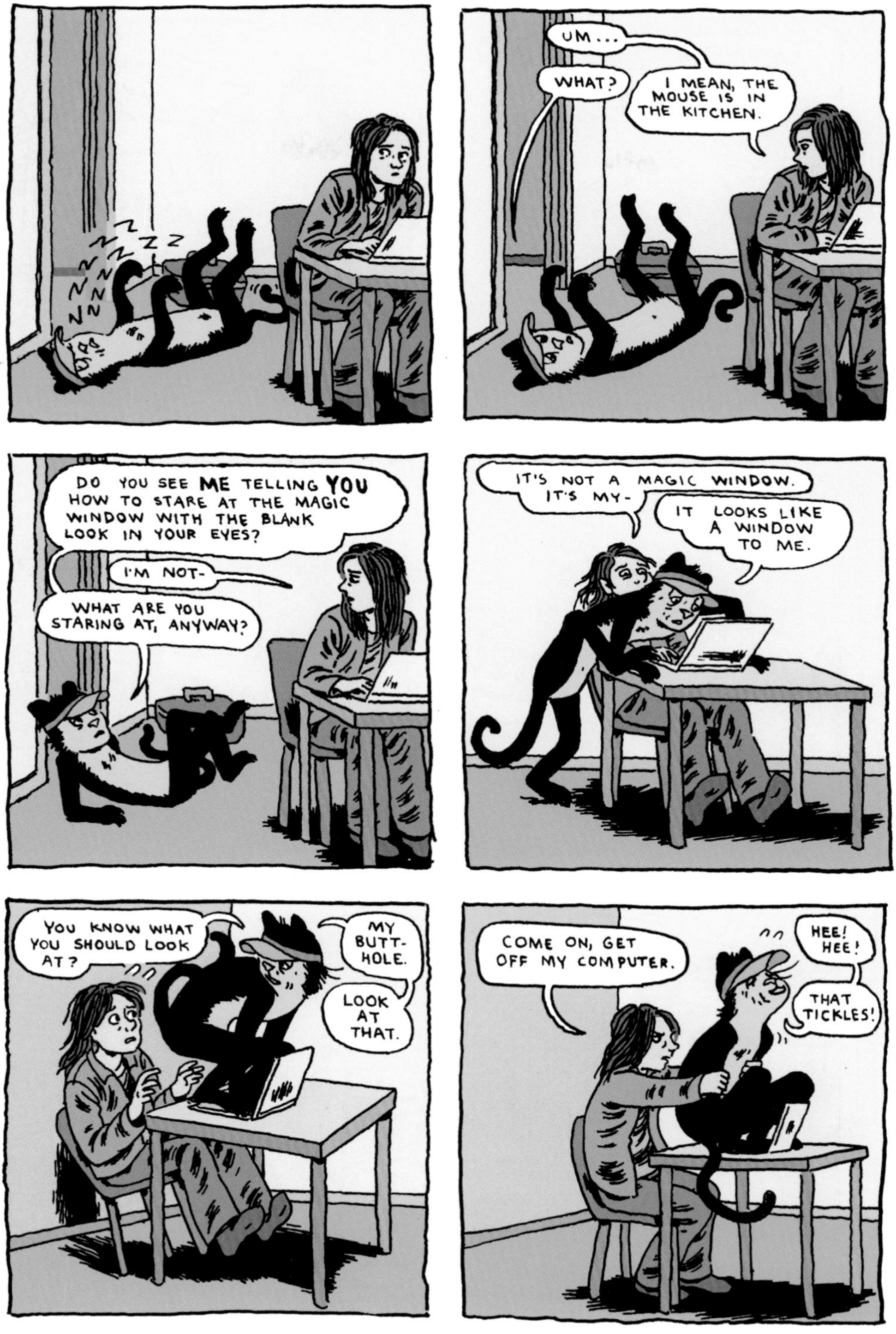
ZZZ
NNNNNN
UM...
WHAT?
I MEAN, THE MOUSE IS IN THE KITCHEN.
DO YOU SEE ME TELLING YOU HOW TO STARE AT THE MAGIC WINDOW WITH THE BLANK LOOK IN YOUR EYES?
I'M NOT-
WHAT ARE YOU STARING AT, ANYWAY?
IT'S NOT A MAGIC WINDOW. IT'S MY-
IT LOOKS LIKE A WINDOW TO ME.
YOU KNOW WHAT YOU SHOULD LOOK AT?
MY BUTT-HOLE.
LOOK AT THAT.
COME ON, GET OFF MY COMPUTER.
HEE! HEE!
THAT TICKLES!

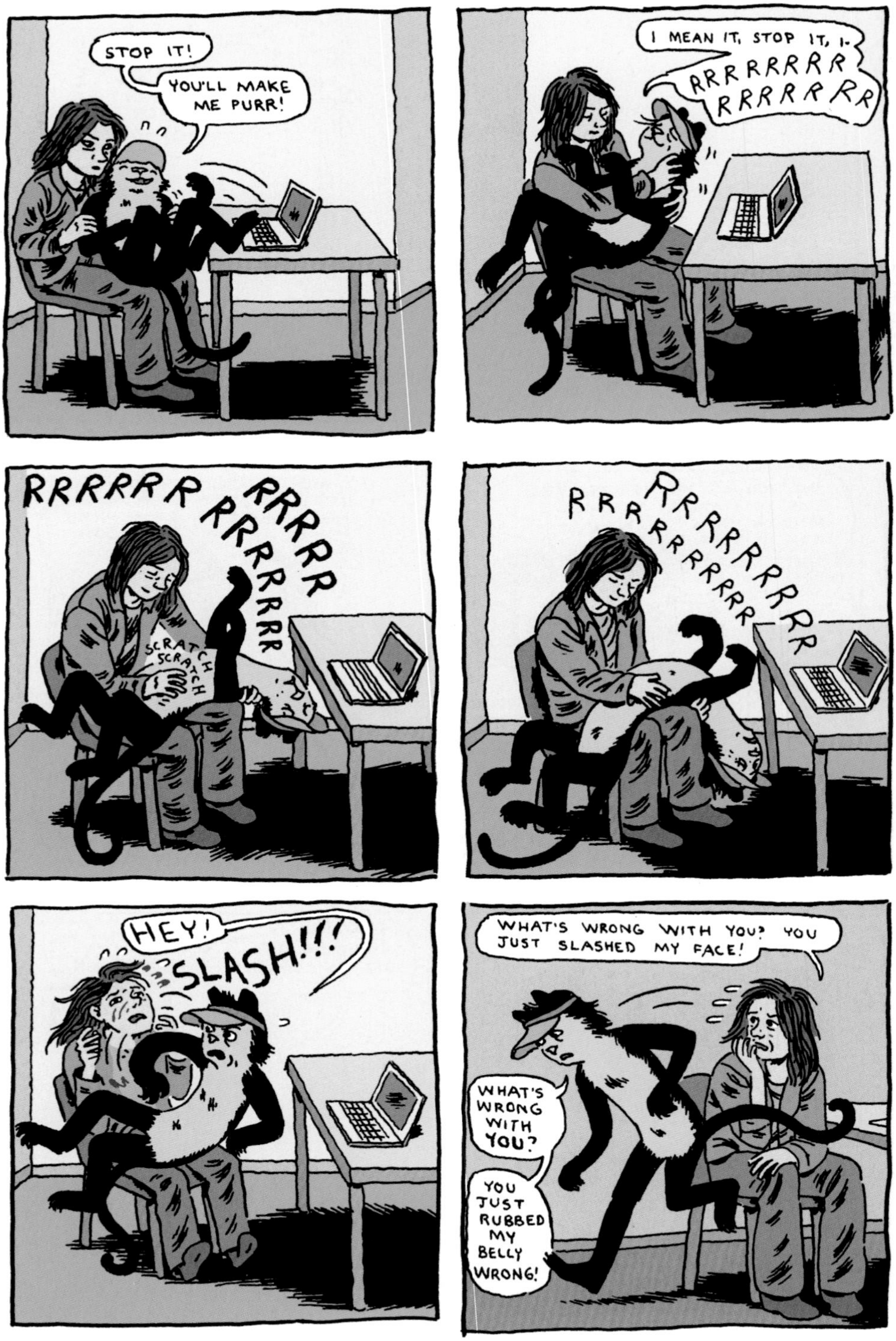
STOP IT!
YOU'LL MAKE ME PURR!
I MEAN IT, STOP IT, I-
RRRRRRRR RRRRRRR
RRRRRR RRRRR RRRRRR RRRRRRR
SCRATCH SCRATCH SCRATCH
RRR RRRRRRRRR RRRRRRRRR
HEY!
SLASH!!!
WHAT'S WRONG WITH YOU? YOU JUST SLASHED MY FACE!
WHAT'S WRONG WITH YOU?
YOU JUST RUBBED MY BELLY WRONG!

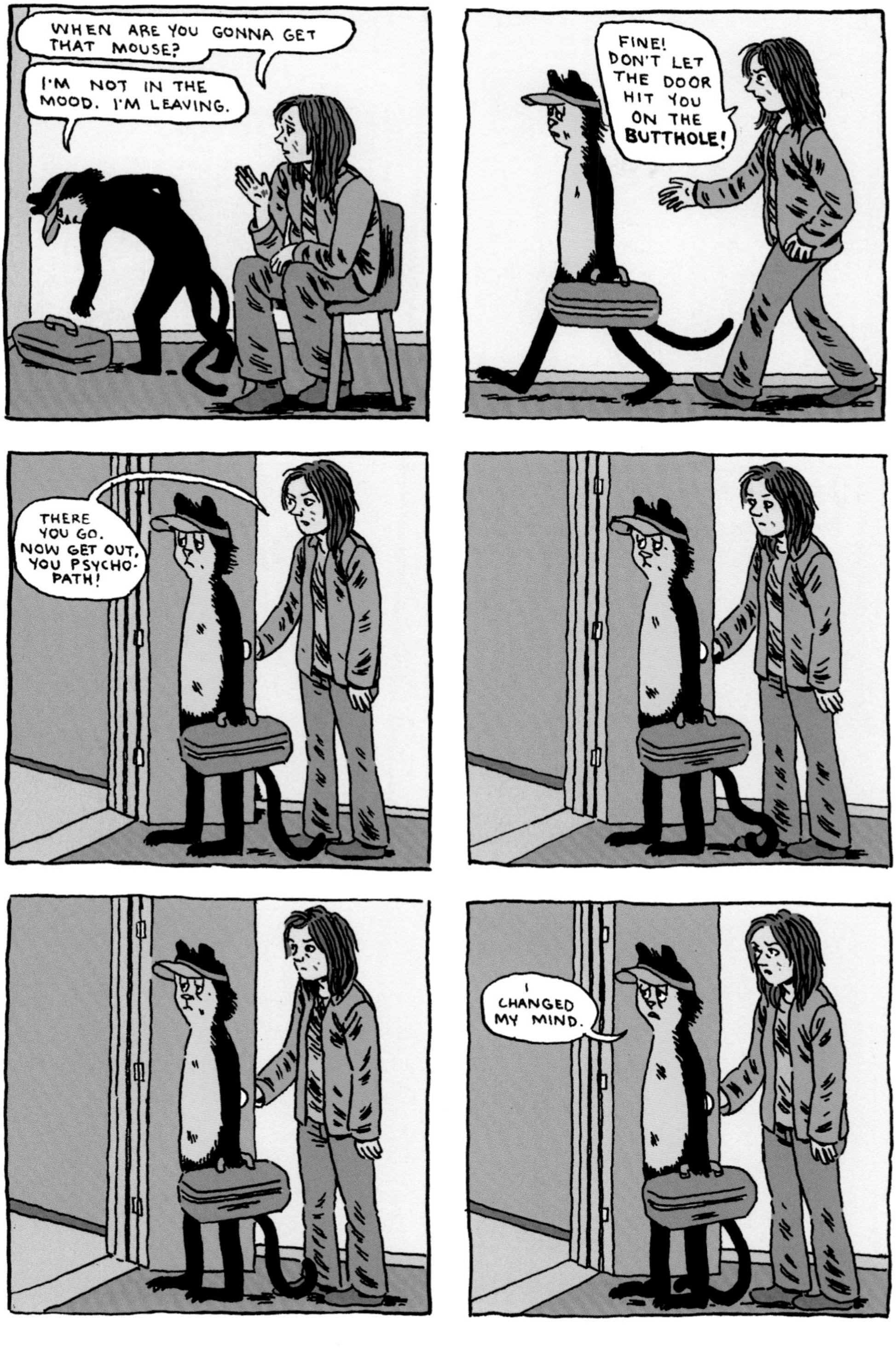
WHEN ARE YOU GONNA GET THAT MOUSE?
I'M NOT IN THE MOOD. I'M LEAVING.
FINE! DON'T LET THE DOOR HIT YOU ON THE BUTTHOLE!
THERE YOU GO. NOW GET OUT, YOU PSYCHO-PATH!
I CHANGED MY MIND.

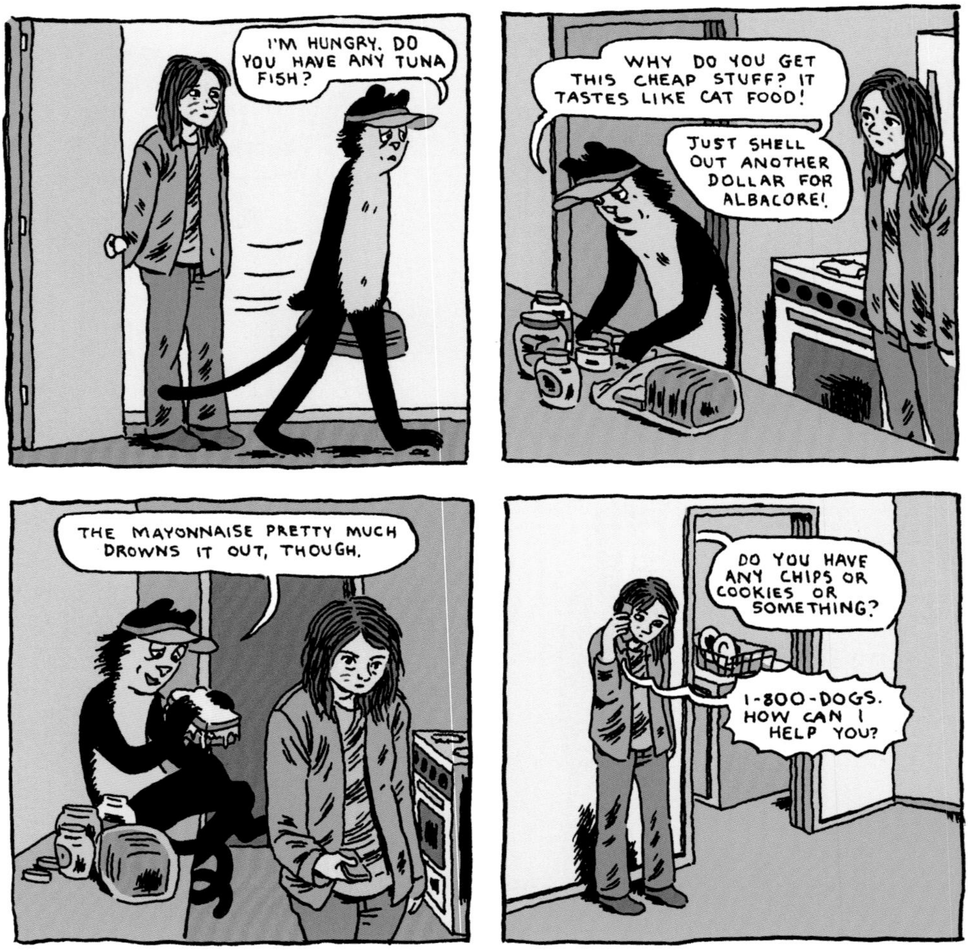
I'M HUNGRY. DO YOU HAVE ANY TUNA FISH?
WHY DO YOU GET THIS CHEAP STUFF? IT TASTES LIKE CAT FOOD!
JUST SHELL OUT ANOTHER DOLLAR FOR ALBACORE!
THE MAYONNAISE PRETTY MUCH DROWNS IT OUT, THOUGH.
DO YOU HAVE ANY CHIPS OR COOKIES OR SOMETHING?
1-800-DOGS. HOW CAN I HELP YOU?

Dreaming

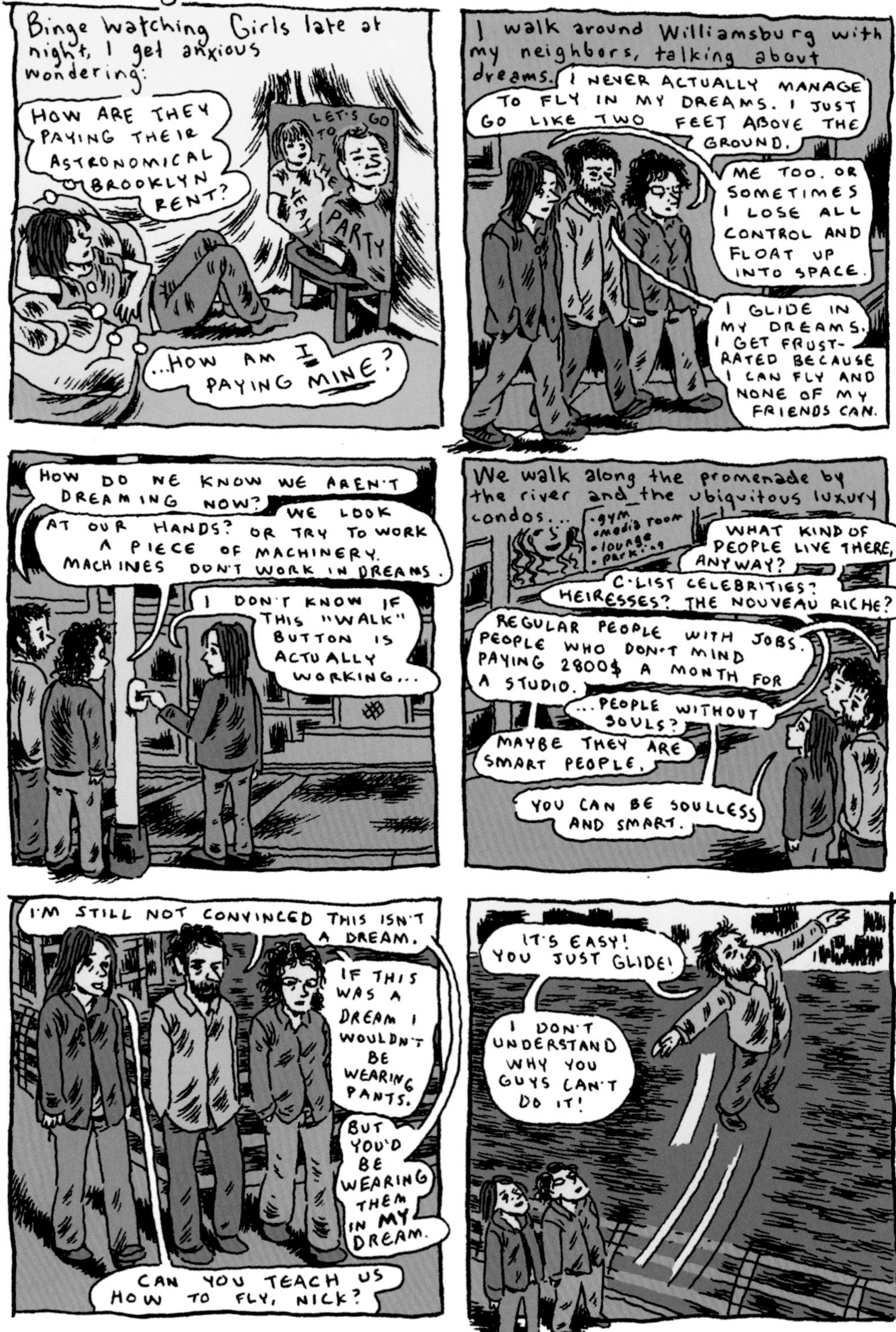
Binge watching Girls late at night, I get anxious wondering:
HOW ARE THEY PAYING THEIR ASTRONOMICAL BROOKLYN RENT?
LET'S GO TO THE PARTY YEAH
...HOW AM I PAYING MINE?
I walk around Williamsburg with my neighbors, talking about dreams.
I NEVER ACTUALLY MANAGE TO FLY IN MY DREAMS. I JUST GO LIKE TWO FEET ABOVE THE GROUND.
ME TOO. OR SOMETIMES I LOSE ALL CONTROL AND FLOAT UP INTO SPACE.
I GLIDE IN MY DREAMS. I GET FRUSTRATED BECAUSE I CAN FLY AND NONE OF MY FRIENDS CAN.
HOW DO WE KNOW WE AREN'T DREAMING NOW?
WE LOOK AT OUR HANDS? OR TRY TO WORK A PIECE OF MACHINERY. MACHINES DON'T WORK IN DREAMS.
I DON'T KNOW IF THIS "WALK" BUTTON IS ACTUALLY WORKING...
We walk along the promenade by the river and the ubiquitous luxury condos...
•gym •media room •lounge •parking
WHAT KIND OF PEOPLE LIVE THERE, ANYWAY?
C-LIST CELEBRITIES? HEIRESSES? THE NOUVEAU RICHE?
REGULAR PEOPLE WITH JOBS. PEOPLE WHO DON'T MIND PAYING 2800$ A MONTH FOR A STUDIO.
...PEOPLE WITHOUT SOULS?
MAYBE THEY ARE SMART PEOPLE.
YOU CAN BE SOULLESS AND SMART.
I'M STILL NOT CONVINCED THIS ISN'T A DREAM.
IF THIS WAS A DREAM I WOULDN'T BE WEARING PANTS.
BUT YOU'D BE WEARING THEM IN MY DREAM.
CAN YOU TEACH US HOW TO FLY, NICK?
IT'S EASY! YOU JUST GLIDE!
I DON'T UNDERSTAND WHY YOU GUYS CAN'T DO IT!

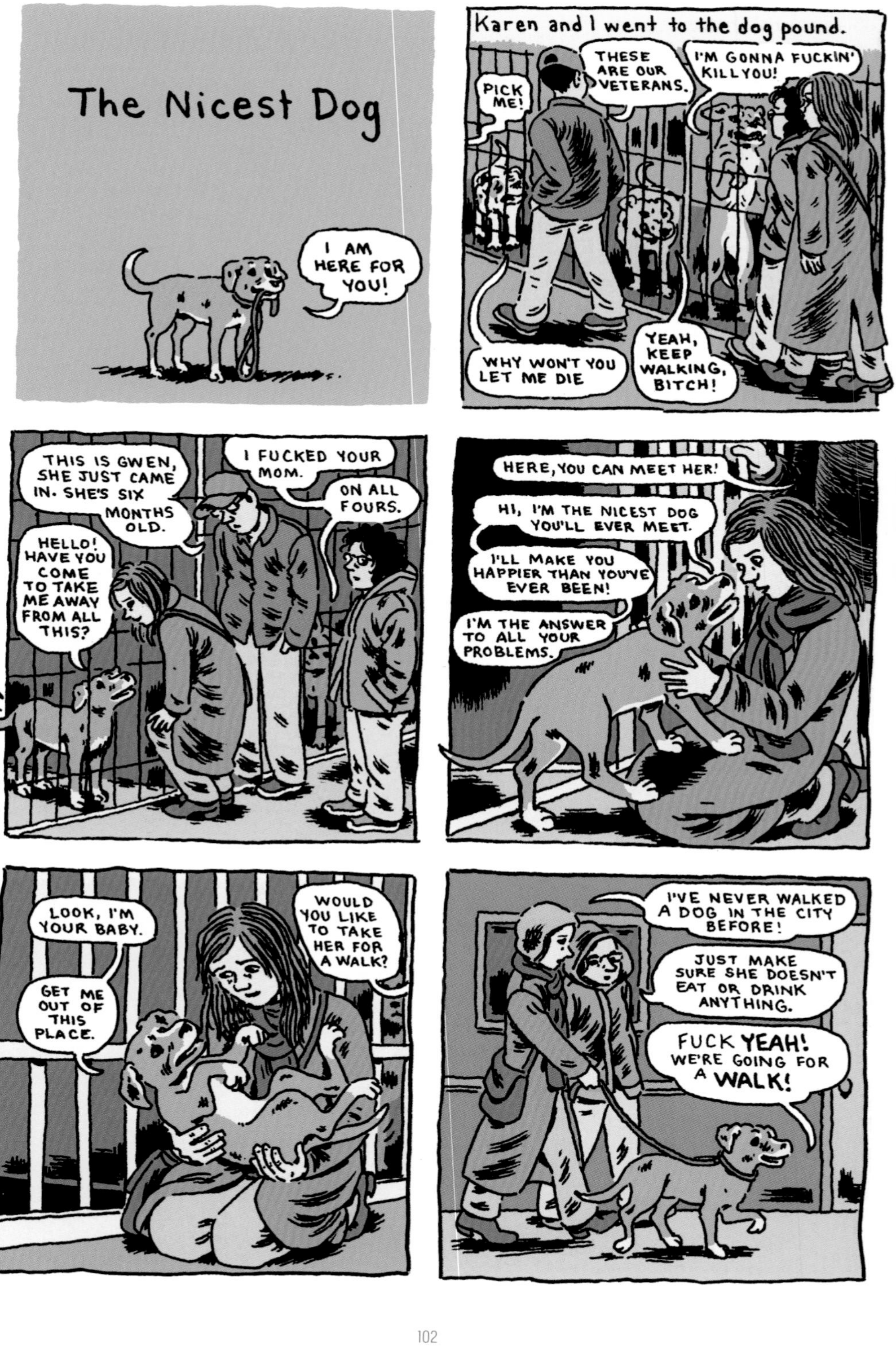

The Nicest Dog
I AM HERE FOR YOU!
Karen and I went to the dog pound.
PICK ME!
THESE ARE OUR VETERANS.
I'M GONNA FUCKIN' KILL YOU!
WHY WON'T YOU LET ME DIE
YEAH, KEEP WALKING, BITCH!
THIS IS GWEN, SHE JUST CAME IN. SHE'S SIX MONTHS OLD.
I FUCKED YOUR MOM.
ON ALL FOURS.
HELLO! HAVE YOU COME TO TAKE ME AWAY FROM ALL THIS?
HERE, YOU CAN MEET HER!
HI, I'M THE NICEST DOG YOU'LL EVER MEET.
I'LL MAKE YOU HAPPIER THAN YOU'VE EVER BEEN!
I'M THE ANSWER TO ALL YOUR PROBLEMS.
LOOK, I'M YOUR BABY.
WOULD YOU LIKE TO TAKE HER FOR A WALK?
GET ME OUT OF THIS PLACE.
I'VE NEVER WALKED A DOG IN THE CITY BEFORE!
JUST MAKE SURE SHE DOESN'T EAT OR DRINK ANYTHING.
FUCK YEAH! WE'RE GOING FOR A WALK!

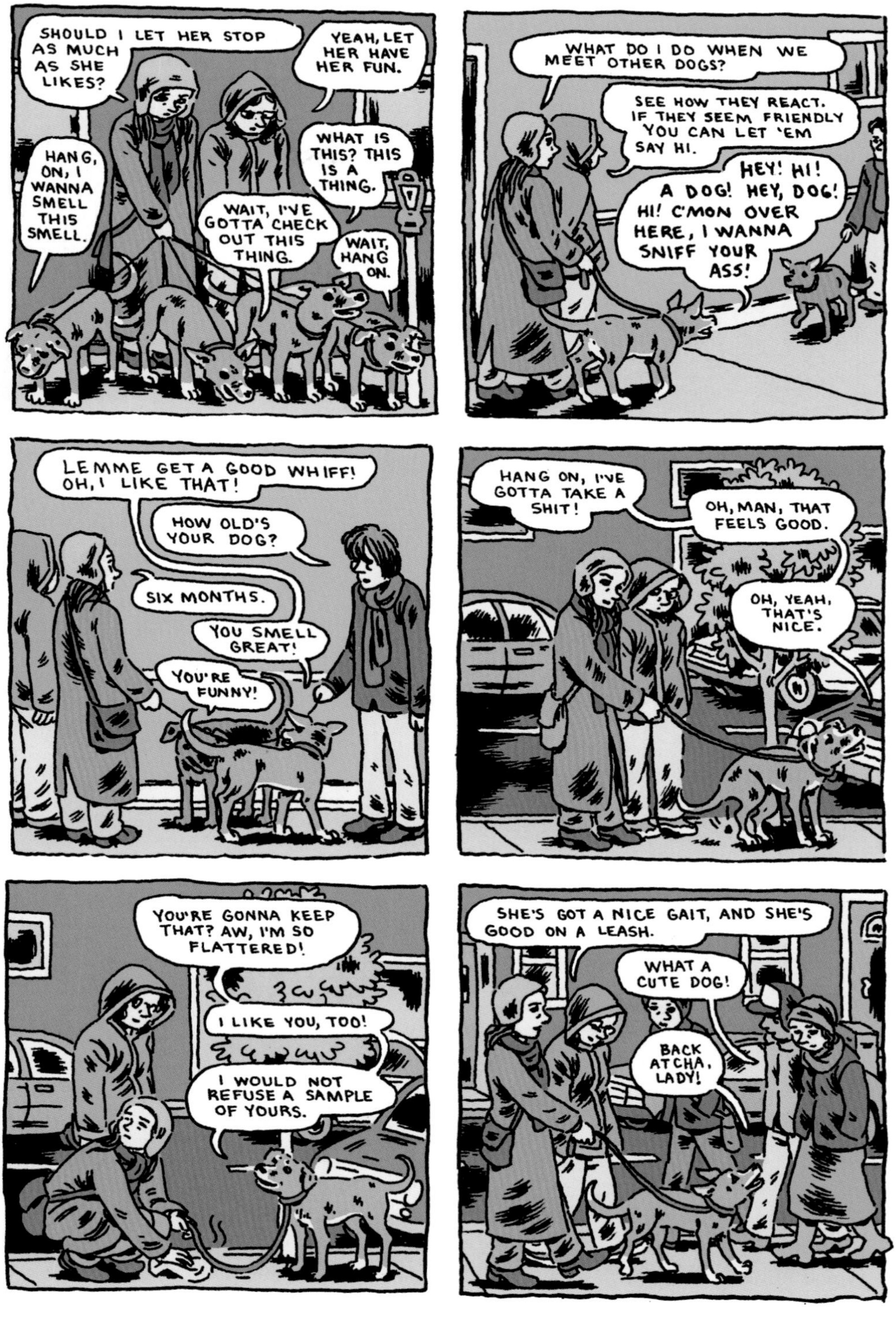
SHOULD I LET HER STOP AS MUCH AS SHE LIKES?
YEAH, LET HER HAVE HER FUN.
HANG, ON, I WANNA SMELL THIS SMELL.
WHAT IS THIS? THIS IS A THING.
WAIT, I'VE GOTTA CHECK OUT THIS THING.
WAIT, HANG ON.
WHAT DO I DO WHEN WE MEET OTHER DOGS?
SEE HOW THEY REACT. IF THEY SEEM FRIENDLY YOU CAN LET 'EM SAY HI.
HEY! HI! A DOG! HEY, DOG! HI! C'MON OVER HERE, I WANNA SNIFF YOUR ASS!
LEMME GET A GOOD WHIFF! OH, I LIKE THAT!
HOW OLD'S YOUR DOG?
SIX MONTHS.
YOU SMELL GREAT!
YOU'RE FUNNY!
HANG ON, I'VE GOTTA TAKE A SHIT!
OH, MAN, THAT FEELS GOOD.
OH, YEAH, THAT'S NICE.
YOU'RE GONNA KEEP THAT? AW, I'M SO FLATTERED!
I LIKE YOU, TOO!
I WOULD NOT REFUSE A SAMPLE OF YOURS.
SHE'S GOT A NICE GAIT, AND SHE'S GOOD ON A LEASH.
WHAT A CUTE DOG!
BACK ATCHA, LADY!

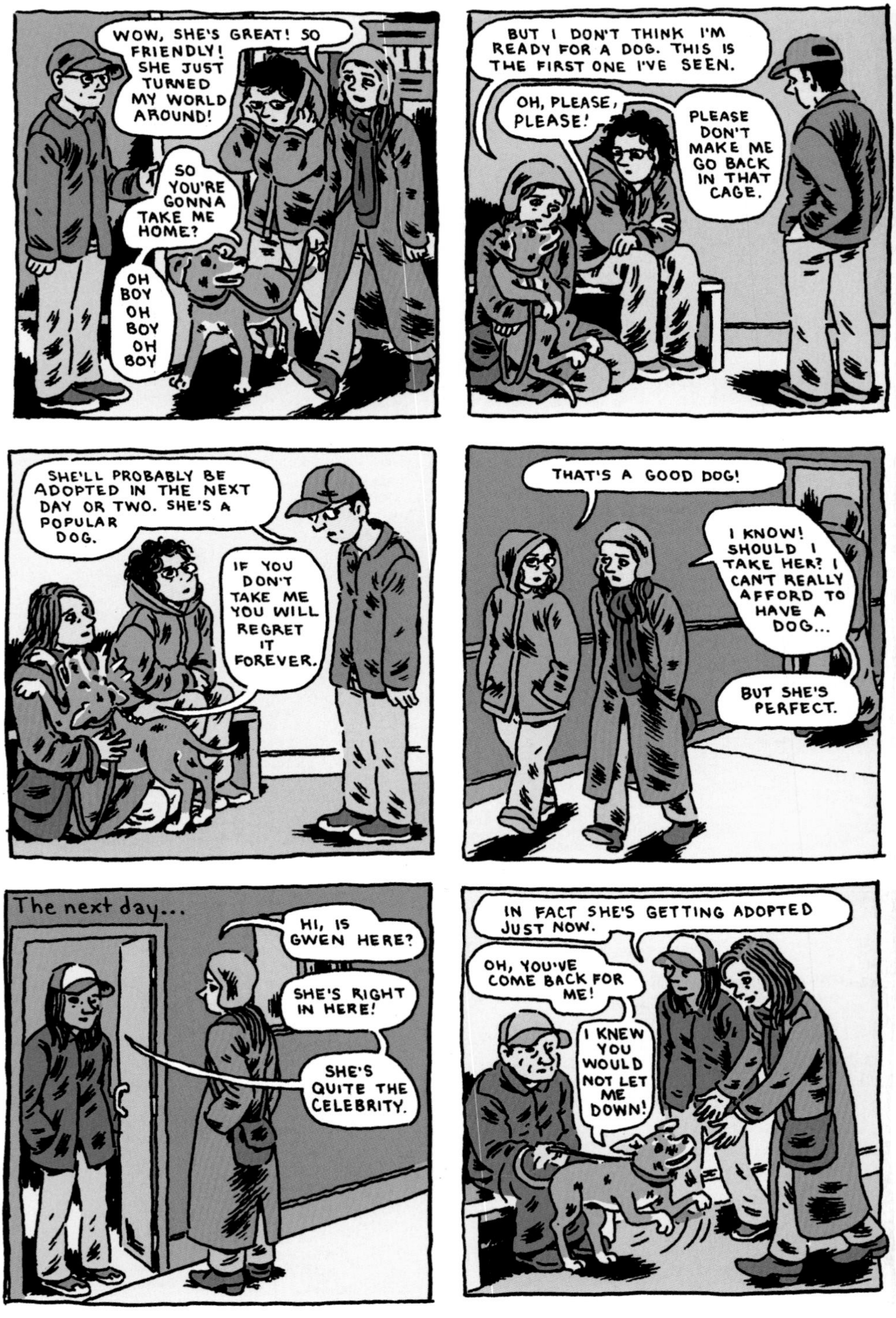
WOW, SHE'S GREAT! SO FRIENDLY! SHE JUST TURNED MY WORLD AROUND!
SO YOU'RE GONNA TAKE ME HOME?
OH BOY OH BOY OH BOY
BUT I DON'T THINK I'M READY FOR A DOG. THIS IS THE FIRST ONE I'VE SEEN.
OH, PLEASE, PLEASE!
PLEASE DON'T MAKE ME GO BACK IN THAT CAGE.
SHE'LL PROBABLY BE ADOPTED IN THE NEXT DAY OR TWO. SHE'S A POPULAR DOG.
IF YOU DON'T TAKE ME YOU WILL REGRET IT FOREVER.
THAT'S A GOOD DOG!
I KNOW! SHOULD I TAKE HER? I CAN'T REALLY AFFORD TO HAVE A DOG...
BUT SHE'S PERFECT.
The next day...
HI, IS GWEN HERE?
SHE'S RIGHT IN HERE!
SHE'S QUITE THE CELEBRITY.
IN FACT SHE'S GETTING ADOPTED JUST NOW.
OH, YOU'VE COME BACK FOR ME!
I KNEW YOU WOULD NOT LET ME DOWN!

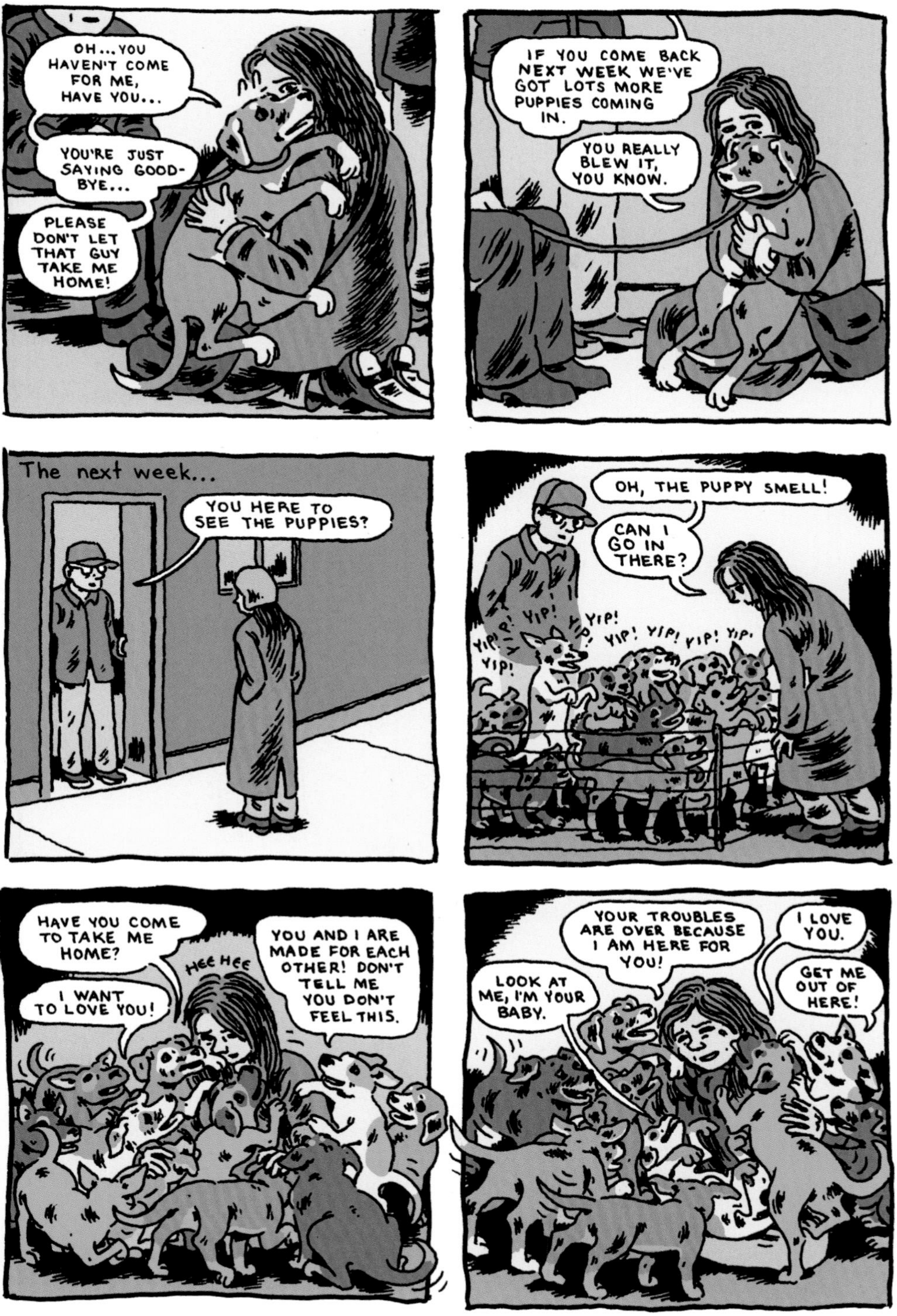
OH... YOU HAVEN'T COME FOR ME, HAVE YOU...
YOU'RE JUST SAYING GOOD-BYE...
PLEASE DON'T LET THAT GUY TAKE ME HOME!
IF YOU COME BACK NEXT WEEK WE'VE GOT LOTS MORE PUPPIES COMING IN.
YOU REALLY BLEW IT, YOU KNOW.
The next week...
YOU HERE TO SEE THE PUPPIES?
OH, THE PUPPY SMELL!
CAN I GO IN THERE?
YIP! YIP! YIP! YIP! YIP! YIP! YIP! YIP! YIP!
HAVE YOU COME TO TAKE ME HOME?
I WANT TO LOVE YOU!
HEE HEE
YOU AND I ARE MADE FOR EACH OTHER! DON'T TELL ME YOU DON'T FEEL THIS.
YOUR TROUBLES ARE OVER BECAUSE I AM HERE FOR YOU!
LOOK AT ME, I'M YOUR BABY.
I LOVE YOU.
GET ME OUT OF HERE!

THESE BOOTS

When I ask for advice on teaching for the first time, I'm told I should make sure I'm well prepared. How does one prepare? All preparation seems to be is thinking things and jotting them down.

How do I know if I'm doing it right?

More substantial is preparing the outfit I will wear. I'm pretty sure that 95% of teaching is looking like a teacher. 97% is looking like a teacher who has taken the train from New York City for the day.

Oh, these boots? I just bought them for twenty dollars at a party/moving sale. I'm not exactly into the Julia Roberts/Pretty Woman style but these would make Carrie Bradshaw jealous.

I used scissors and glue to turn them from above-the-knee boots to below-the-knee boots.

Then I discovered that these were Prada.

I imagine that the feeling of wearing designer footwear must be similar to how some men describe driving a luxury sports car. You'll never understand it unless you get to try it.

What I'm trying to say is I've spent far more time thinking about these boots than the class I will teach.

The night before class, as soon as I fell asleep, I dreamed that I stood on some sort of balcony and watched helplessly while an evil man one floor up beat my two little brothers.

N-N-N

When I tried to scream I woke myself up with my own choked grunts.

UNGH!

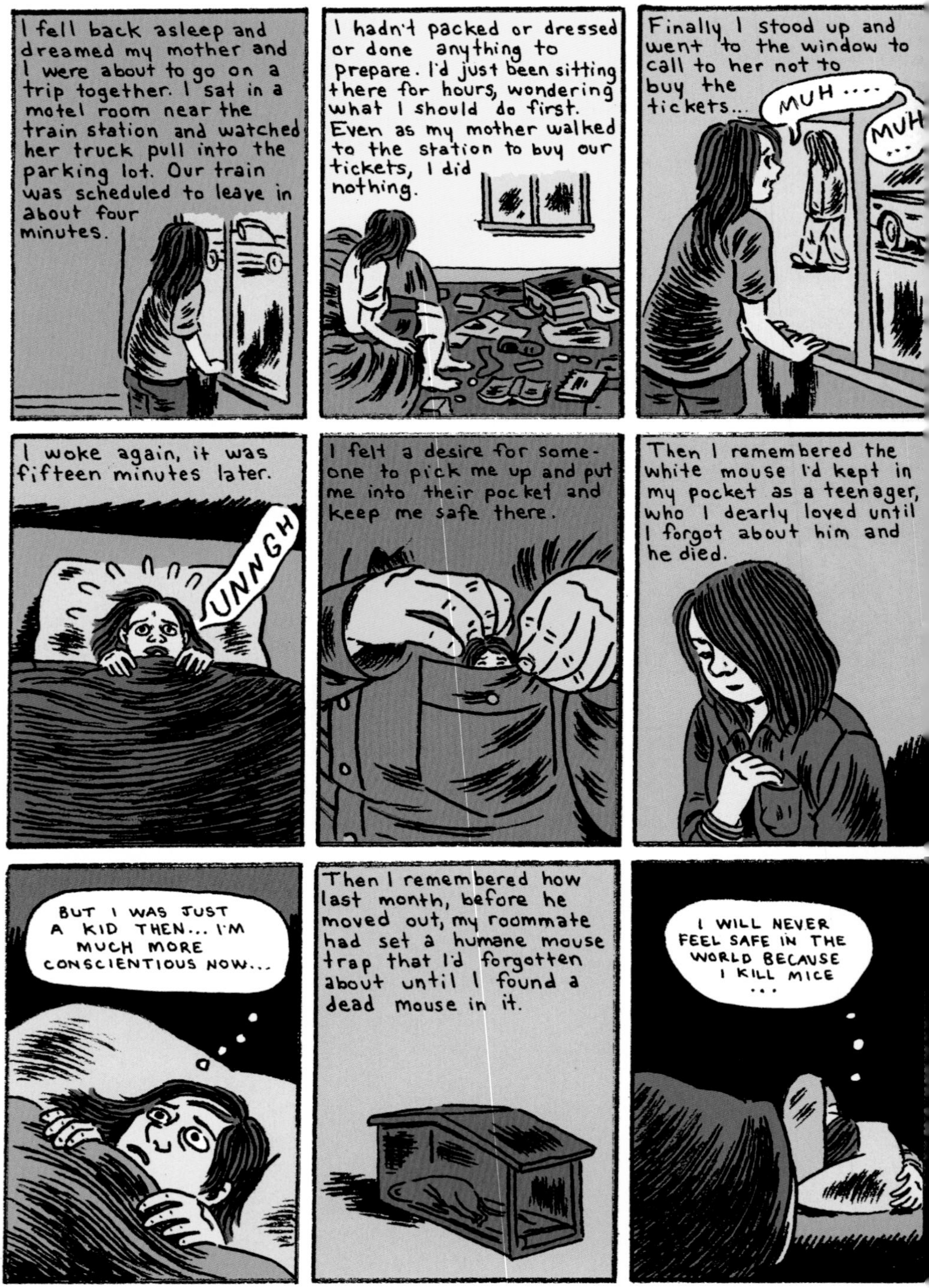

I fell back asleep and dreamed my mother and I were about to go on a trip together. I sat in a motel room near the train station and watched her truck pull into the parking lot. Our train was scheduled to leave in about four minutes.
I hadn't packed or dressed or done anything to prepare. I'd just been sitting there for hours, wondering what I should do first. Even as my mother walked to the station to buy our tickets, I did nothing.
Finally I stood up and went to the window to call to her not to buy the tickets...
MUH....
MUH...
I woke again, it was fifteen minutes later.
UNNGH
I felt a desire for someone to pick me up and put me into their pocket and keep me safe there.
Then I remembered the white mouse I'd kept in my pocket as a teenager, who I dearly loved until I forgot about him and he died.
BUT I WAS JUST A KID THEN... I'M MUCH MORE CONSCIENTIOUS NOW...
Then I remembered how last month, before he moved out, my roommate had set a humane mouse trap that I'd forgotten about until I found a dead mouse in it.
I WILL NEVER FEEL SAFE IN THE WORLD BECAUSE I KILL MICE...

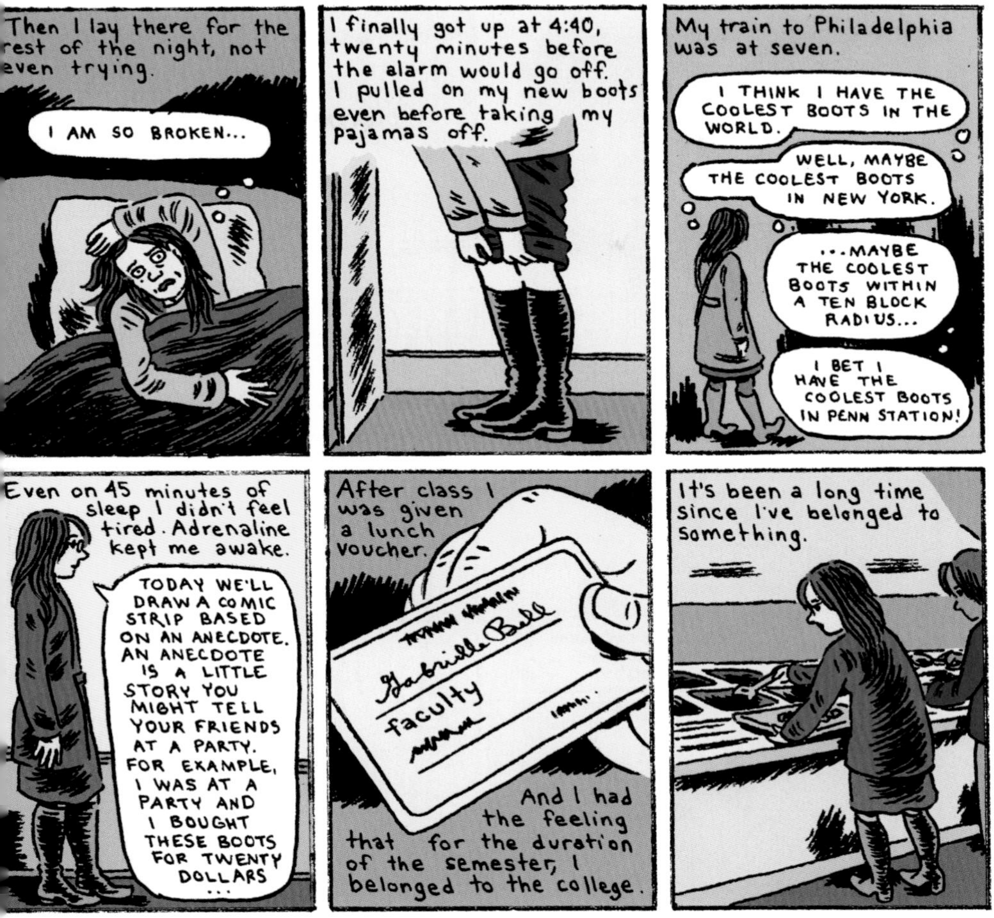
Then I lay there for the rest of the night, not even trying.
I AM SO BROKEN...
I finally got up at 4:40, twenty minutes before the alarm would go off. I pulled on my new boots even before taking my pajamas off.
My train to Philadelphia was at seven.
I THINK I HAVE THE COOLEST BOOTS IN THE WORLD.
WELL, MAYBE THE COOLEST BOOTS IN NEW YORK.
...MAYBE THE COOLEST BOOTS WITHIN A TEN BLOCK RADIUS...
I BET I HAVE THE COOLEST BOOTS IN PENN STATION!
Even on 45 minutes of sleep I didn't feel tired. Adrenaline kept me awake.
TODAY WE'LL DRAW A COMIC STRIP BASED ON AN ANECDOTE. AN ANECDOTE IS A LITTLE STORY YOU MIGHT TELL YOUR FRIENDS AT A PARTY. FOR EXAMPLE, I WAS AT A PARTY AND I BOUGHT THESE BOOTS FOR TWENTY DOLLARS ...
After class I was given a lunch voucher.
Gabrielle Bell
faculty
And I had the feeling that for the duration of the semester, I belonged to the college.
It's been a long time since I've belonged to something.

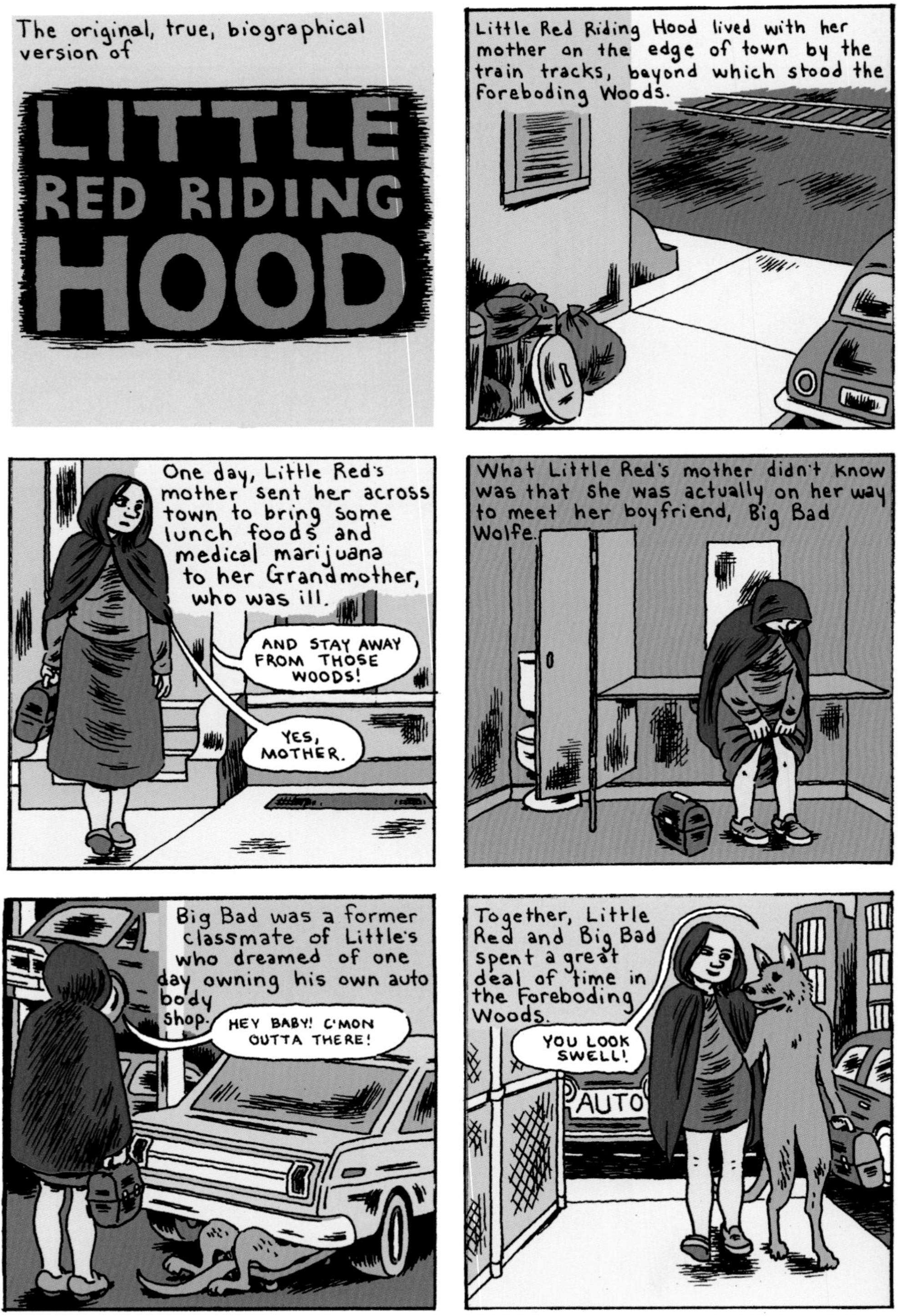
The original, true, biographical version of
LITTLE RED RIDING HOOD
Little Red Riding Hood lived with her mother on the edge of town by the train tracks, beyond which stood the Foreboding Woods.
One day, Little Red's mother sent her across town to bring some lunch foods and medical marijuana to her Grandmother, who was ill.
AND STAY AWAY FROM THOSE WOODS!
YES, MOTHER.
What Little Red's mother didn't know was that she was actually on her way to meet her boyfriend, Big Bad Wolfe.
Big Bad was a former classmate of Little's who dreamed of one day owning his own auto body shop.
HEY BABY! C'MON OUTTA THERE!
Together, Little Red and Big Bad spent a great deal of time in the Foreboding Woods.
YOU LOOK SWELL!
AUTO

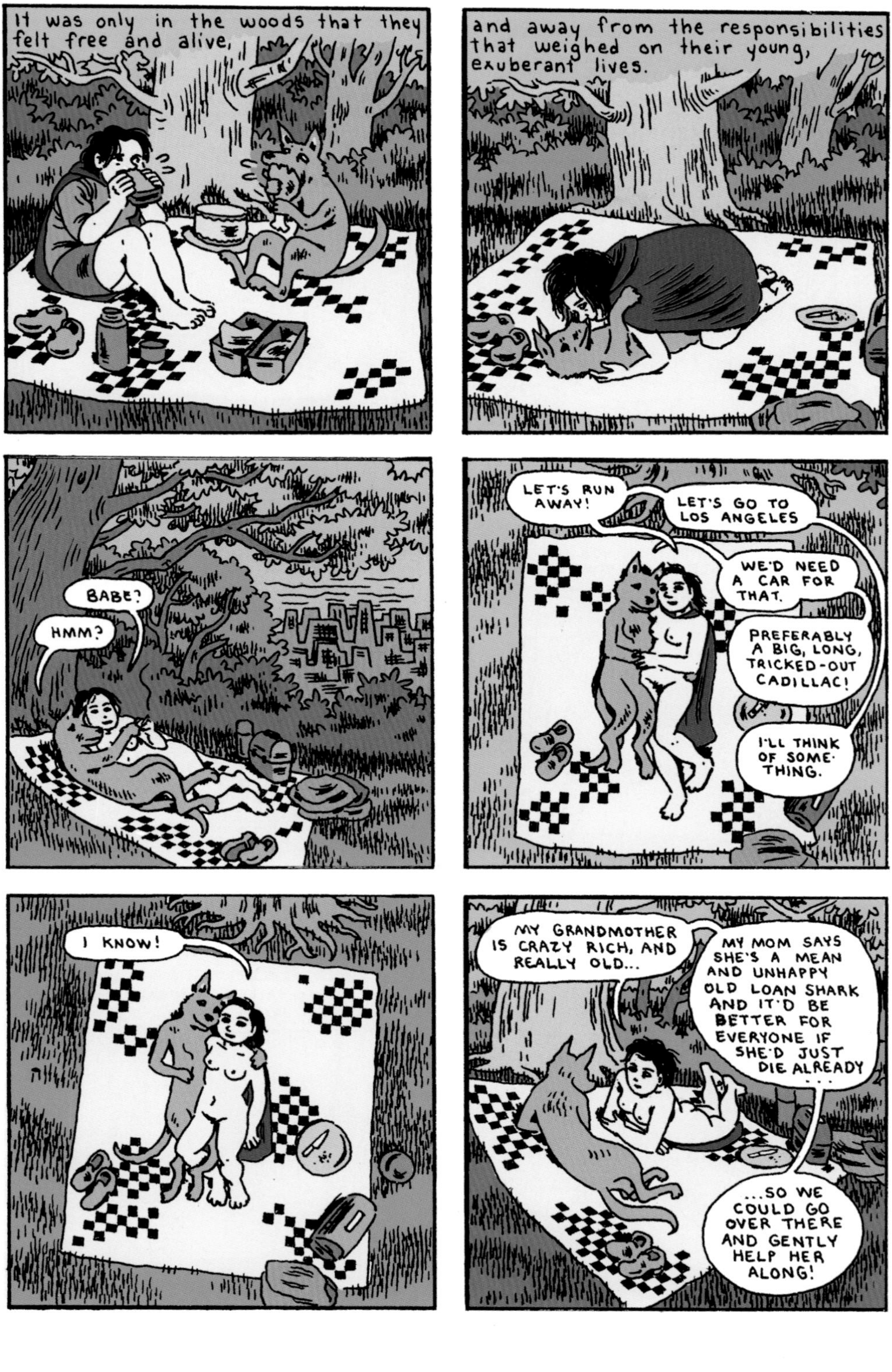
It was only in the woods that they felt free and alive,
and away from the responsibilities that weighed on their young, exuberant lives.
BABE?
HMM?
LET'S RUN AWAY!
LET'S GO TO LOS ANGELES
WE'D NEED A CAR FOR THAT.
PREFERABLY A BIG, LONG, TRICKED-OUT CADILLAC!
I'LL THINK OF SOMETHING.
I KNOW!
MY GRANDMOTHER IS CRAZY RICH, AND REALLY OLD...
MY MOM SAYS SHE'S A MEAN AND UNHAPPY OLD LOAN SHARK AND IT'D BE BETTER FOR EVERYONE IF SHE'D JUST DIE ALREADY...
...SO WE COULD GO OVER THERE AND GENTLY HELP HER ALONG!

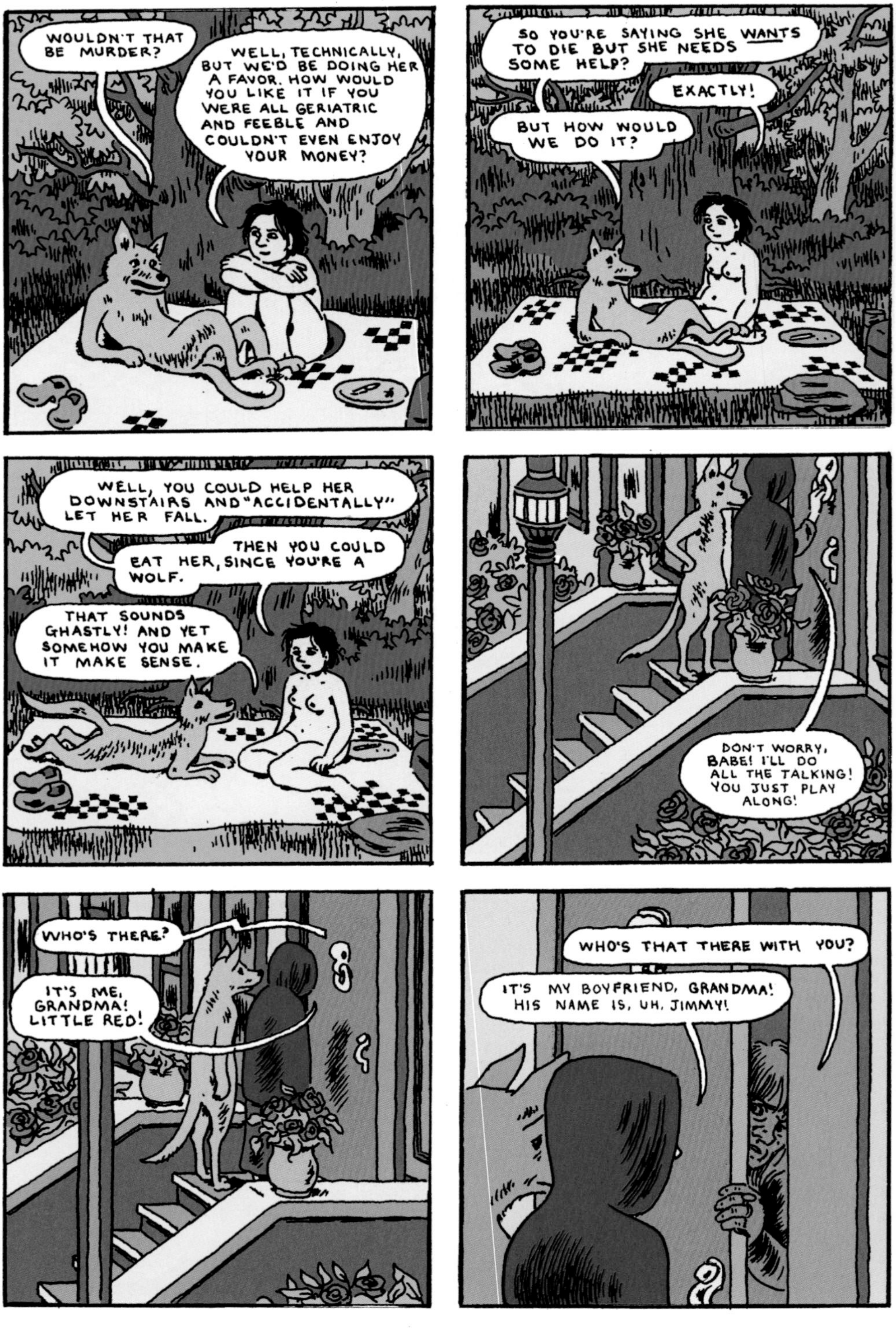
WOULDN'T THAT BE MURDER?
WELL, TECHNICALLY, BUT WE'D BE DOING HER A FAVOR. HOW WOULD YOU LIKE IT IF YOU WERE ALL GERIATRIC AND FEEBLE AND COULDN'T EVEN ENJOY YOUR MONEY?
SO YOU'RE SAYING SHE WANTS TO DIE BUT SHE NEEDS SOME HELP?
EXACTLY!
BUT HOW WOULD WE DO IT?
WELL, YOU COULD HELP HER DOWNSTAIRS AND "ACCIDENTALLY" LET HER FALL.
THEN YOU COULD EAT HER, SINCE YOU'RE A WOLF.
THAT SOUNDS GHASTLY! AND YET SOMEHOW YOU MAKE IT MAKE SENSE.
DON'T WORRY, BABE! I'LL DO ALL THE TALKING! YOU JUST PLAY ALONG!
WHO'S THERE?
IT'S ME, GRANDMA! LITTLE RED!
WHO'S THAT THERE WITH YOU?
IT'S MY BOYFRIEND, GRANDMA! HIS NAME IS, UH, JIMMY!

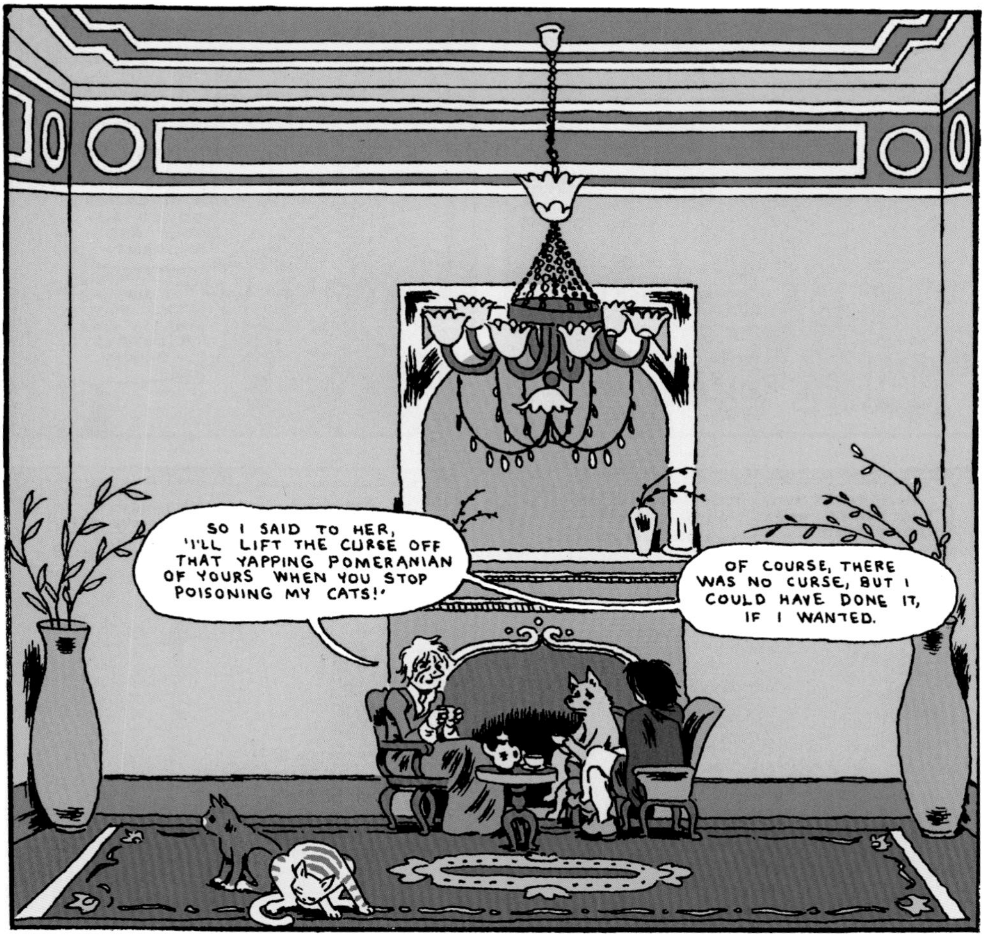
SO I SAID TO HER, 'I'LL LIFT THE CURSE OFF THAT YAPPING POMERANIAN OF YOURS WHEN YOU STOP POISONING MY CATS!'
OF COURSE, THERE WAS NO CURSE, BUT I COULD HAVE DONE IT, IF I WANTED.

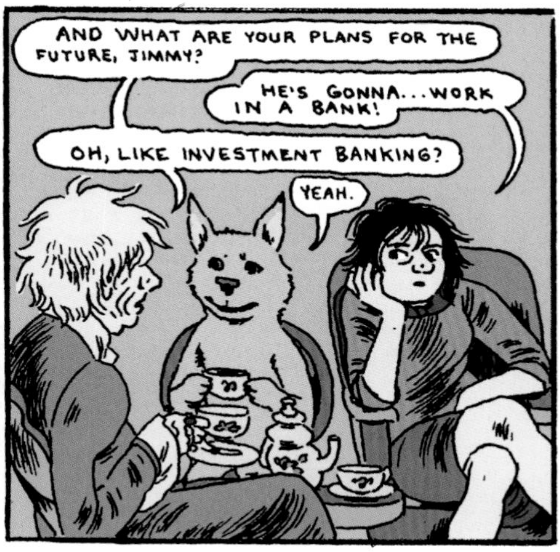
AND WHAT ARE YOUR PLANS FOR THE FUTURE, JIMMY?
HE'S GONNA... WORK IN A BANK!
OH, LIKE INVESTMENT BANKING?
YEAH.

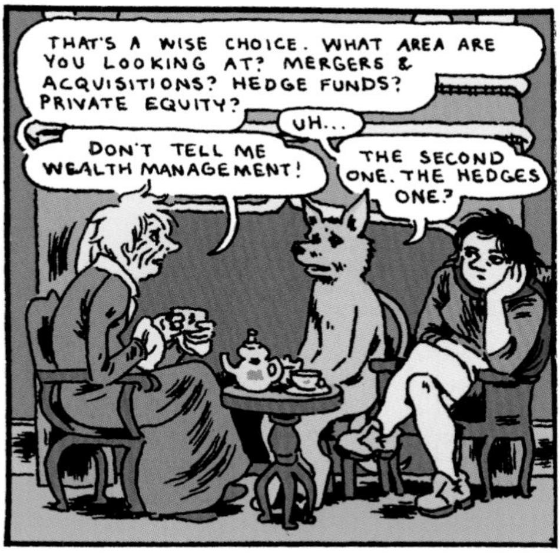
THAT'S A WISE CHOICE. WHAT AREA ARE YOU LOOKING AT? MERGERS & ACQUISITIONS? HEDGE FUNDS? PRIVATE EQUITY?
UH...
DON'T TELL ME WEALTH MANAGEMENT!
THE SECOND ONE. THE HEDGES ONE?

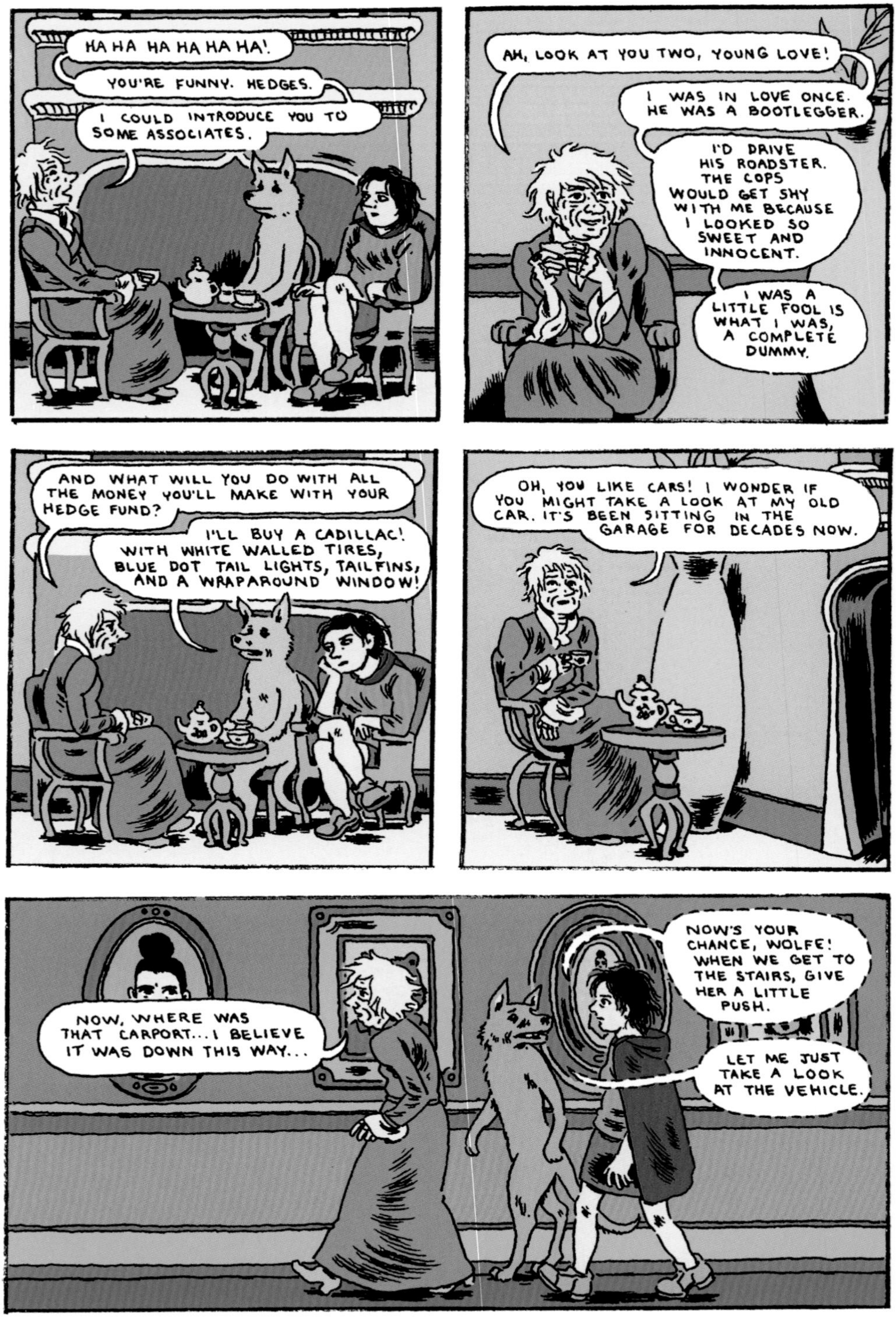
HA HA HA HA HA HA!
YOU'RE FUNNY. HEDGES.
I COULD INTRODUCE YOU TO SOME ASSOCIATES.
AH, LOOK AT YOU TWO, YOUNG LOVE!
I WAS IN LOVE ONCE. HE WAS A BOOTLEGGER.
I'D DRIVE HIS ROADSTER. THE COPS WOULD GET SHY WITH ME BECAUSE I LOOKED SO SWEET AND INNOCENT.
I WAS A LITTLE FOOL IS WHAT I WAS, A COMPLETE DUMMY.
AND WHAT WILL YOU DO WITH ALL THE MONEY YOU'LL MAKE WITH YOUR HEDGE FUND?
I'LL BUY A CADILLAC! WITH WHITE WALLED TIRES, BLUE DOT TAIL LIGHTS, TAILFINS, AND A WRAPAROUND WINDOW!
OH, YOU LIKE CARS! I WONDER IF YOU MIGHT TAKE A LOOK AT MY OLD CAR. IT'S BEEN SITTING IN THE GARAGE FOR DECADES NOW.
NOW, WHERE WAS THAT CARPORT... I BELIEVE IT WAS DOWN THIS WAY...
NOW'S YOUR CHANCE, WOLFE! WHEN WE GET TO THE STAIRS, GIVE HER A LITTLE PUSH.
LET ME JUST TAKE A LOOK AT THE VEHICLE.

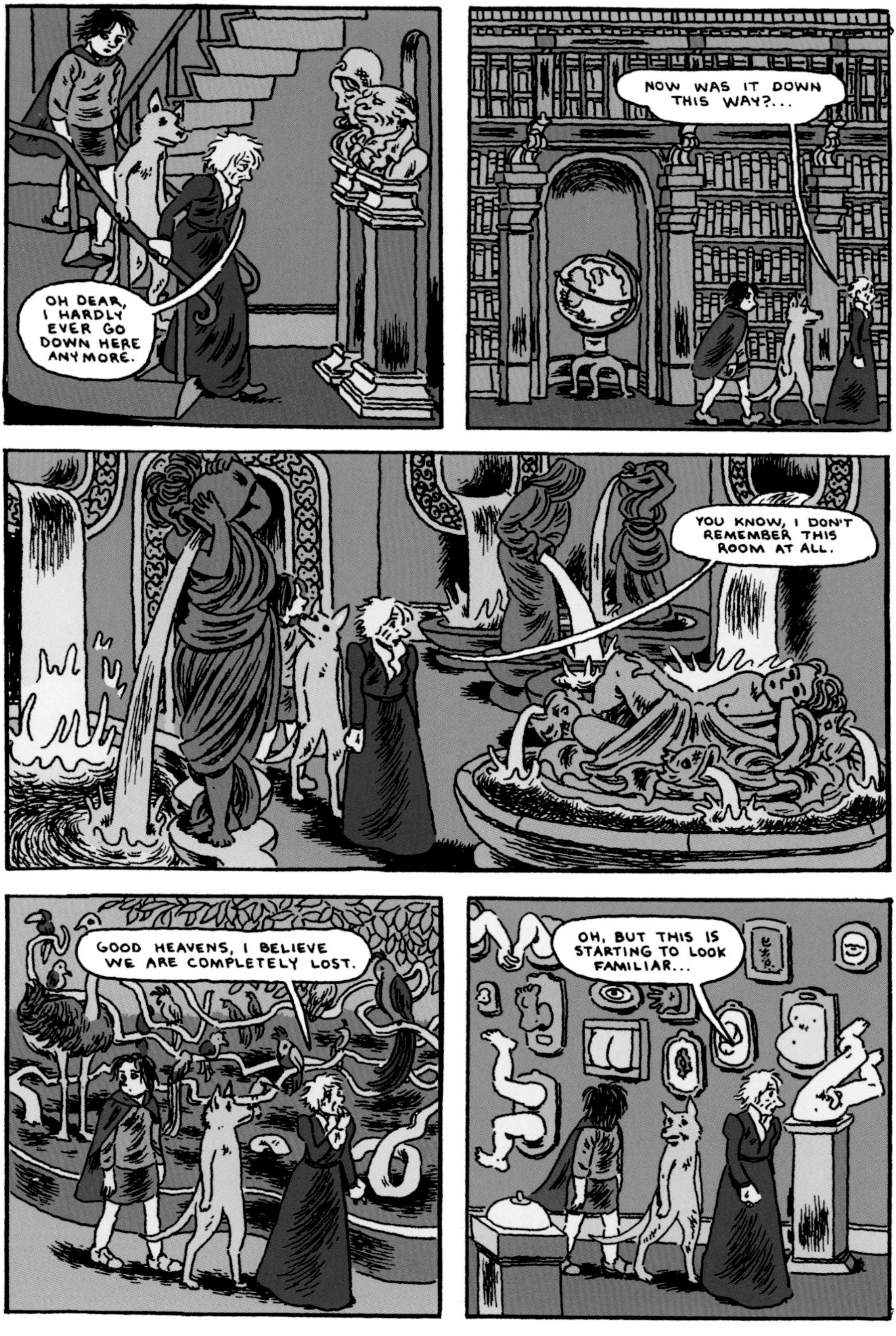
OH DEAR, I HARDLY EVER GO DOWN HERE ANYMORE.
NOW WAS IT DOWN THIS WAY?...
YOU KNOW, I DON'T REMEMBER THIS ROOM AT ALL.
GOOD HEAVENS, I BELIEVE WE ARE COMPLETELY LOST.
OH, BUT THIS IS STARTING TO LOOK FAMILIAR...

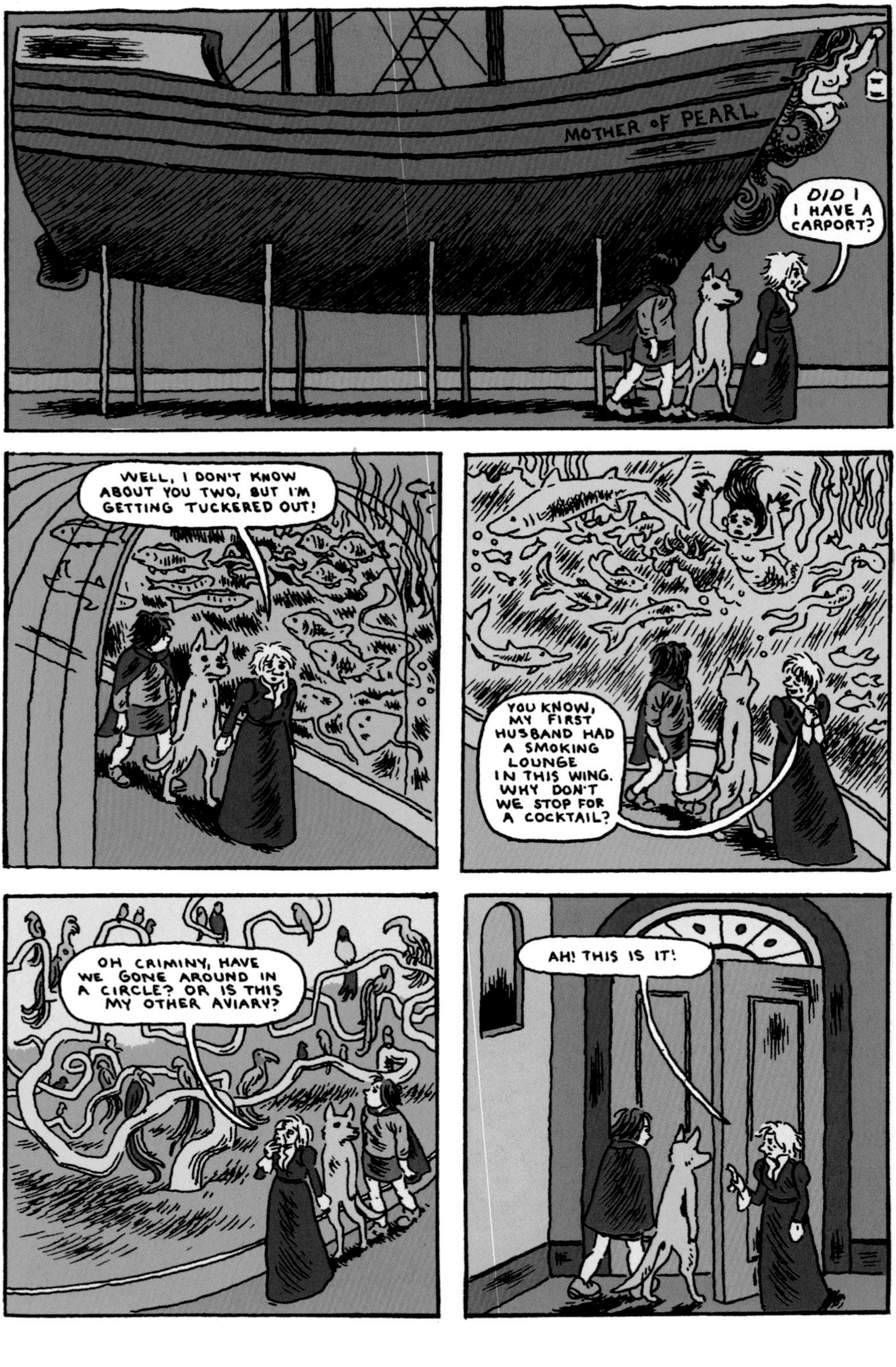
MOTHER OF PEARL
DID I I HAVE A CARPORT?
WELL, I DON'T KNOW ABOUT YOU TWO, BUT I'M GETTING TUCKERED OUT!
YOU KNOW, MY FIRST HUSBAND HAD A SMOKING LOUNGE IN THIS WING. WHY DON'T WE STOP FOR A COCKTAIL?
OH CRIMINY, HAVE WE GONE AROUND IN A CIRCLE? OR IS THIS MY OTHER AVIARY?
AH! THIS IS IT!

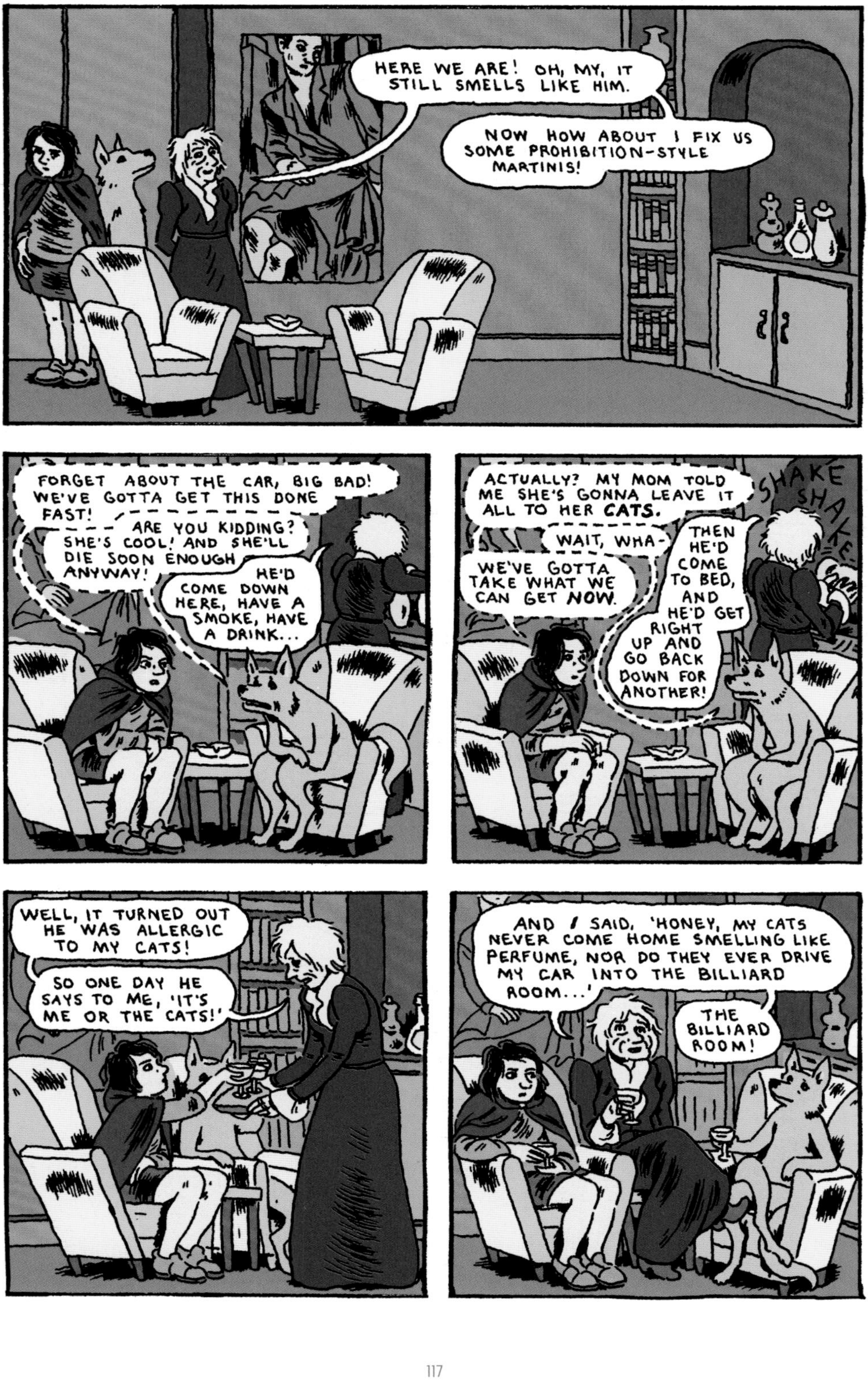
HERE WE ARE! OH, MY, IT STILL SMELLS LIKE HIM.
NOW HOW ABOUT I FIX US SOME PROHIBITION-STYLE MARTINIS!
FORGET ABOUT THE CAR, BIG BAD! WE'VE GOTTA GET THIS DONE FAST!
ARE YOU KIDDING? SHE'S COOL! AND SHE'LL DIE SOON ENOUGH ANYWAY!
HE'D COME DOWN HERE, HAVE A SMOKE, HAVE A DRINK...
ACTUALLY? MY MOM TOLD ME SHE'S GONNA LEAVE IT ALL TO HER **CATS.**
WAIT, WHA-
WE'VE GOTTA TAKE WHAT WE CAN GET **NOW**.
THEN HE'D COME TO BED, AND HE'D GET RIGHT UP AND GO BACK DOWN FOR ANOTHER!
SHAKE SHAKE
WELL, IT TURNED OUT HE WAS ALLERGIC TO MY CATS!
SO ONE DAY HE SAYS TO ME, 'IT'S ME OR THE CATS!'
AND I SAID, 'HONEY, MY CATS NEVER COME HOME SMELLING LIKE PERFUME, NOR DO THEY EVER DRIVE MY CAR INTO THE BILLIARD ROOM...'
THE BILLIARD ROOM!

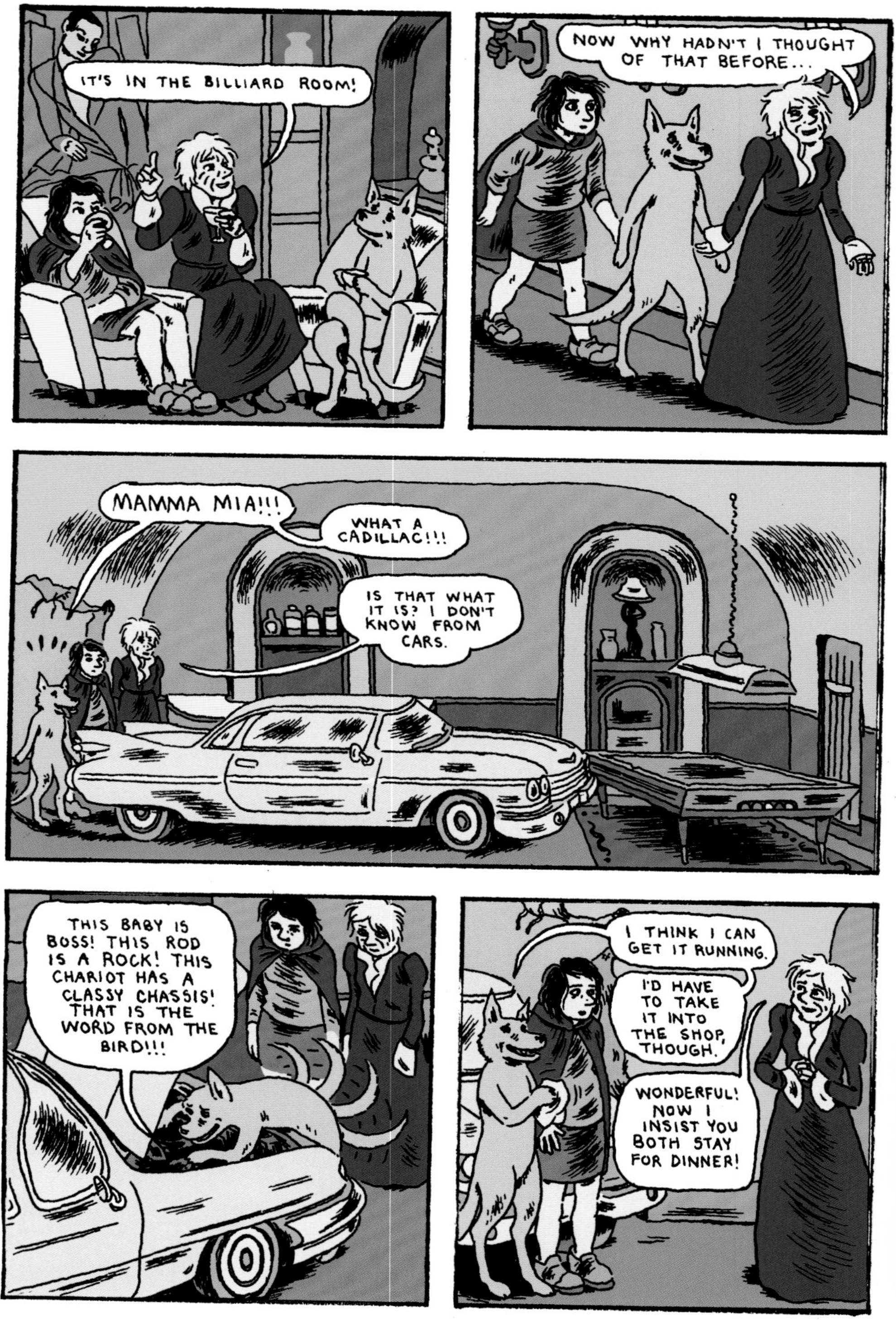
IT'S IN THE BILLIARD ROOM!
NOW WHY HADN'T I THOUGHT OF THAT BEFORE...
MAMMA MIA!!!
WHAT A CADILLAC!!!
IS THAT WHAT IT IS? I DON'T KNOW FROM CARS.
THIS BABY IS BOSS! THIS ROD IS A ROCK! THIS CHARIOT HAS A CLASSY CHASSIS! THAT IS THE WORD FROM THE BIRD!!!
I THINK I CAN GET IT RUNNING.
I'D HAVE TO TAKE IT INTO THE SHOP, THOUGH.
WONDERFUL! NOW I INSIST YOU BOTH STAY FOR DINNER!

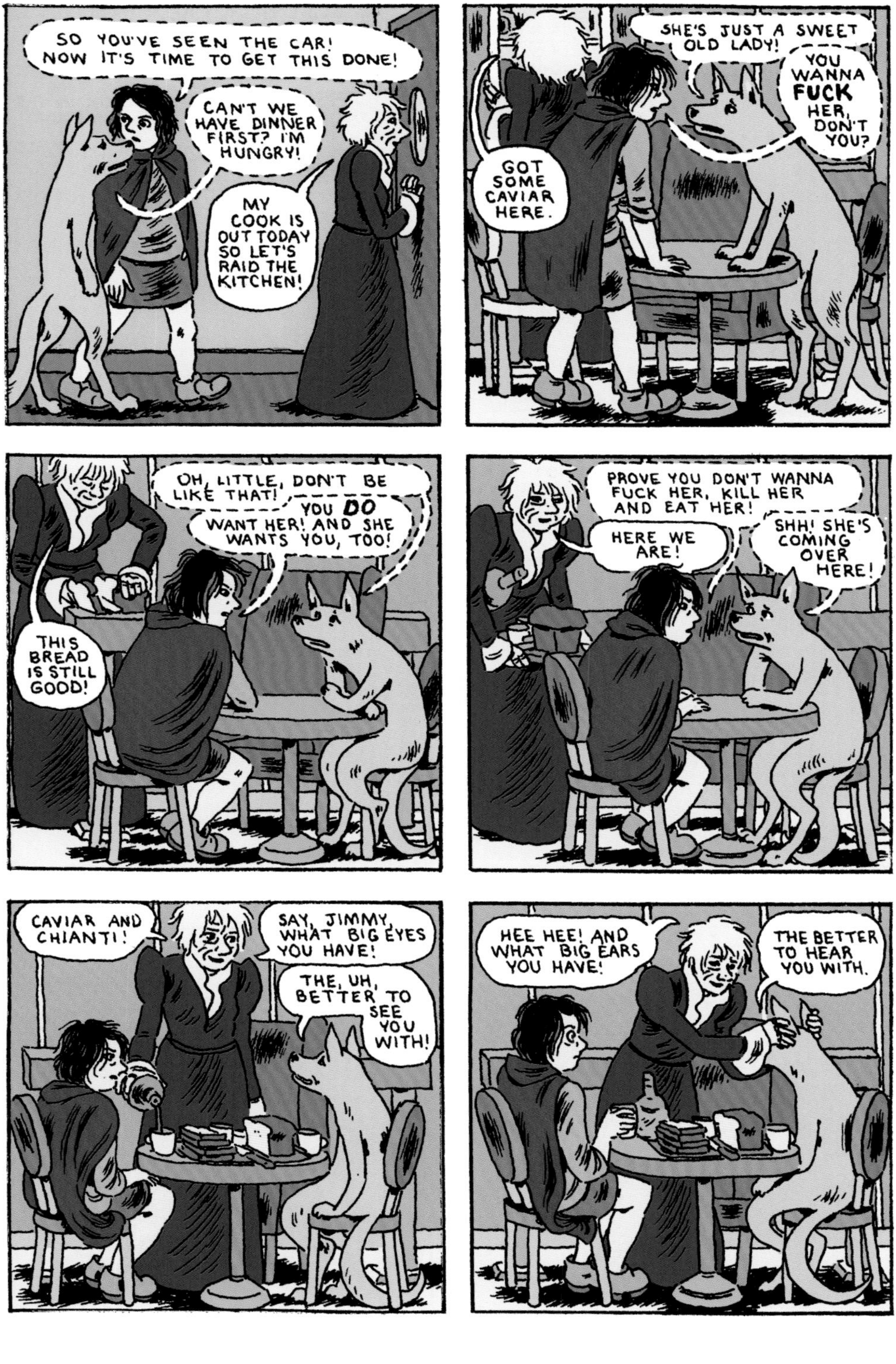
SO YOU'VE SEEN THE CAR! NOW IT'S TIME TO GET THIS DONE!
CAN'T WE HAVE DINNER FIRST? I'M HUNGRY!
MY COOK IS OUT TODAY SO LET'S RAID THE KITCHEN!
SHE'S JUST A SWEET OLD LADY!
YOU WANNA FUCK HER, DON'T YOU?
GOT SOME CAVIAR HERE.
OH, LITTLE, DON'T BE LIKE THAT!
YOU DO WANT HER! AND SHE WANTS YOU, TOO!
THIS BREAD IS STILL GOOD!
PROVE YOU DON'T WANNA FUCK HER, KILL HER AND EAT HER!
HERE WE ARE!
SHH! SHE'S COMING OVER HERE!
CAVIAR AND CHIANTI!
SAY, JIMMY, WHAT BIG EYES YOU HAVE!
THE, UH, BETTER TO SEE YOU WITH!
HEE HEE! AND WHAT BIG EARS YOU HAVE!
THE BETTER TO HEAR YOU WITH.

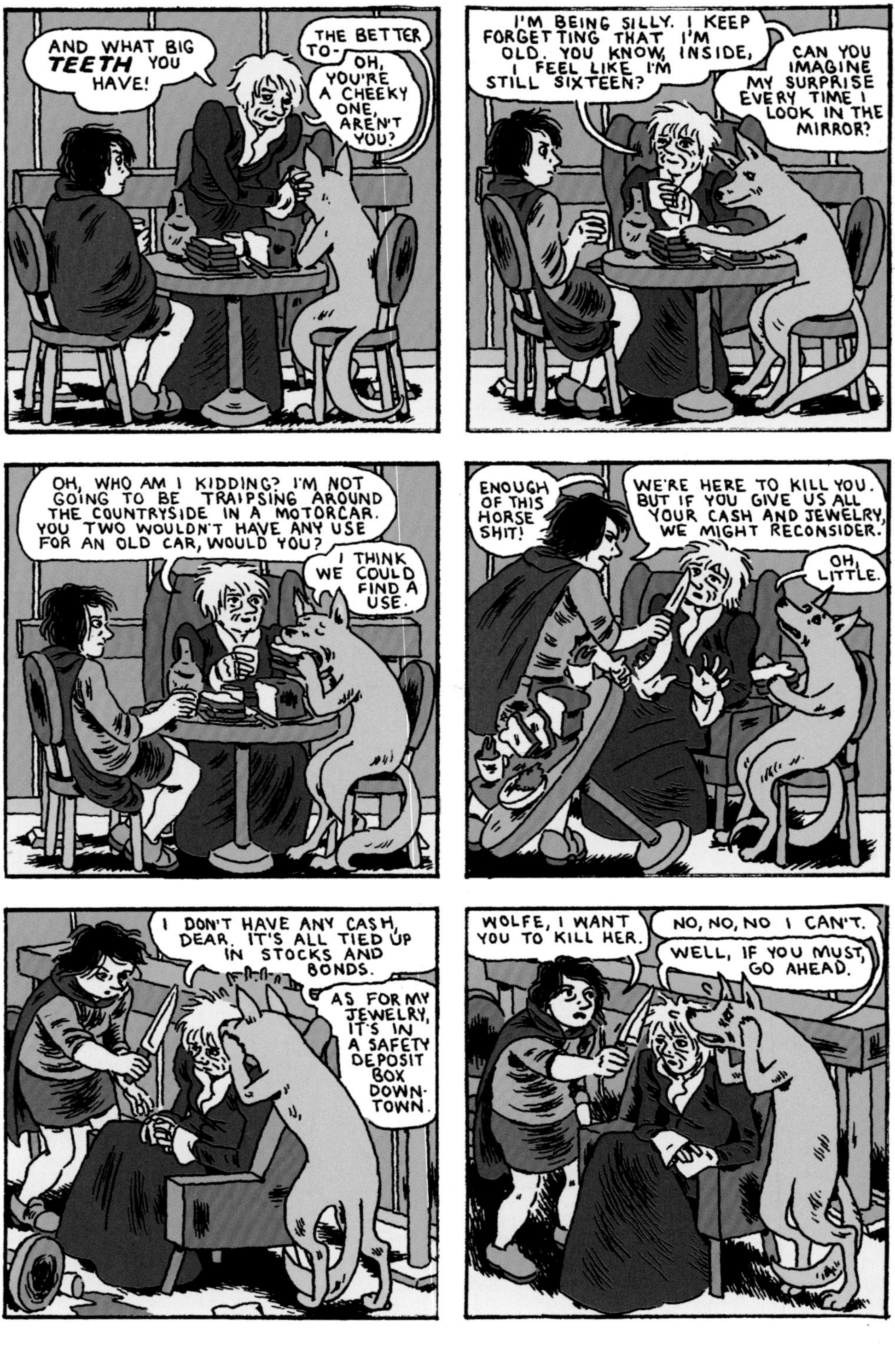
AND WHAT BIG TEETH YOU HAVE!
THE BETTER TO-
OH, YOU'RE A CHEEKY ONE, AREN'T YOU?
I'M BEING SILLY. I KEEP FORGETTING THAT I'M OLD. YOU KNOW, INSIDE, I FEEL LIKE I'M STILL SIXTEEN?
CAN YOU IMAGINE MY SURPRISE EVERY TIME I LOOK IN THE MIRROR?
OH, WHO AM I KIDDING? I'M NOT GOING TO BE TRAIPSING AROUND THE COUNTRYSIDE IN A MOTORCAR. YOU TWO WOULDN'T HAVE ANY USE FOR AN OLD CAR, WOULD YOU?
I THINK WE COULD FIND A USE.
ENOUGH OF THIS HORSE SHIT!
WE'RE HERE TO KILL YOU. BUT IF YOU GIVE US ALL YOUR CASH AND JEWELRY, WE MIGHT RECONSIDER.
OH, LITTLE.
I DON'T HAVE ANY CASH, DEAR. IT'S ALL TIED UP IN STOCKS AND BONDS.
AS FOR MY JEWELRY, IT'S IN A SAFETY DEPOSIT BOX DOWNTOWN.
WOLFE, I WANT YOU TO KILL HER.
NO, NO, NO I CAN'T.
WELL, IF YOU MUST, GO AHEAD.

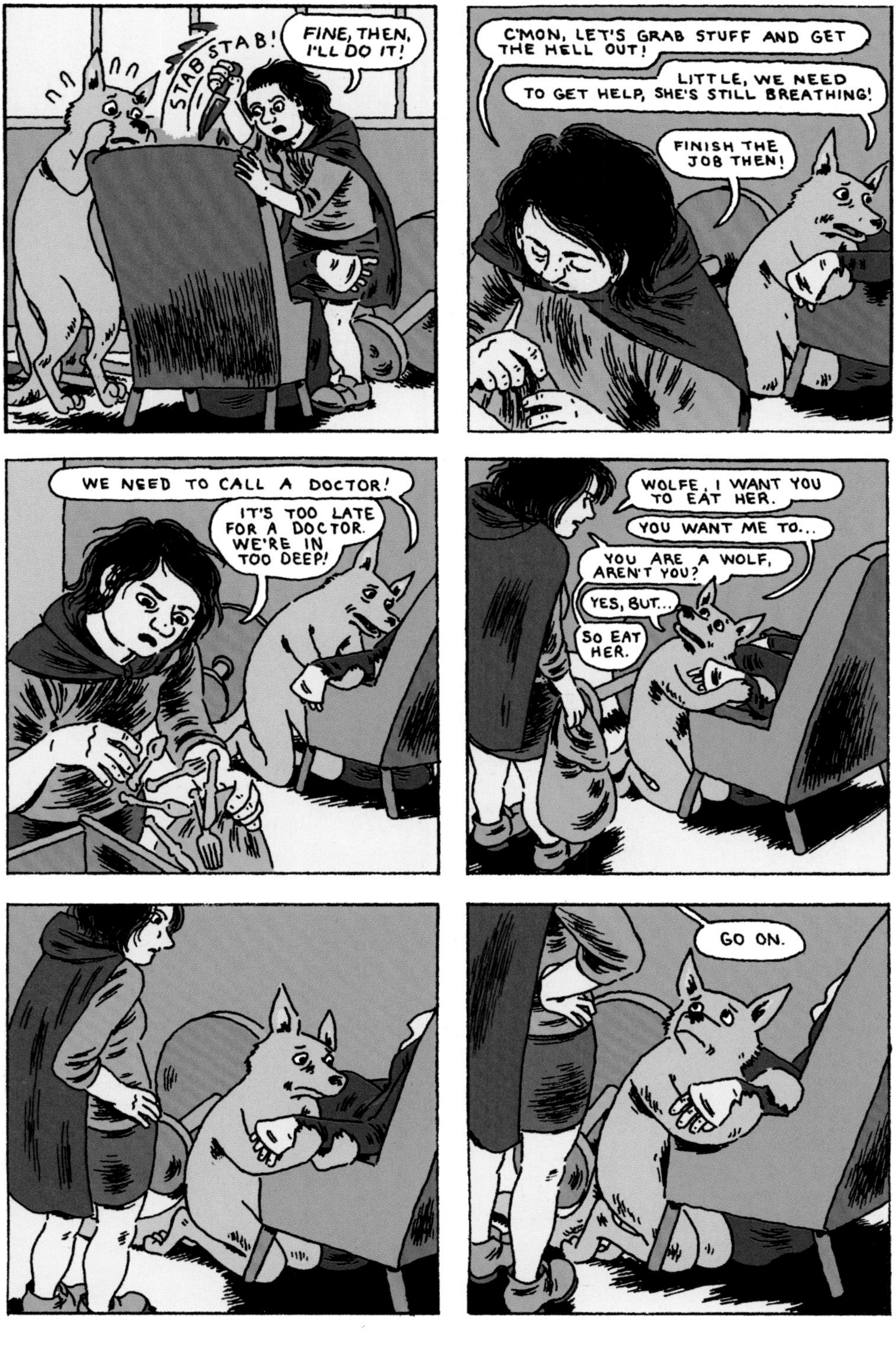
STAB STAB!
FINE, THEN, I'LL DO IT!
C'MON, LET'S GRAB STUFF AND GET THE HELL OUT!
LITTLE, WE NEED TO GET HELP, SHE'S STILL BREATHING!
FINISH THE JOB THEN!
WE NEED TO CALL A DOCTOR!
IT'S TOO LATE FOR A DOCTOR. WE'RE IN TOO DEEP!
WOLFE, I WANT YOU TO EAT HER.
YOU WANT ME TO...
YOU ARE A WOLF, AREN'T YOU?
YES, BUT...
SO EAT HER.
GO ON.

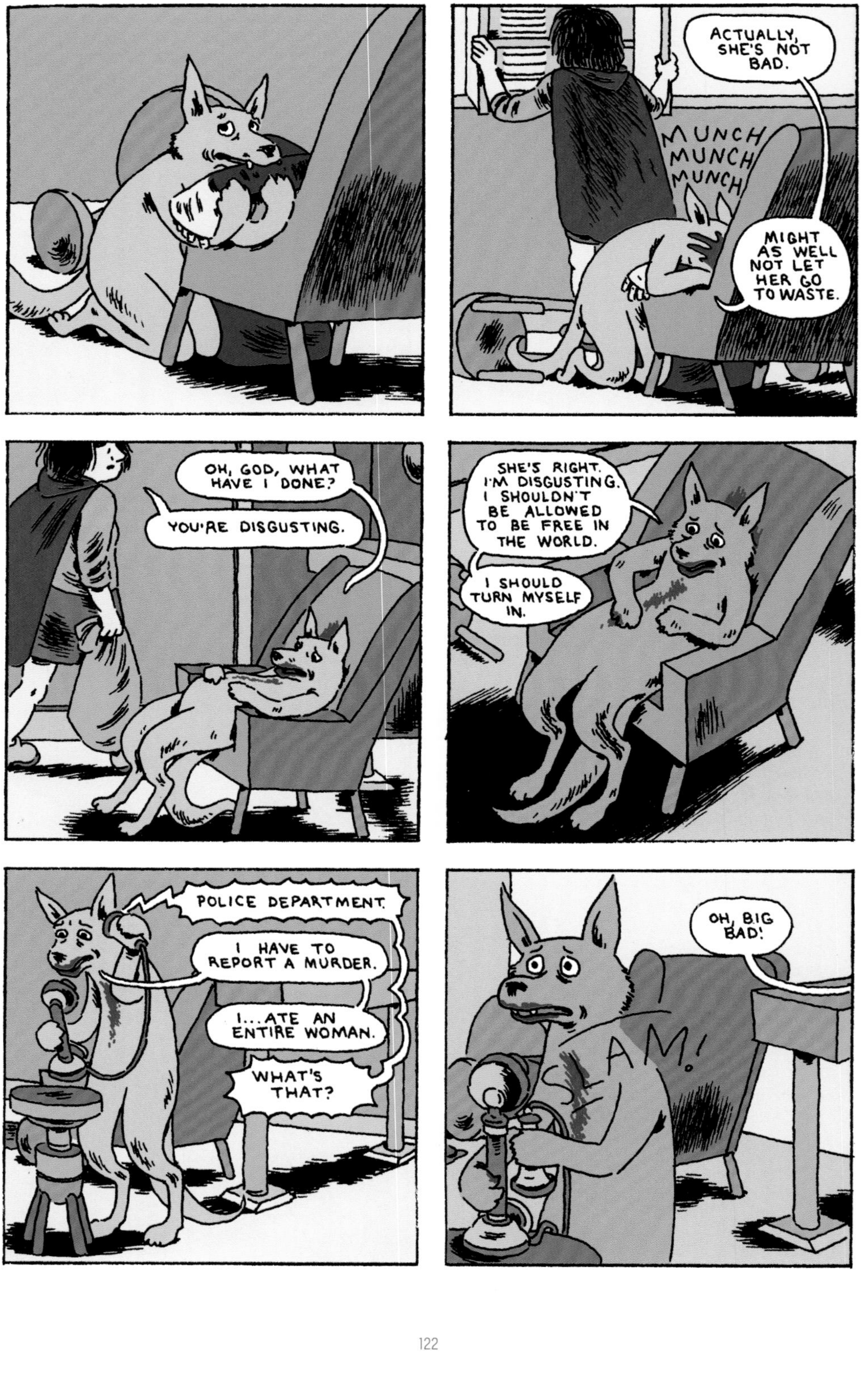
ACTUALLY, SHE'S NOT BAD.
MUNCH MUNCH MUNCH
MIGHT AS WELL NOT LET HER GO TO WASTE.
OH, GOD, WHAT HAVE I DONE?
YOU'RE DISGUSTING.
SHE'S RIGHT. I'M DISGUSTING. I SHOULDN'T BE ALLOWED TO BE FREE IN THE WORLD.
I SHOULD TURN MYSELF IN.
POLICE DEPARTMENT.
I HAVE TO REPORT A MURDER.
I... ATE AN ENTIRE WOMAN.
WHAT'S THAT?
OH, BIG BAD!
SLAM!

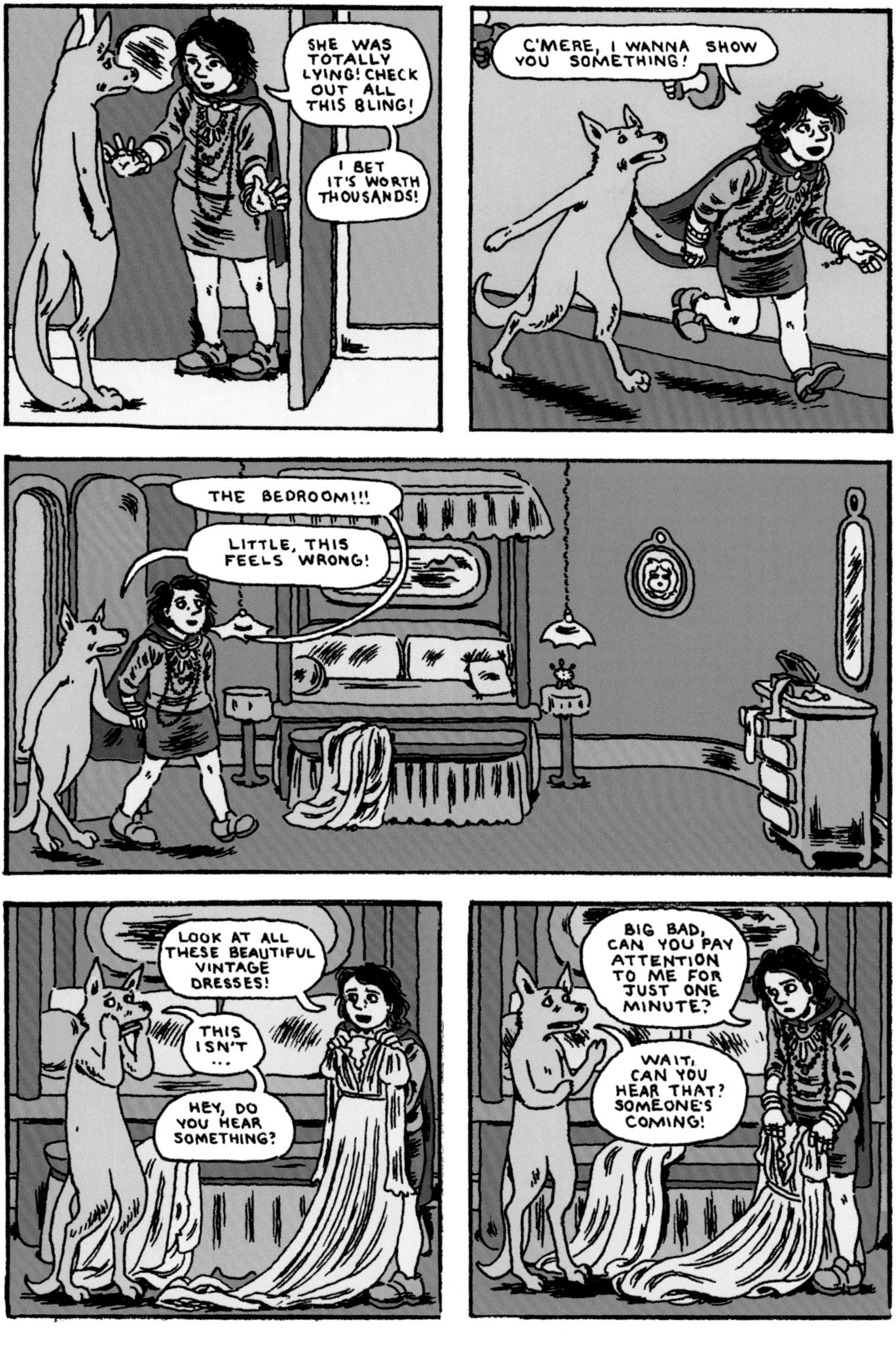
SHE WAS TOTALLY LYING! CHECK OUT ALL THIS BLING!
I BET IT'S WORTH THOUSANDS!
C'MERE, I WANNA SHOW YOU SOMETHING!
THE BEDROOM!!!
LITTLE, THIS FEELS WRONG!
LOOK AT ALL THESE BEAUTIFUL VINTAGE DRESSES!
THIS ISN'T ...
HEY, DO YOU HEAR SOMETHING?
BIG BAD, CAN YOU PAY ATTENTION TO ME FOR JUST ONE MINUTE?
WAIT, CAN YOU HEAR THAT? SOMEONE'S COMING!

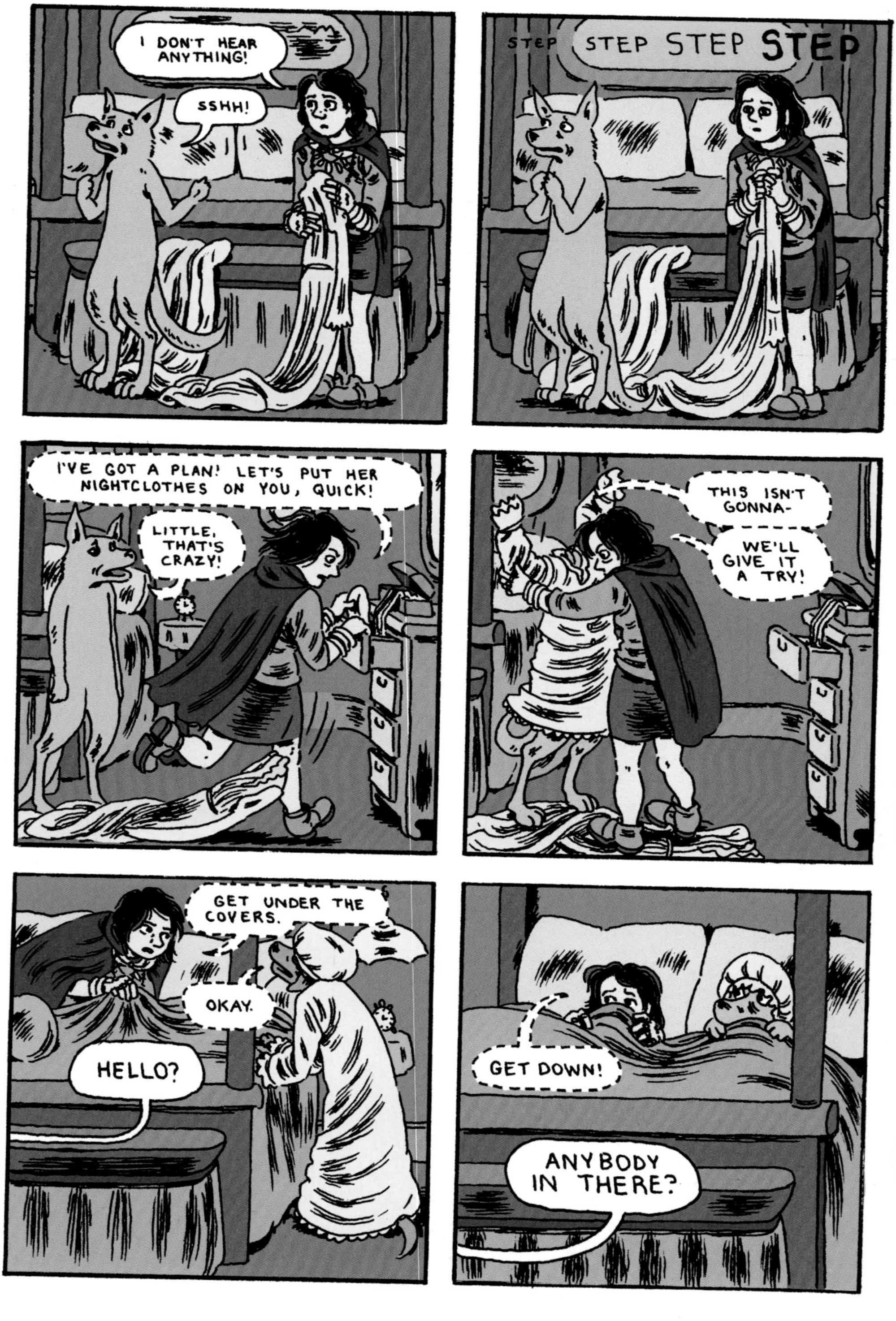
I DON'T HEAR ANYTHING!
SSHH!
STEP STEP STEP STEP
I'VE GOT A PLAN! LET'S PUT HER NIGHTCLOTHES ON YOU, QUICK!
LITTLE, THAT'S CRAZY!
THIS ISN'T GONNA-
WE'LL GIVE IT A TRY!
GET UNDER THE COVERS.
OKAY.
HELLO?
GET DOWN!
ANYBODY IN THERE?

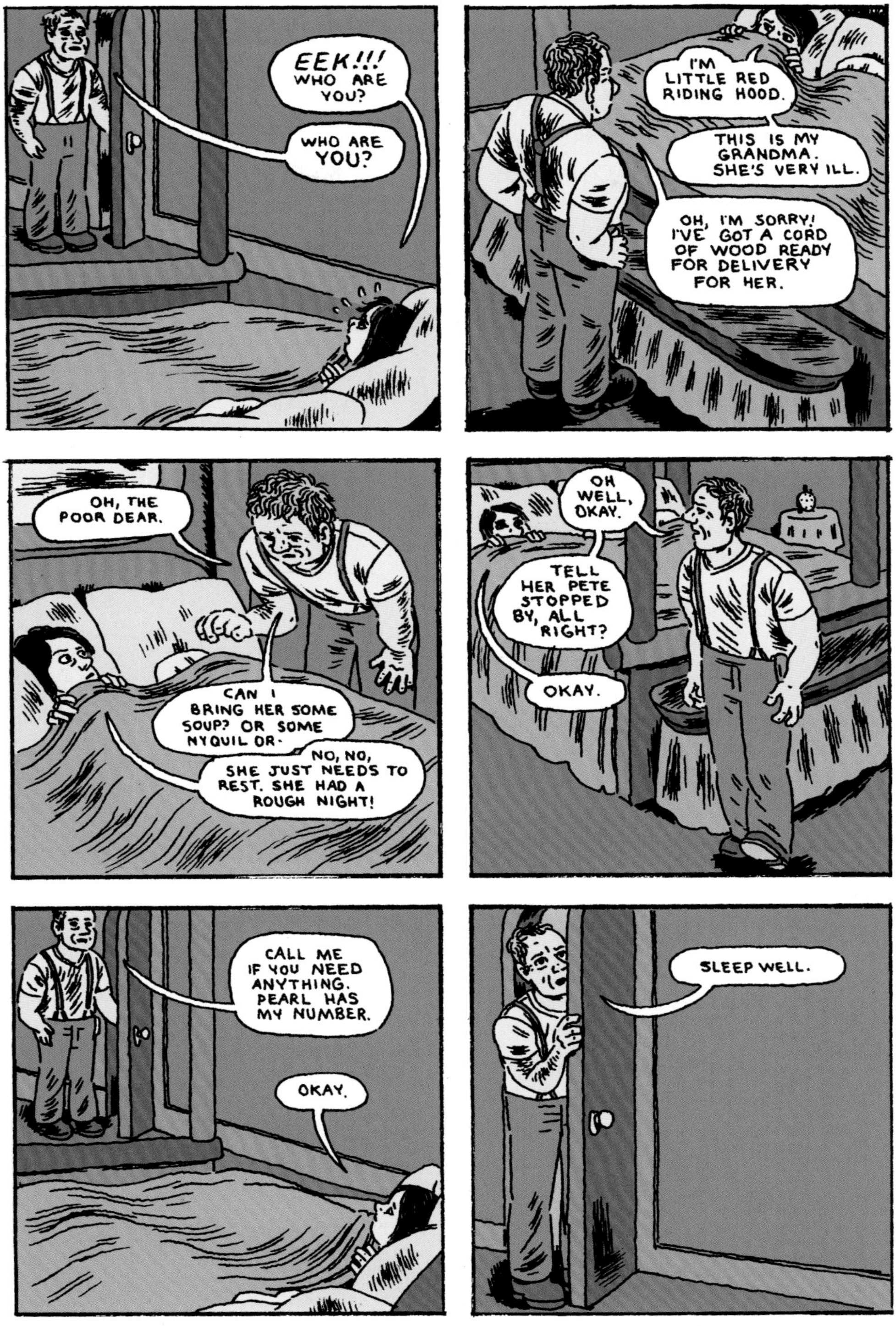
EEK!!! WHO ARE YOU?
WHO ARE YOU?
I'M LITTLE RED RIDING HOOD.
THIS IS MY GRANDMA. SHE'S VERY ILL.
OH, I'M SORRY! I'VE GOT A CORD OF WOOD READY FOR DELIVERY FOR HER.
OH, THE POOR DEAR.
CAN I BRING HER SOME SOUP? OR SOME NYQUIL OR-
NO, NO, SHE JUST NEEDS TO REST. SHE HAD A ROUGH NIGHT!
OH WELL, OKAY.
TELL HER PETE STOPPED BY, ALL RIGHT?
OKAY.
CALL ME IF YOU NEED ANYTHING. PEARL HAS MY NUMBER.
OKAY.
SLEEP WELL.

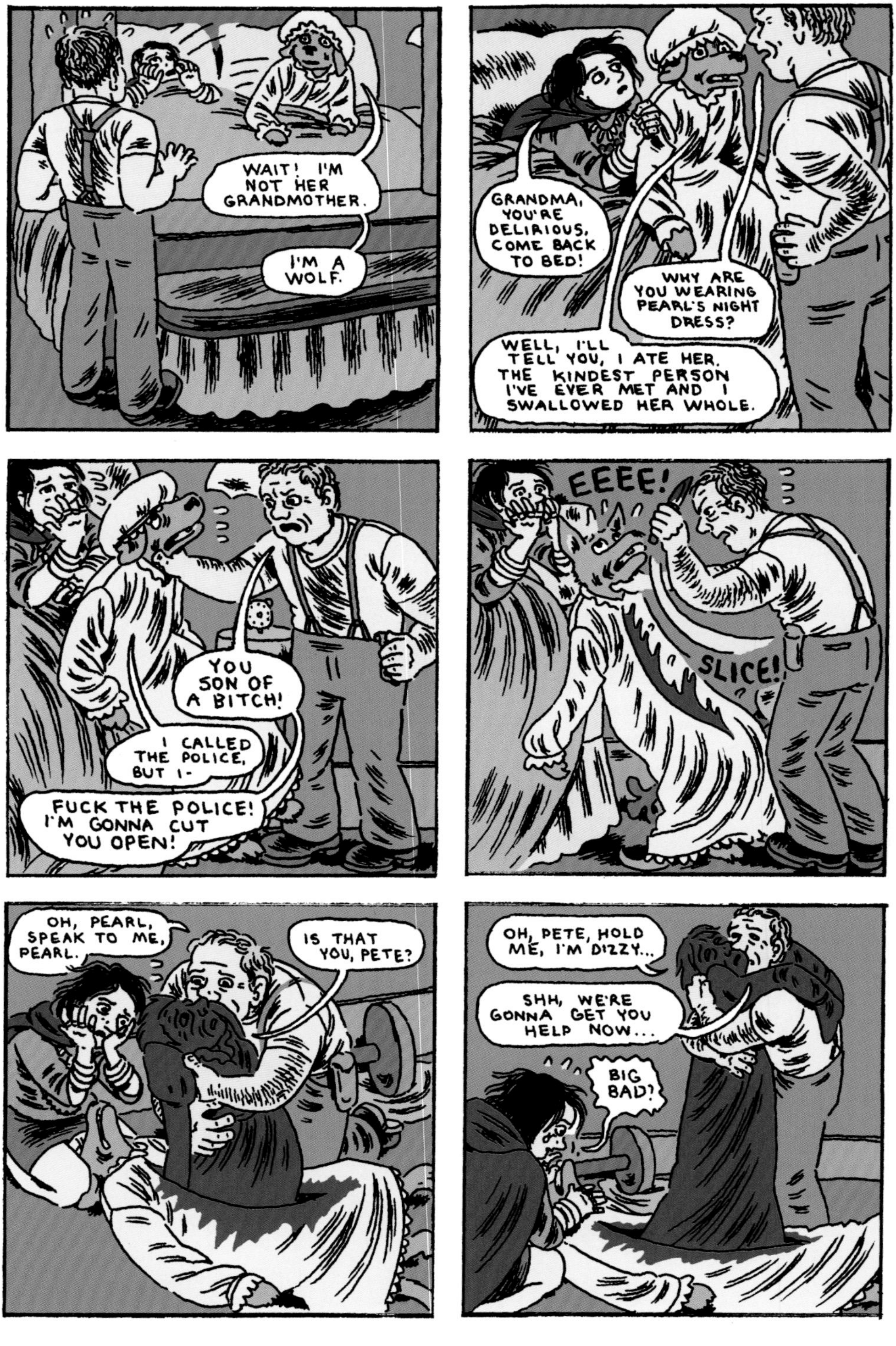
WAIT! I'M NOT HER GRANDMOTHER.
I'M A WOLF.
GRANDMA, YOU'RE DELIRIOUS. COME BACK TO BED!
WHY ARE YOU WEARING PEARL'S NIGHT DRESS?
WELL, I'LL TELL YOU, I ATE HER. THE KINDEST PERSON I'VE EVER MET AND I SWALLOWED HER WHOLE.
YOU SON OF A BITCH!
I CALLED THE POLICE, BUT I-
FUCK THE POLICE! I'M GONNA CUT YOU OPEN!
EEEE!
SLICE!
OH, PEARL, SPEAK TO ME, PEARL.
IS THAT YOU, PETE?
OH, PETE, HOLD ME, I'M DIZZY...
SHH, WE'RE GONNA GET YOU HELP NOW...
BIG BAD?

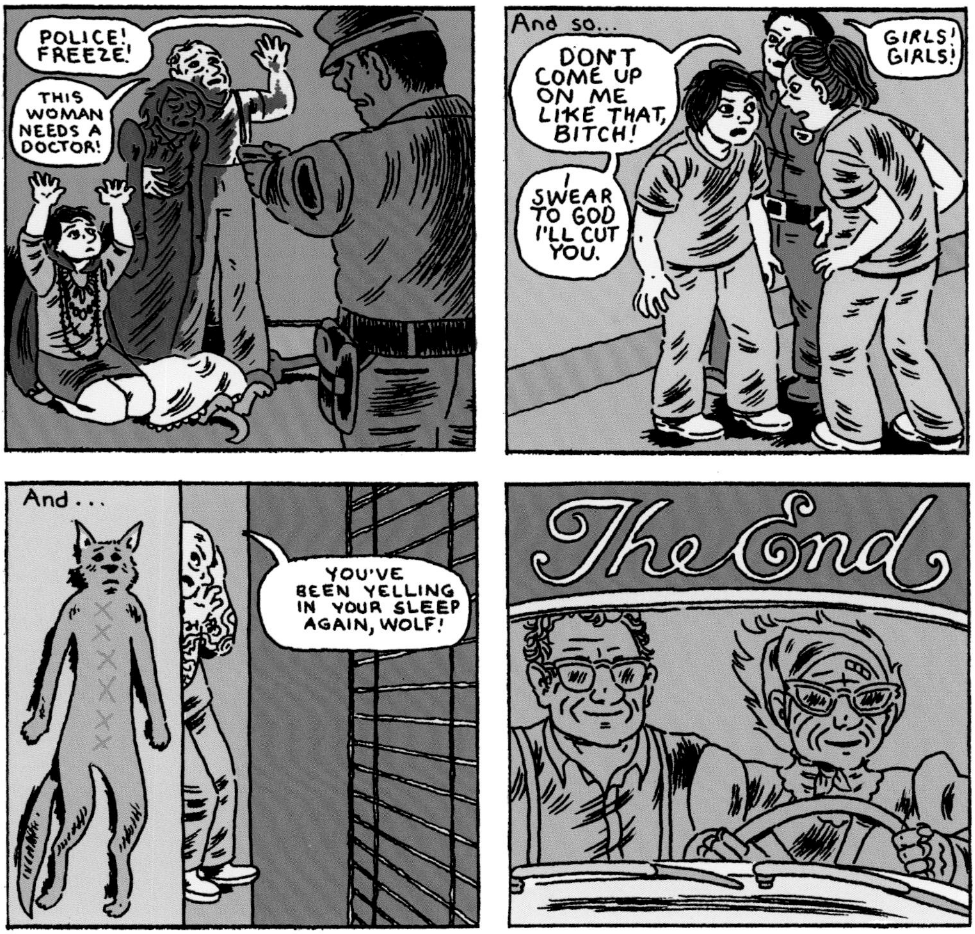
POLICE! FREEZE!
THIS WOMAN NEEDS A DOCTOR!
And so...
DON'T COME UP ON ME LIKE THAT, BITCH!
I SWEAR TO GOD I'LL CUT YOU.
GIRLS! GIRLS!
And...
YOU'VE BEEN YELLING IN YOUR SLEEP AGAIN, WOLF!
The End

I Love You

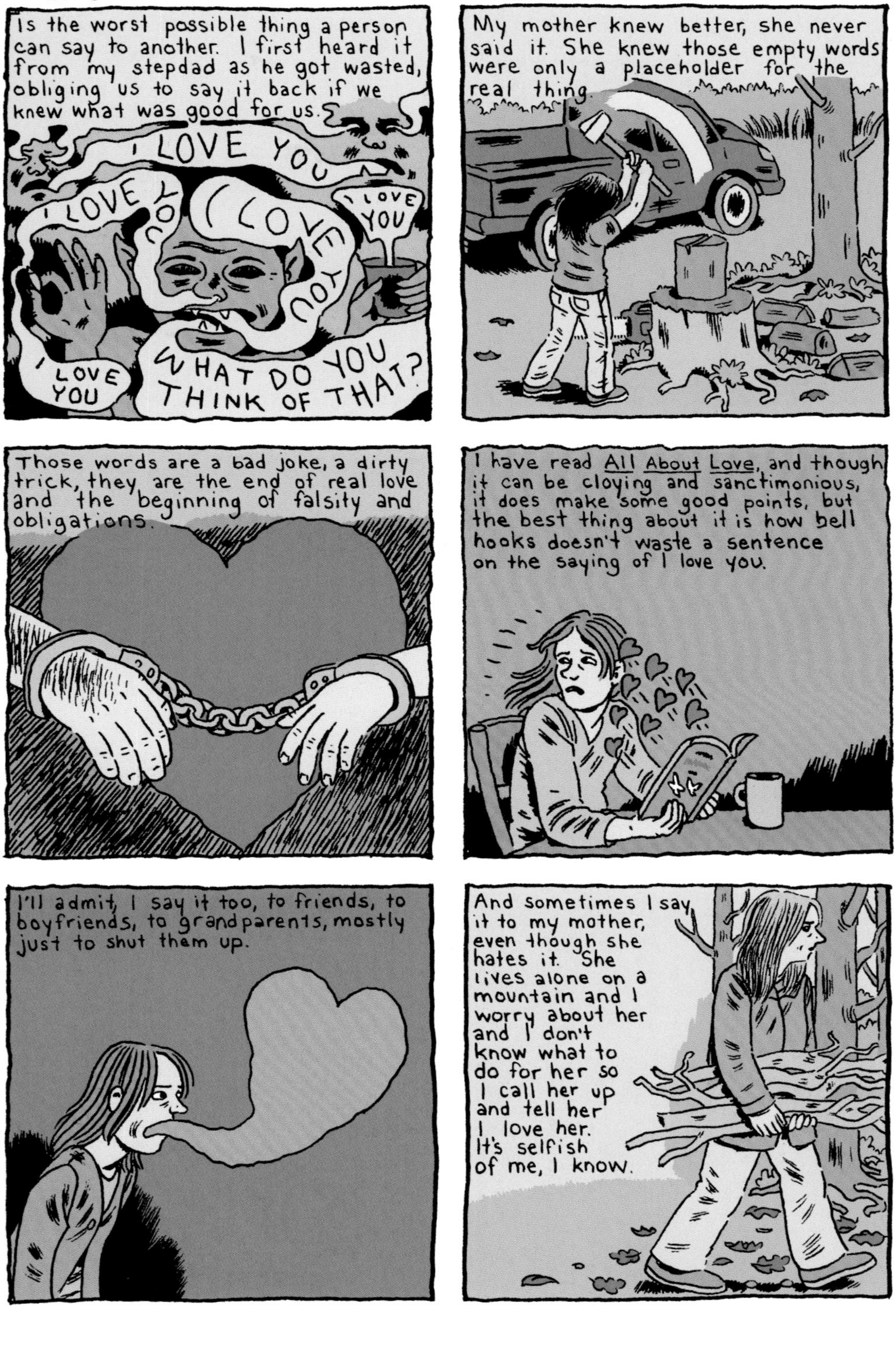

Is the worst possible thing a person can say to another. I first heard it from my stepdad as he got wasted, obliging us to say it back if we knew what was good for us.
I LOVE YOU
I LOVE YOU
I LOVE YOU
I LOVE YOU
I LOVE YOU
WHAT DO YOU THINK OF THAT?
My mother knew better, she never said it. She knew those empty words were only a placeholder for the real thing.
Those words are a bad joke, a dirty trick, they are the end of real love and the beginning of falsity and obligations.
I have read All About Love, and though it can be cloying and sanctimonious, it does make some good points, but the best thing about it is how bell hooks doesn't waste a sentence on the saying of I love you.
I'll admit, I say it too, to friends, to boyfriends, to grandparents, mostly just to shut them up.
And sometimes I say it to my mother, even though she hates it. She lives alone on a mountain and I worry about her and I don't know what to do for her so I call her up and tell her I love her. It's selfish of me, I know.

BUCKET

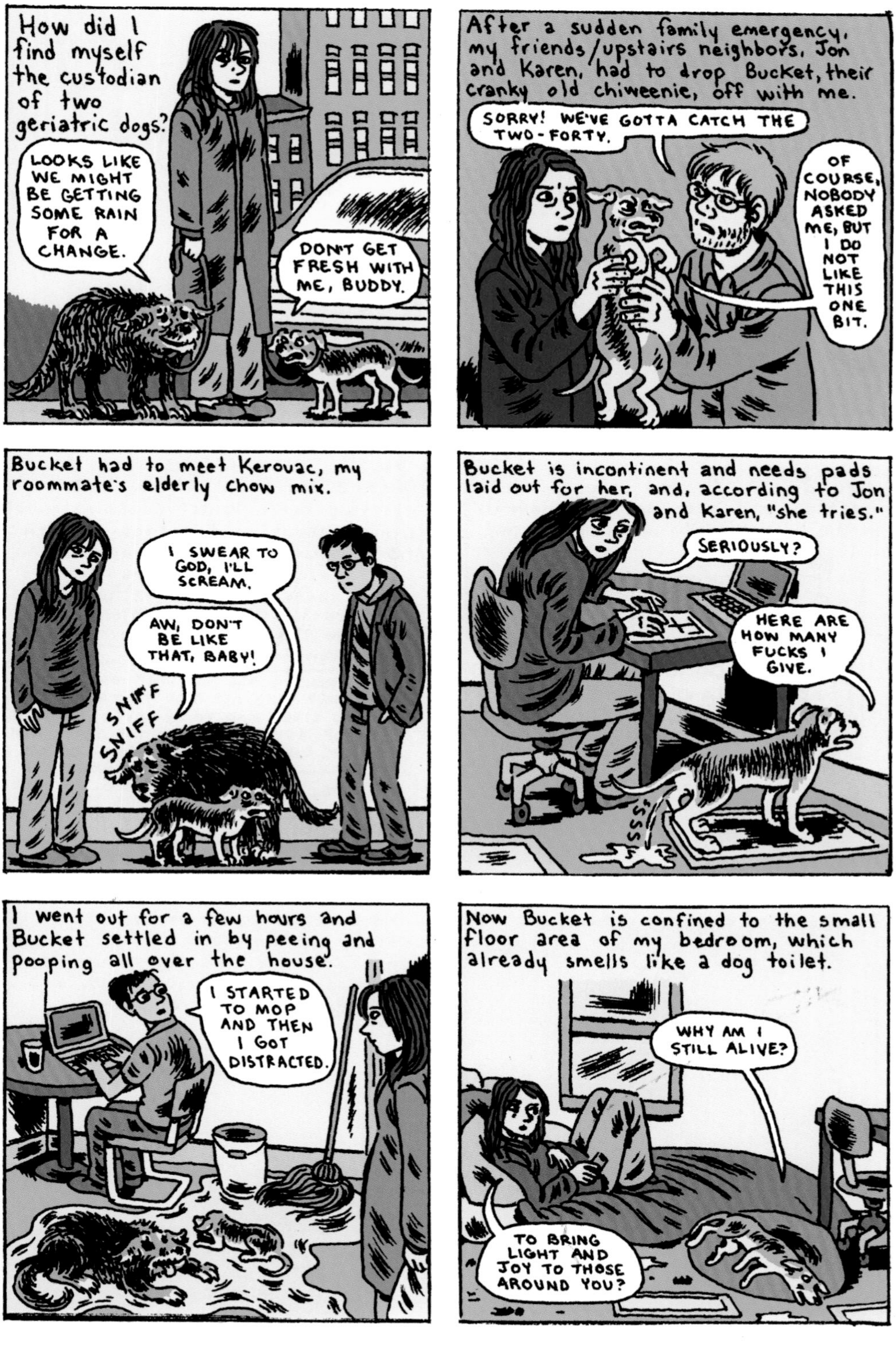
How did I find myself the custodian of two geriatric dogs?
LOOKS LIKE WE MIGHT BE GETTING SOME RAIN FOR A CHANGE.
DON'T GET FRESH WITH ME, BUDDY.
After a sudden family emergency, my friends/upstairs neighbors, Jon and Karen, had to drop Bucket, their cranky old chiweenie, off with me.
SORRY! WE'VE GOTTA CATCH THE TWO-FORTY.
OF COURSE, NOBODY ASKED ME, BUT I DO NOT LIKE THIS ONE BIT.
Bucket had to meet Kerouac, my roommate's elderly chow mix.
I SWEAR TO GOD, I'LL SCREAM.
AW, DON'T BE LIKE THAT, BABY!
SNIFF SNIFF
Bucket is incontinent and needs pads laid out for her, and, according to Jon and Karen, "she tries."
SERIOUSLY?
HERE ARE HOW MANY FUCKS I GIVE.
SSSS
I went out for a few hours and Bucket settled in by peeing and pooping all over the house.
I STARTED TO MOP AND THEN I GOT DISTRACTED.
Now Bucket is confined to the small floor area of my bedroom, which already smells like a dog toilet.
WHY AM I STILL ALIVE?
TO BRING LIGHT AND JOY TO THOSE AROUND YOU?

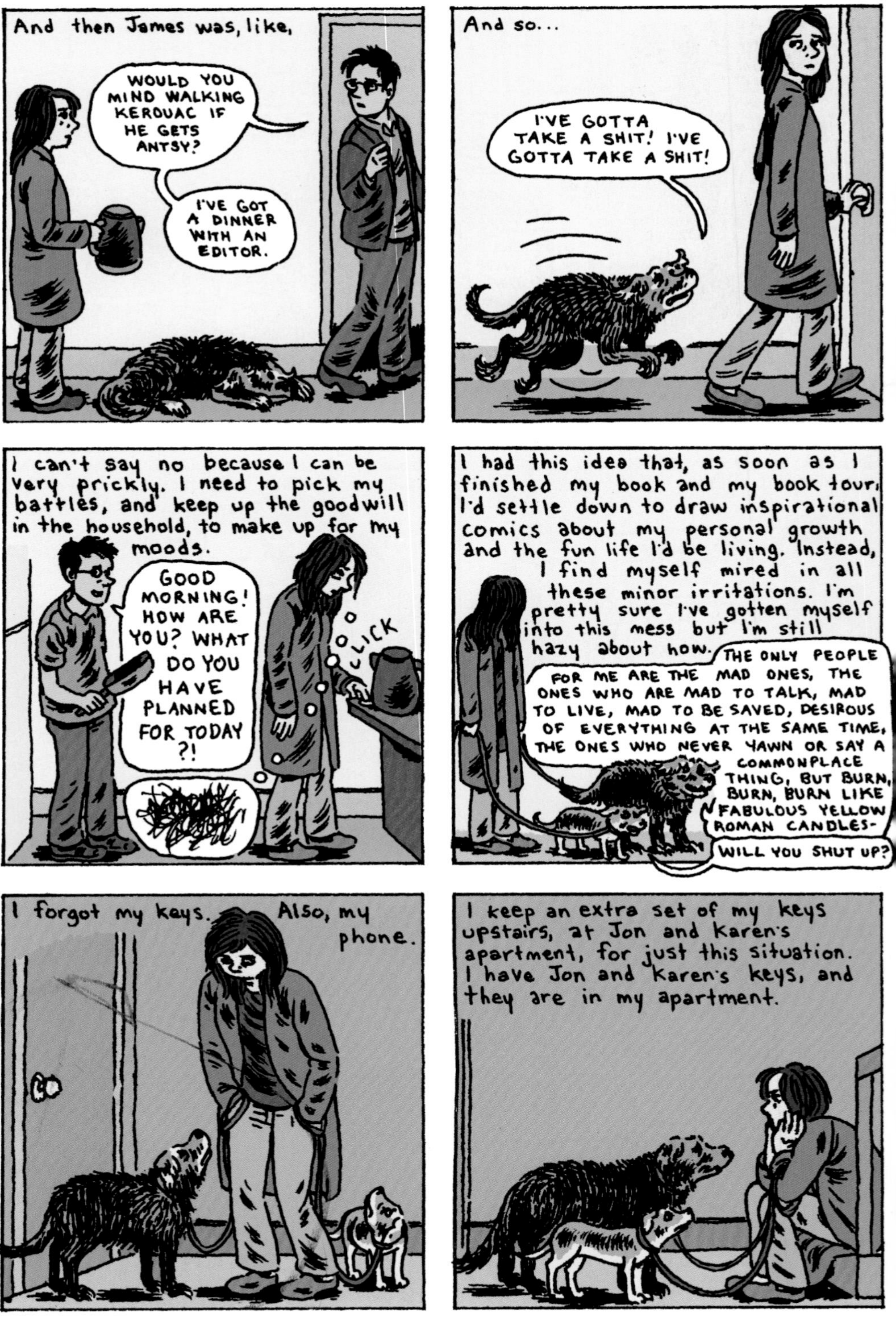
And then James was, like,
WOULD YOU MIND WALKING KEROUAC IF HE GETS ANTSY?
I'VE GOT A DINNER WITH AN EDITOR.
And so...
I'VE GOTTA TAKE A SHIT! I'VE GOTTA TAKE A SHIT!
I can't say no because I can be very prickly. I need to pick my battles, and keep up the goodwill in the household, to make up for my moods.
GOOD MORNING! HOW ARE YOU? WHAT DO YOU HAVE PLANNED FOR TODAY?!
CLICK
I had this idea that, as soon as I finished my book and my book tour, I'd settle down to draw inspirational comics about my personal growth and the fun life I'd be living. Instead, I find myself mired in all these minor irritations. I'm pretty sure I've gotten myself into this mess but I'm still hazy about how.
THE ONLY PEOPLE FOR ME ARE THE MAD ONES, THE ONES WHO ARE MAD TO TALK, MAD TO LIVE, MAD TO BE SAVED, DESIROUS OF EVERYTHING AT THE SAME TIME, THE ONES WHO NEVER YAWN OR SAY A COMMONPLACE THING, BUT BURN, BURN, BURN LIKE FABULOUS YELLOW ROMAN CANDLES-
WILL YOU SHUT UP?
I forgot my keys.
Also, my phone.
I keep an extra set of my keys upstairs, at Jon and Karen's apartment, for just this situation. I have Jon and Karen's keys, and they are in my apartment.

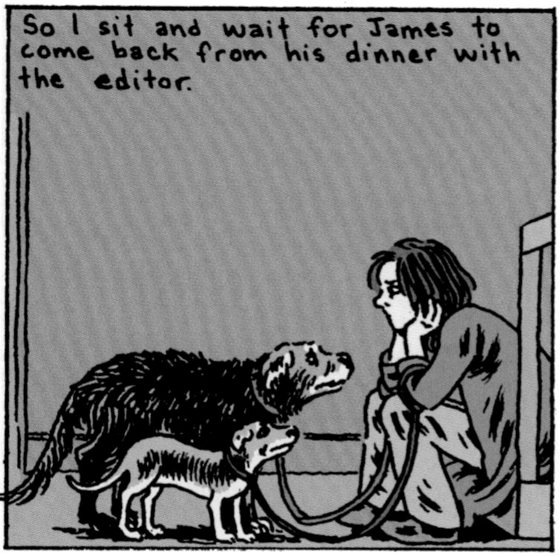
So I sit and wait for James to come back from his dinner with the editor.

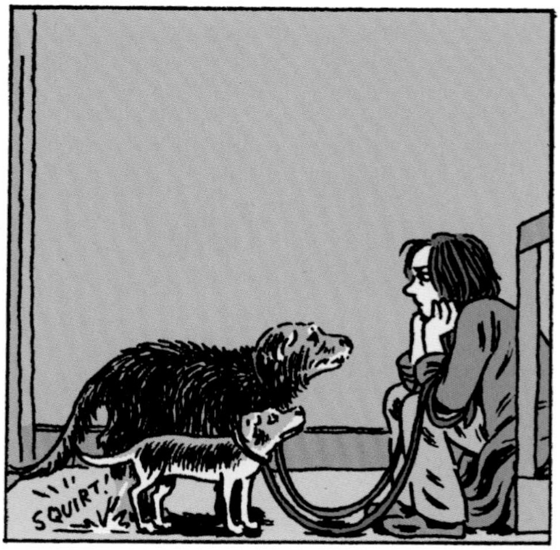
SQUIRT!

HOSPICE

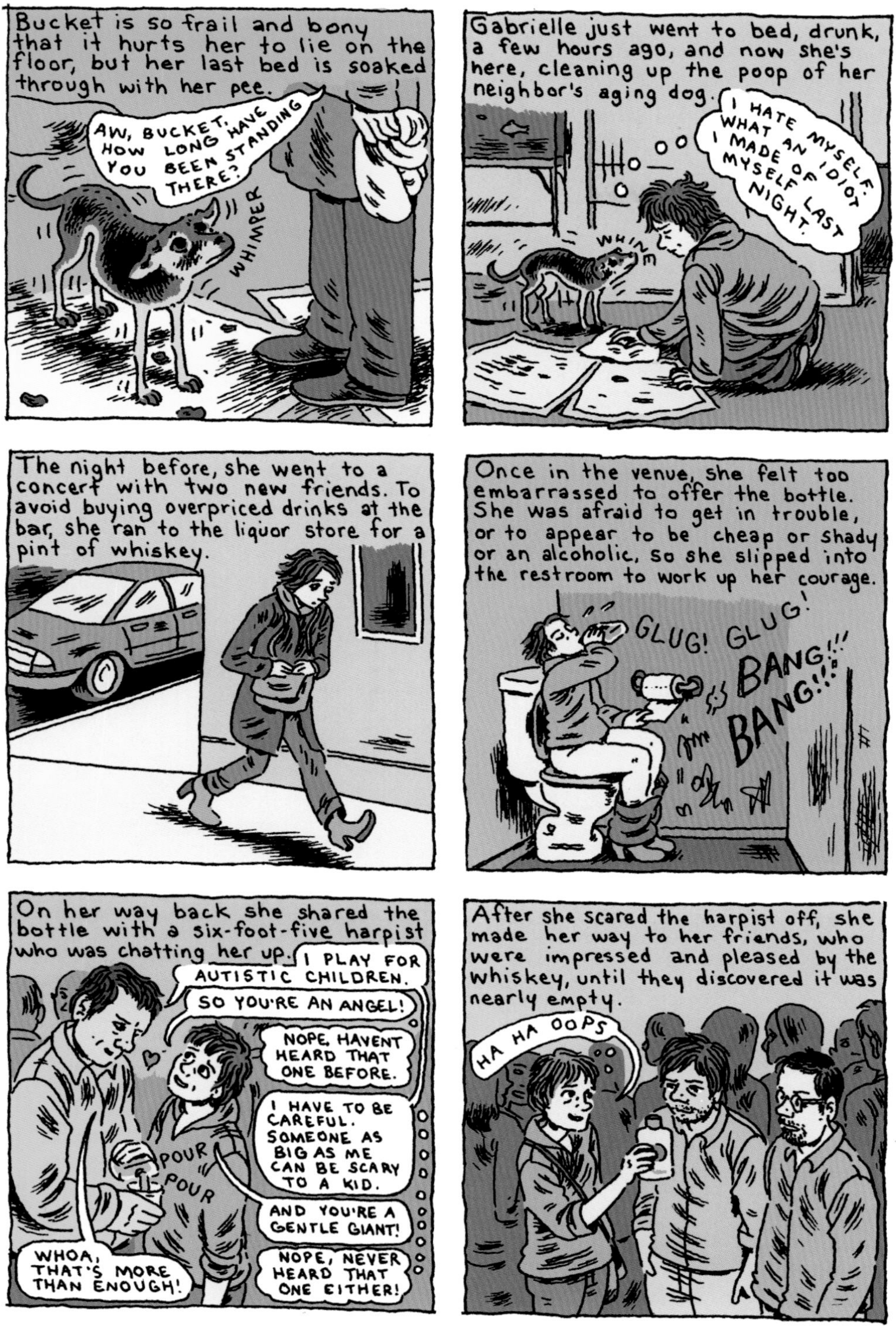
Bucket is so frail and bony that it hurts her to lie on the floor, but her last bed is soaked through with her pee.
AW, BUCKET. HOW LONG HAVE YOU BEEN STANDING THERE?
WHIMPER
Gabrielle just went to bed, drunk, a few hours ago, and now she's here, cleaning up the poop of her neighbor's aging dog.
I HATE MYSELF. WHAT AN IDIOT I MADE OF MYSELF LAST NIGHT.
WHINE
The night before, she went to a concert with two new friends. To avoid buying overpriced drinks at the bar, she ran to the liquor store for a pint of whiskey.
Once in the venue, she felt too embarrassed to offer the bottle. She was afraid to get in trouble, or to appear to be cheap or shady or an alcoholic, so she slipped into the restroom to work up her courage.
GLUG! GLUG!
BANG!!!
BANG!!!
On her way back she shared the bottle with a six-foot-five harpist who was chatting her up.
I PLAY FOR AUTISTIC CHILDREN.
SO YOU'RE AN ANGEL!
NOPE, HAVENT HEARD THAT ONE BEFORE.
I HAVE TO BE CAREFUL. SOMEONE AS BIG AS ME CAN BE SCARY TO A KID.
POUR
POUR
AND YOU'RE A GENTLE GIANT!
WHOA, THAT'S MORE THAN ENOUGH!
NOPE, NEVER HEARD THAT ONE EITHER!
After she scared the harpist off, she made her way to her friends, who were impressed and pleased by the whiskey, until they discovered it was nearly empty.
HA HA OOPS

Gabrielle spent a good amount of time in the sparsely populated dance tent, peopled by only the diehards. These were the extreme weirdos, alongside the truly good dancers. Gabrielle did not allow herself to think too much about where she stood on that spectrum.

Once, her friend Tony said to her,

YOU HAVE A PECULIAR WAY OF DANCING. ME AND SADIE WERE WATCHING YOU AND DISCUSSING IT. IT TAKES AN IMAGINATIVE PERSON TO APPRECIATE IT.

WAIT, WHAT?

NO, IT'S KIND OF WEIRD, BUT IN A GOOD WAY.

Bucket has given Karen and Jon seventeen years of joy, and now they uncomplainingly clean up after her non-stop incontinence, launder and switch out her beds, administer pills, and endure the unending smell of poop, pee, and a cranky old dog.

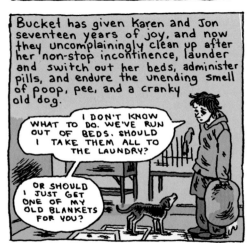

I DON'T KNOW WHAT TO DO. WE'VE RUN OUT OF BEDS. SHOULD I TAKE THEM ALL TO THE LAUNDRY?

OR SHOULD I JUST GET ONE OF MY OLD BLANKETS FOR YOU?

On her way downstairs to get a blanket, she overhears her other upstairs neighbors, whose elderly cat she also occasionally cares for, laughing with their infant daughter.

GIGGLE! HA HA! DA DA

On her way back up, she marvels at their joyfulness and energy at eight in the morning, when she herself wishes that she weren't alive.

GIGGLE! COME HERE, SILLY

She realizes that she's never heard these neighbors fight, and that they always seem so happy and kind. She imagines them in another seventeen years, seeing their daughter off to college.

I CAN'T BELIEVE THIS DAY HAS COME. WE WILL MISS YOU SO MUCH!

MOM, I'M GOING TO COLUMBIA. IT'S A SUBWAY RIDE AWAY!

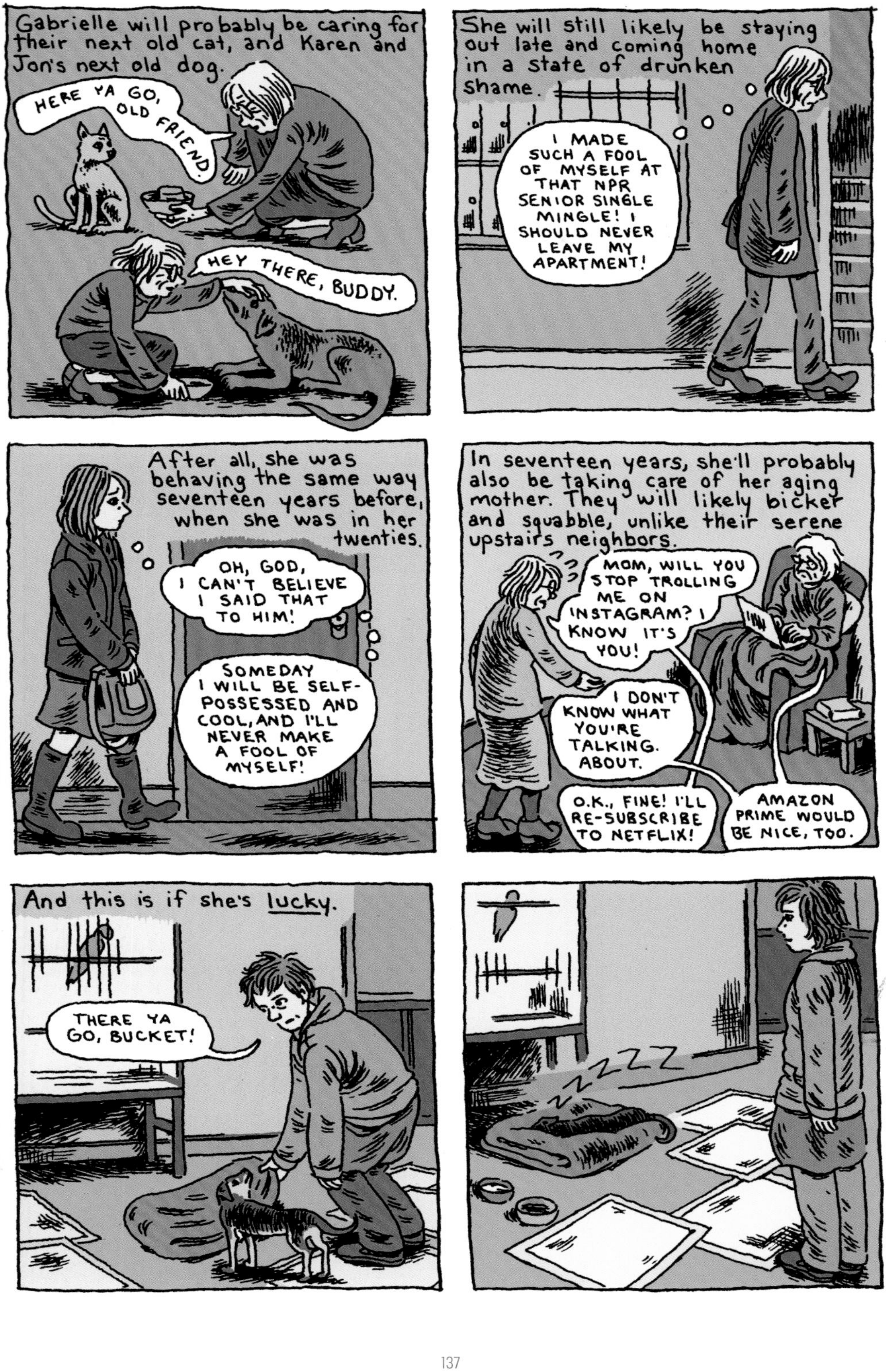
Gabrielle will probably be caring for their next old cat, and Karen and Jon's next old dog.
HERE YA GO, OLD FRIEND.
HEY THERE, BUDDY.
She will still likely be staying out late and coming home in a state of drunken shame.
I MADE SUCH A FOOL OF MYSELF AT THAT NPR SENIOR SINGLE MINGLE! I SHOULD NEVER LEAVE MY APARTMENT!
After all, she was behaving the same way seventeen years before, when she was in her twenties.
OH, GOD, I CAN'T BELIEVE I SAID THAT TO HIM!
SOMEDAY I WILL BE SELF-POSSESSED AND COOL, AND I'LL NEVER MAKE A FOOL OF MYSELF!
In seventeen years, she'll probably also be taking care of her aging mother. They will likely bicker and squabble, unlike their serene upstairs neighbors.
MOM, WILL YOU STOP TROLLING ME ON INSTAGRAM? I KNOW IT'S YOU!
I DON'T KNOW WHAT YOU'RE TALKING ABOUT.
O.K., FINE! I'LL RE-SUBSCRIBE TO NETFLIX!
AMAZON PRIME WOULD BE NICE, TOO.
And this is if she's lucky.
THERE YA GO, BUCKET!
ZZZZZ

NOTES

My Prince, **The Story of Number Sixteen, The Forty-Three-Year-Old Spider**, **John Porcellino**, and **These Boots** were originally published on *Spiralbound.com*.

Cody was originally published in *Kramers Ergot*.

1-800-CATS, **Bucket**, and **Hospice** were originally published for *The New Yorker*.

Little Red and Big Bad was originally published for *The Paris Review*.

Talking Rats, **How Do You Do Things**, **Don't Talk To Strangers** and **Dreaming** were published in *Kuš!*

The Nicest Dog and **Dentist** were originally published for *Vice Magazine*.

Photo by Joseph Radoccia

THANK YOU

Tomasz Kaczynski & Nikki Weispfenning, Emma Ruddock, Jordan Shiveley, Kevin Huizenga, Az Sperry, Jon & Karen, Liana, Lauren, Julia, Julia, Ariel, Tania, Sarah, Tony, Larry, Stefano, Steve, Patrick Allaby, Sanika Phawde, Emma Allen, Edith Zimmerman, & Margaret Hayes